# Animals

a children's
encyclopedia

A DORLING
KINDERSLEY
BOOK

**LONDON, NEW YORK,
MELBOURNE, MUNICH, and DELHI**

**Project editors** Carrie Love, Caroline Stamps
**Project designer** Rachael Smith
**Editors** Ann Baggaley, Elinor Greenwood, Wendy Horobin,
Cécile Landau, Lorrie Mack, and Penny Smith
**Designers** Sadie Thomas, Clemence De Molliens,
Gemma Fletcher, and Joanna Pocock
**Picture researcher** Liz Moore

Packaging services supplied by **Bookwork**

**Publishing manager** Bridget Giles
**Art director** Rachael Foster
**Production controller** Claire Pearson
**Production editor** Sean Daly
**Jacket designer** Natalie Godwin
**Jacket editor** Mariza O'Keeffe

**Consultants** Dr Mark Fox, Dr John Friel,
Matthew Robertson , and Eileen Westwig MS

First published in Great Britain in 2008 by
Dorling Kindersley Limited,
80 Strand, London, WC2R 0RL

A CIP catalogue record for this book
is available from the British Library

ISBN: 978-1-40532-875-3

Colour reproduction by Colourscan, Singapore
Printed and bound by Tlaciarne BB s.r.o, Slovakia

Discover more at
**www.dk.com**

# Contents

# *Foreword*

We share our planet with a wonderful array of diverse and fascinating creatures. From the tiniest insect to the mighty blue whale, animals have adapted to fill every niche in the ecosystem. There are so many different types (species), that even after hundreds of years of scientific study people have still not managed to catalogue every species that exists. Even the most familiar animals have aspects of their behaviour, lifestyle, or biology that remain to be discovered. However, it is a sad fact that many species will vanish through habitat loss, pollution, and human exploitation before their true value to biodiversity is known.

This comprehensive guide aims to introduce children to the exciting world of animals. All the major groups are represented: mammals, birds, fish, reptiles, amphibians, and invertebrates. Each section introduces the reader to the main characteristics of the groups, families, and species that follow. Individual entries focus on particularly interesting or common species, detailing their habitat, geographic location, relative size, lifespan, and conservation status. Stunning photographs accompany the text, revealing the spectacular colours and fabulous decorations displayed by many animals, as well as insights into their behaviour in the wild. From the biggest to the baddest and the beautiful to the bizarre, the wonders of the animal kingdom are revealed here to amaze and inform young minds.

Dr John P. Friel
Curator of Fishes, Amphibians, & Reptiles
Cornell University Museum of Vertebrates

## ANIMALS IN DANGER

Many animals face the threat of extinction. An animal is said to be extinct when the last known specimen has died. Scientists monitor how close an animal may be to extinction using a classification system devised by the International Union for the Conservation of Nature (IUCN). Under this system, animals that have been evaluated are put into the following categories:

- **Extinct in the wild:** the animal only exists in captivity or as a naturalized population outside its normal range.
- **Critically endangered:** the animal is facing an extremely high risk of extinction.
- **Endangered:** the animal is facing a very high risk of extinction.

- **Vulnerable:** the animal is facing a high risk of extinction.
- **Near threatened:** the animal is likely to qualify for one of the above categories in the near future, or depends on conservation efforts for its survival.

- **Least concern:** the animal has been assessed but is regarded as widespread and abundant.

- **Data deficient/Not evaluated:** there is not enough information to assess the animal fully or it has not been assessed. Some of these animals, such as earthworms, fall within this category even though they are known to be common.
  IUCN does not classify animals that are domesticated or farmed, such as cattle, sheep, dromedary camels, goldfish, and household pets.

## KEY TO SYMBOLS

All the animals featured in this book are coded with symbols that indicate their usual habitats, maximum size relative to a human, lifespan, and conservation status. Caves are one habitat not denoted by an icon, as relatively few species spend their entire lives there. Urban habitats have also not been included as such animals have a natural home in the wild. Animals with a lifespan of less than one year do not have an icon. A question mark indicates that the lifespan, though longer than a year, is unknown. Animal sizes are shown by comparing the animal to an average-height adult man for large species, or an adult human hand for smaller species.

### ICONS

| | |
|---|---|
| ⚠ | ANIMAL NOT ENDANGERED |
| ⚠ | ANIMAL NUMBERS ARE DECLINING |
| ⚠ | ANIMAL ENDANGERED |
| ? | ANIMAL STATUS UNKNOWN |
| ♥ | ANIMAL LIFESPAN |
| | TROPICAL FOREST AND RAINFOREST |
| | TEMPERATE FOREST, INCLUDING WOODLAND |
| | CONIFEROUS FOREST, INCLUDING WOODLAND |
| | SEAS AND OCEANS |
| | COASTAL AREAS, INCLUDING BEACHES AND CLIFFS |
| | POLAR REGIONS AND TUNDRA |
| | RIVERS, STREAMS, AND ALL FLOWING WATER |
| | WETLANDS AND STILL WATER: LAKES, PONDS, MARSHES, BOGS, AND SWAMPS |
| | MANGROVE SWAMPS, ABOVE AND BELOW THE WATERLINE |
| | MOUNTAINS, HIGHLANDS, SCREE SLOPES |
| | DESERT AND SEMI-DESERT |
| | CORAL REEFS AND WATERS IMMEDIATELY AROUND THEM |
| | GRASSLAND HABITATS: MOOR, SAVANNA, FIELDS, SCRUBLAND |
| | SIZE OF ANIMAL COMPARED WITH ADULT HUMAN |

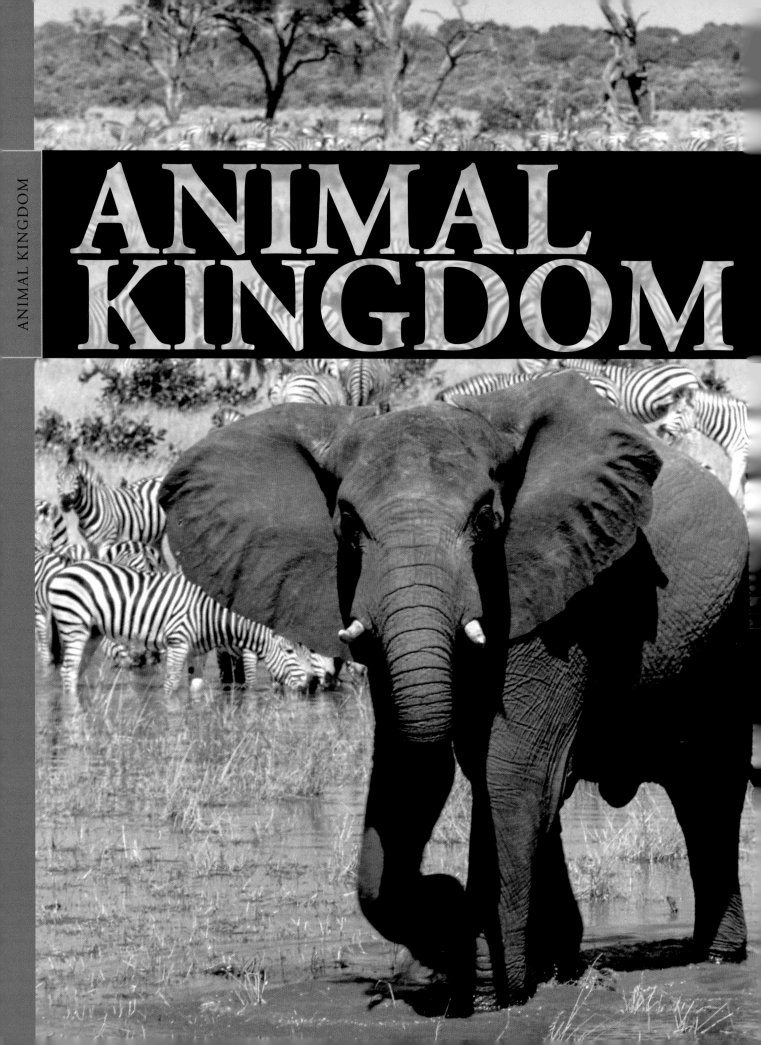

# ANIMAL KINGDOM

# *What* is an ANIMAL?

The animal kingdom is a vast collection of weird and wonderful creatures. Members of this group come in many different shapes and sizes, but they are all made up of cells, and they all have nerves and muscles to move and respond to the world around them. Most importantly, all animals eat food to make energy.

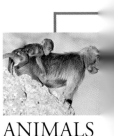

ANIMALS

**Warm and cold blood** Birds and mammals are warm-blooded animals, which means they make their own body heat using the energy from their food. Other animals, such as amphibians, fish, insects, and reptiles, are cold-blooded creatures, which means they cannot make their own body heat. Instead, cold-blooded animals rely on outside sources of heat, such as the warmth of the Sun, to raise their body temperature and carry on their daily lives.

VERTEBRATES
*are animals with backbones and include amphibians, birds, fish, mammals, and reptiles.*

MAMMALS
*Mammals have fur and feed their young with milk from the mother's mammary glands.*

BIRDS
*Birds have feathers and produce young by laying eggs. Most birds move using their wings to fly.*

REPTILES
*Reptiles have dry skin covered with scales or horny plates. Most produce young by laying eggs.*

AMPHIBIANS
*Amphibians spend most of their adult lives on land and breathe air, but return to water to breed.*

FISH
*Fish have fins scales and spen of their lives in water. They br using gills.*

**FOOD CHAINS** When animals eat other animals, the energy in the food passes through a food chain. The first link in the chain is a plant. Plants create food using the energy from the Sun. When an animal eats the plant, the energy passes up the chain. The food chain continues as animals eat other animals.

ENERGY FLOW *These simple food chains show the feeding relationships between different animals. Energy flows up each chain until it reaches an animal that has no natural predators – represented here by a serval, an orca, and a cougar.*

Orca (killer whale)

Sea lion

Serval cat

Starling

Spider

Herring

Mouse

Cougar

Raccoon

Snake

 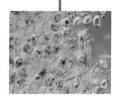

LIFE

**ACTERIA**

**PLANTS**

**FUNGI**

**PROTISTS**
*are a group of organisms that include some seaweeds and moulds. Many are single-celled.*

**INVERTEBRATES**
*make up 95 per cent of the animal kingdom. They are animals that do not have a bony skeleton. They include insects, spiders and many marine creatures such as crabs and starfish.*

**ORMS**
*rious related ups.*

**ARACHNIDS**
*Scorpions, spiders, ticks, mites.*

**CRUSTACEANS**
*Crabs, lobsters, woodlice.*

**MOLLUSCS**
*Clams, octopuses, oysters, squid, slugs, snails.*

**SPONGES**

**CNIDARIANS**
*Sea anemones, corals, jellyfish, hydroids.*

**HORSESHOE CRAB**

**INSECTS**
*Butterflies, moths, mosquitoes, flies, dragonflies, beetles.*

**ECHINODERMS**
*Starfish, sea urchins, sand dollars.*

---

*Feathers (left), fur (centre), and scales (right).*

**Animal overcoats** Animals keep warm and protect their skin and bodies in different ways. Birds are covered with feathers, mammals have coats of fur, while scales or horny plates grow out of the skin of fish and reptiles.

## CLASSIFICATION

Scientists around the world organize the living world into groups. A species is a type that can breed fertile offspring. Related species are grouped into a genus, and genera are grouped into families. This grouping system carries on through order, class, and phylum to kingdom at the top of the classification system. The following shows an example of scientific classification for the lion. The genus name is always written in italics with a capital first letter; the species name is written in italics but does not have a capital first letter.

- **Order:** Carnivora
  Animals with cheek teeth for slicing meat.

- **Family:** Felidae
  Includes every type of cat, both large and small.

- **Genus:** *Panthera*
  Large cats that can roar as well as purr. Includes lions, tigers, panthers.

- **Species:** *leo*
  Identifies the large cat specifically as a lion.

# ANIMAL *behaviour*

Anything an animal does is its behaviour. This ranges from simple things such as eating and keeping clean to more complex activities such as attracting a mate. Some behaviour is instinctive, while other behaviour develops through experience.

## LIVING ALONE

Many animals choose to live and hunt alone and only come together to mate during the breeding season. As soon as the mating takes place, the two sexes part company again.

## LIVING TOGETHER

Animals choose to live together for many different reasons. One of the main benefits is safety in numbers. You might think that a group of animals offers a predator a wider choice of prey. In fact, the predator often finds it hard to single out its victim. So for any one animal, the chance of being eaten is less.

**Feeding time** Animals spend a lot of time looking for food. Some predators hunt alone and rely on speed or stealth to capture prey. Others hunt in groups. Scavengers feed on the remains that other animals leave behind.

▲ LIFE IN THE HERD
*Living in a herd offers a better chance of survival for zebras since there are more eyes on the lookout for predators such as lions.*

▲ BEE COLONIES
*Within a bee colony, one female, called the queen, produces all the young. It's her job, and she is helped by all the bees in the colony.*

▲ HOME TO ROOST
*During the day, large numbers of bats gather to rest at roosting sites, such as caves. They emerge at dusk to feed.*

▲ NESTING SITES
*During the breeding season, seabirds such as gannets and gulls make their nests in dense colonies along the coast.*

▲ ON THE PROWL
*Female lions and their cubs live in groups called prides. Male lions live alongside the females either alone or in small groups.*

# SENDING A MESSAGE

Animals keep in touch in different ways. They may make noisy calls, use body language and other visual cues, or leave scent marks. Animals communicate in these ways for many reasons, such as finding food and finding each other.

◄ SMILE *When a chimpanzee is frightened, it bares its teeth. So what looks like a smile to us is actually a chimpanzee's grin of fear.*

*A smile?*

◄ BIRD SONG *Birds use a range of melodic songs and calls to "speak" to each other. They use these calls in many ways, perhaps to warn of danger or mark out a territory.*

▼ TONGUE TASTER *The snake's forked tongue brings smells and tastes into its mouth. These are then detected in two pits, called "Jacobson's organs", on the roof of its mouth.*

Mangrove snake
*Boiga dendrophila*

## Danger signals

Animals use a range of defensive tactics when they feel threatened. Some rely on their speed to escape from danger, while others puff up their bodies to exaggerate their size and look more dangerous. In some cases, these threats are real.

◄ BROWN BEAR *These bears can be aggressive, especially when a mother is protecting her cubs. Brown bears stand upright to look as threatening as possible, growling and baring their teeth.*

▶ COBRA *When threatened, the Indian cobra spreads its broad hood to look more menacing. This display is usually enough to deter the potential threat.*

▶ POISON DART FROG *The bright colour of the poison dart frog is a warning to all animals that it contains some deadly poisons.*

▶ BUTTERFLY *The large eye spots on the wings of some butterflies and moths may startle predators by resembling the eyes of larger animals.*

▶ OPOSSUM *When threatened, the opossum sinks to the ground, bares its teeth, and lolls its tongue to one side in a convincing display of death.*

# ANIMAL IQ

It is incredibly difficult for people to measure the intelligence of an animal. Some apparently intelligent behaviour comes naturally, such as the beaver's ability to build a dam. Better examples of animal intelligence are the abilities to learn from experiences and solve problems. Unfortunately, these are rare in the animal world.

▶ TOOLS OF THE TRADE *These chimpanzees are using a thin twig to probe a termite mound for the insects inside. The use of tools is unusual in the animal kingdom.*

◄ MENTAL MAPS *The Eurasian jay buries acorns as a food store for the winter. Rarely do these birds forget the location of the burial sites.*

# An ANIMAL'S *life cycle*

The whole of an animal's life has just one purpose: survival of the species. Staying alive long enough to find a mate and produce young is all that really matters. Each species has its own special life cycle that is repeated as one generation follows another.

## GOING COURTING

Some animals mate at any time of year. Others breed only in particular seasons, such as spring and autumn. Attracting a mate can mean putting in a lot of effort, especially for the males. Fancy plumage, shows of strength, and love songs are just some of the ploys animals use.

▶ DISPLAY *The more impressive his tail, the more females a peacock will entice into his harem.*

▶ FROG SONGS *Frogs and toads inflate their throat sacs to make love calls to mates.*

▲ LOCKING ANTLERS *These deer are having a wrestling match to decide which one of them wins the females.*

▲ BOXING GLOVES *In spring, male hares who are rivals for the same mate often settle the matter with a fierce boxing match.*

CARING MUM
*This mother orang-utan is bringing up her infant without any help from her mate. Over the next ten years she will teach the youngster survival skills, such as how to live safely in the forests and where to find food.*

## The way young develop

Most mammals give birth to live young. Animals such as birds, insects, and many reptiles and fish, lay eggs. The time it takes for young to develop independent life, inside the womb or inside an egg, or by passing through larval stages, varies enormously. A small mammal such as a vole is pregnant for two or three weeks, while an elephant's pregnancy lasts about 22 months. Some insects stay at an early stage of development for years.

◀ IN THE EGG *An embryo chick may not begin to develop until the parent birds start sitting on the eggs. The growing chick is nourished by the egg yolk.*

▶ IN THE WOMB *At this early stage a kitten looks much the same as a human embryo. Its body systems will be developed long before birth.*

# CHILDCARE

Some newborn animals receive lavish childcare. For example, a mother ape carries her young everywhere; an infant kangaroo always has a mother's pouch to shelter in; parent birds feed their nestlings on demand. On the other hand, the young of hares and some deer survive on one short daily visit from their mother, when she turns up to feed them. Often, animals such as insects, fish, and reptiles never meet their parents at all.

▶ A NEST FULL *of chicks is hard work. Many parent birds exhaust themselves feeding their hungry brood.*

◀ KING PENGUINS *carry their single egg on their feet, tucked under a warm tummy fold. Both parent birds share the duty.*

◀ YOUNG KANGAROOS *stay in their mother's pouch for six months. They feed from a nipple inside the pouch.*

▲ PUPS *are ready to be weaned from their mother's milk when they are about three weeks old.*

◀ TADPOLES *know nothing about parents. When they hatch, they must fend for themselves.*

◀ A NEWLY BORN ANTEATER *climbs straight up on to its mother's back. It rides around, clinging to the mother's fur, until it is about one year old.*

## A continuing cycle

In some species of animals, mothers and their young stay together as a group for life. Among animals as widely different as lions, monkeys, and killer whales family ties remain unbroken in this way, though the male offspring will leave the group when mature so that only one dominant male remains with the females. Other young male and female animals, such as pandas, move on to a largely solitary existence.

▲ ELEPHANT AUNTS
*All the females in an elephant herd help a mother to look after her calf.*

◀ LIFE TIES
*The close bond between dolphins and their offspring lasts for life.*

## WHERE IN THE WORLD?

Habitats are places where animals live and mix with other animals and their surroundings. Most animals can move from place to place, so they have spread to every part of the world. Many thrive in warm, wet tropical forests, while other hardy types live in some of the harshest places on our planet, from arid deserts to the darkest ocean depths.

The following symbols are used throughout the book.

| | |
|---|---|
| | *Tropical forest and rainforest* |
| | *Temperate forest, including woodland* |
| | *Coniferous forest, including woodland* |
| | *Mountains, highlands, scree slopes* |
| | *Desert and semi desert* |
| | *Open habitats including grassland, moorland, heathland, savanna, fields, scrub* |
| | *Rivers, streams, and all flowing water* |
| | *Wetlands and all still bodies of water* |
| | *Mangrove swamps above or below waterline* |
| | *Seas and oceans* |
| | *Coastal areas* |
| | *Coral reefs and waters immediately around them* |
| | *Polar regions, including tundra and icebergs* |
| | *Mediterranean-type biomes* |

# World habitats

Our planet is home to a range of landscapes and some equally varied weather patterns. Months go by in the desert without a single drop of rain, while rainforests soaked daily by tropical storms. Little wonder then th earth supports such an amazing diversity of life.

## Wetlands and mangroves

In some wetlands, plants form a thin carpet over the waterlogged soil, while in others stretches of open water mix with patches of dense vegetation. Wetlands are homes for land-based swimmers such as snakes, as well as many insects, fish and waterbirds. Mangrove swamps (see inset) are flooded with salt water when the tide comes in and left exposed when the water retreats. These swamps contain many fish, and the dense forests provide excellent nesting sites for birds.

*Tropic of Can*

*Equator*

*Tropic of Capr*

## Temperate and coniferous forest

In the northern hemisphere, temperate forests of deciduous trees eventually give way to coniferous forests that stretch across the far north, deep inside the Arctic Circle, where the temperatures rarely rise above freezing. Further south, the temperate forests of evergreen trees have warm summers and mild winters. These forests are home to many different animals. Bears, birds of prey, and wolves live in the coniferous forests of the far north, while deer, lizards, squirrels, and many forest birds are found farther south.

## Tundra

The tundra is a vast, frozen landscape north of the Arctic Circle. It is so cold that the soil is frozen for most of the year. In the spring, the tundra bursts into life as snow and ice melt. Alpine plants appear, and birds arrive to breed. As the soil starts to freeze again, the plants wither and the birds depart, marking the end of the short summer.

## Grassland

Grasslands go by different names in different places. They are prairies in North America, pampas or paramo in South America, steppes in Europe and Asia, and the outback in Australia. The tropical and subtropical grassland of Africa is known as the savanna. In all these areas, grasses are the dominant plants and the main source of food for huge herds of grazing mammals, such as the wildebeest and zebras of Africa. In turn, these grazers are the food for predators such as the big cats and wild dogs.

Arctic Ocean

NORTH AMERICA

EUROPE

ASIA

Atlantic Ocean

AFRICA

Pacific Ocean

SOUTH AMERICA

Indian Ocean

Atlantic Ocean

AUSTRALIA

DESERT LIFE
*The world's deserts
are places of extreme
climate, with very
high temperatures
and little moisture.*

ANTARCTICA

## Mountain

Few habitats experience such a variation in conditions as the mountains. Lower down the slopes, in the foothills, the conditions usually match that of the surrounding area. Many animals make their home here, including forest birds and large mammals, such as apes, bears, deer, and monkeys. Higher up the slopes, the air gets thinner and the temperature drops rapidly. Only the hardiest animals, such as birds of prey and mountain goats, can cope with the harsh conditions.

## Coastal areas

The coast is a natural barrier between land and sea. It is one of the few places on earth where the landscape constantly changes. Animals that live here must adapt to the rhythm of the tides. Rocky coasts, mudflats, and sandy beaches abound with marine invertebrates and the wading birds that feed on them.

The **rainforest** is warm and wet, creating the perfect conditions for plant growth. This rich vegetation provides the foundations for abundant animal life.

## Hot forests

Rainforests enjoy plenty of warmth and moisture. The rainforests that lie on the equator are hot and humid all year round. They are some of the most productive habitats on Earth. The seasonal forests on either side of the equator – the so-called monsoon forests – experience a yearly cycle of rain and sun. They are home to a wide variety of animal life.

## Rainforest layers

A tropical rainforest grows in distinct layers. Each layer consists of plants and animals that have adapted to living in that particular part of the rainforest. The top, or emergent, layer consists of the tallest trees. Here it is hot and windy. Below this level is the canopy, a dense layer of branches that is home to most of the forest's animals. The dark understorey of shrubs and seedlings is the next level down, followed by the leaf litter on the forest floor, which supports fungi and new plant growth.

## TROPICAL RAINFOREST

**MEALY PARROT**
*These large parrots live in pairs or small flocks in the Amazon rainforest, where they feast on the abundant fruits, seeds, and nuts.*

**TREE DWELLERS**
*White-faced capuchins live in complex social groups called troops, which patrol the rainforests of Central and South America.*

**LEAF CUTTERS**
*Leafcutter ants live in complex colonies in almost every part of the rainforest, from the tallest treetops down to the leaf litter.*

**NIGHT CAT**
*The ocelot lives on the floor of the rainforest, where it hunts birds, small mammals, and reptiles under the cover of darkness.*

**WATER LOVER**
*The capybara is the largest of all the rodents. It lives in densely forested areas near lakes, rivers, and swamps of the South American rainforest.*

### HABITATS LARGE AND SMALL

**Macrohabitat** A typical example of a macrohabitat would be all the regions within a large, complex environment such as a coastal region. For example, the intertidal zone, rocky pools, and sand dunes along the shore would all make up the coastal macrohabitat.

**Microhabitat** Within each macrohabitat there are many smaller microhabitats. These regions may be no bigger than a small, rotting log within the vast expanse of a rainforest. Each tiny environment harbours animals that may not be found anywhere else in the macrohabitat.

## Dry desert heat

For most of the time, the world's deserts are dry, barren habitats, where the intense heat results in less than 15 cm (6 in) of rain each year. When it comes, rain soaks the parched soil and may lead to local flooding. Few creatures can adapt to these extreme conditions, so the desert is home to a bunch of extremely hardy animals and plants.

### DESERT

**FOOD TIME** *The golden eagle uses its keen sense of sight to hunt animals such as rabbits, hares, squirrels, and mice.*

**NESTING HOLE** *The gila woodpecker lives in the desert of southwestern United States. It builds its nest in holes made in saguaro cacti or mesquite trees.*

**DESERT CAT** *The desert-dwelling bobcat lives in the southerly part of North America, where it hunts birds, hares, rabbits, and other small mammals.*

**DEATH RATTLE** *The rattle on the end of a rattlesnake's tail gives this venomous snake its name. If threatened, the snake shakes its rattle as a warning to steer clear.*

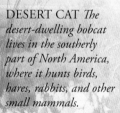

**STINGING TAIL** *Scorpions have large, hook-shaped stings on the ends of their tails. These act as defensive weapons but can be used to stun prey.*

## Life in the cold poles

The world's deserts and polar regions have one thing in common. Both get little in the way of rainfall each year. While deserts are scorching hot, the polar regions are some of the coldest places on Earth. Few creatures can survive in these extremes, so the ones that do, adapt to overcome the frozen conditions. Sea mammals have thick skin, called blubber, while some fish even have an "antifreeze" element in their blood.

### POLAR REGIONS

**ARCTIC TERN** *Arctic terns migrate between the Arctic and Antarctic each year, making full use of the daylight hours at each pole.*

**POLAR BEAR** *Seals are the main food source for these Arctic predators. The polar bear's blubber and thick fur keep it warm under water and on the ice.*

**SWIMMERS** *These superb swimmers are adapted for a life under water. They use their flipper-like wings to chase fish – a favourite food.*

**LEOPARD SEAL** *The fearsome leopard seal roams the southern oceans in search of food such as seabirds, smaller seals, and penguins.*

**KRILL** *These tiny crustaceans thrive in cold Arctic and Antarctic waters, where they feed on plankton. They are eaten by seals and whales.*

## SAVANNA

### GLIDING EYE

*The African white-backed vulture glides high over the vast, open savanna in search of the remains of dead animals.*

### TREE SNAKE

*The boomslang is a highly poisonous tree-dwelling snake that lives in savanna and scrub south of the Sahara Desert.*

### AFRICAN GIANT

*Herds of up to 30 African elephants wander across the savanna in search of food and water holes.*

### TOP PREDATOR

*Female lions hunt together, targeting weak or young zebra and wildebeest from the vast herds that roam the savanna.*

### DUNG DEALERS

*Revolting as it may sound, dung beetles eat poo! They roll the dung into balls and bury them in the soil to feed their young.*

## URBAN HABITATS

Many animals have chosen to make their homes alongside our own. Towns and cities provide plenty of hiding places for these adaptable animals. The vast amounts of rubbish we produce are rich pickings for the hungry scavengers that can cope with the hustle and bustle of city life.

◄ MONKEY PALACE
*Rhesus macaques patrol the walls of the Hawa Mahal temple (Palace of the Winds) in Jaipur, India. These monkeys thrive in urban areas and rely on handouts or human rubbish. They have become a serious pest in some countries.*

## CORAL REEF

### SEA PIRATES
*Frigatebirds are famous for stealing food. They attack other seabirds in flight and force them to release their food.*

### REEF SHARK
*The whitetip reef shark is harmless to people. It patrols the reef, searching for food such as crustaceans, octopus, and fish.*

### SEA TURTLE
*The hawksbill turtle uses its narrow beak to forage for sponges, molluscs, and other marine animals among the coral reef.*

### CLEANER CRAB
*The scarlet reef hermit crab is a domestic goddess. Its appetite for hairy and slime algae helps keep the reef clean and tidy.*

### REEF FISH
*With their bold patterns and bright colours, angelfish are some of the most spectacular fish of the coral reef.*

## FRESH WATER HABITATS

### FISHING BIRD
*Herons are expert fishing birds. They use their keen sense of sight to pluck fish from below the water's surface.*

### DRAGONFLIES
*These skilled aerial hunters skim over the surface of lakes and rivers, using their big, compound eyes to search for smaller insect prey.*

### WATER VOLES
*These rat-like rodents make burrows in the banks of rivers and streams, where they feed on grasses and other plant material.*

### WATER LOVERS
*Tadpoles spend all their time in the water, but most adult frogs and toads usually live on land, only returning to the water to breed.*

### PERCH PREY
*These freshwater fish live in lakes, ponds and slow-moving streams, where they hunt invertebrates and other small fish.*

ANIMAL KINGDOM

### ◄ MOUSE HOUSE
*This adaptable rodent, like its relative the rat, has successfully infiltrated urban living. As cute as they look, they are very troublesome, damaging food stores and spreading disease.*

### ◄ FOX FACTS
*The red fox is a common sight in many city centres. Outside the city centre, red foxes mainly eat rabbits and hares. Urban foxes raid rubbish bags for food scraps.*

### ⚠ CONSERVATION

It's a hard life living with people, and animals will either adapt to life in the city or die very quickly. Most deaths come from encounters with traffic, especially among nocturnal species. Other hazards include the bright lights, noise, and lack of space.

## WHAT'S GOING WRONG?

The greatest threat to animals comes from humans. People are destroying habitats to make room for their own activities. They are poisoning the land, seas, and air with toxic chemicals; they are even changing the climate. And, sometimes, the animals that survive all this are killed to meet human demand.

◀ LOGGING
*Clearance for timber and land development has destroyed vast areas of forest, with large-scale damage to the environment.*

◀ WARMING
*Gases released from burning fossil fuels trap heat in the atmosphere. This warming alters habitats in ways that affect animal survival.*

◀ POLLUTION
*The dumping of poisonous chemicals in the oceans is harming marine life and destroying habitats such as coral reefs.*

◀ SLAUGHTER
*Despite laws that ban trading in animal furs and body parts, the illegal killing of species such as the leopard is difficult to control.*

◀ CAPTURE
*Caught wild birds, such as these young African grey parrots, fetch high prices in the exotic bird trade. Many birds die in transit between countries.*

# Animals in DANGER

Every year, wonderful animals disappear from the Earth – for good. They vanish mostly because their natural habitat has been spoiled or destroyed. When an animal loses its special niche in the world, it will die if it cannot find anywhere else suitable to live.

**Melting ice** Climate warming is melting the Arctic sea ice. Polar bears spend most of the Arctic summer living on the ice, where they hunt seals and mate. Now their habitat is shrinking.

*Fewer polar bear cubs are surviving in the Arctic.*

# GLOBAL CLIMATE

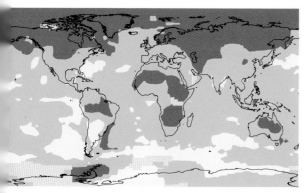

◄ WARMING UP
*Based on climate records for the last 50 years, this map shows the rise of surface temperatures worldwide. The pattern of warming is variable and at present the effects are most noticeable in the polar regions.*

| | |
|---|---|
| ■ 1°C (34°F) TO 3.4°C (38°F) INCREASE | ■ 1°C (34°F) TO 2°C (36°F) INCREASE |
| ■ 0°C (32°F) TO 1°C (34°F) INCREASE | ■ NO DATA |

**World weather** In the last century, the Earth has warmed up. As temperatures continue to rise, there will be permanent climate changes around the world. Summers will be hotter and drier. The type of plants growing in particular areas may die out. Sea levels will rise as the ice caps melt, and land may be flooded. Warming is already beginning to affect wildlife habitats both on land and in the oceans.

**Oil and gas** exploration in the Arctic pollutes the polar bears' habitat and splits up their hunting grounds. Another hazard is the release of toxic industrial chemicals, carried south by winds and currents. These poisons enter the Arctic food web and are seriously damaging the health not only of polar bears but of the native Inuit people.

## FACTFILE

- An estimated 6,000 m² (64,585 ft²) of rainforest are lost every second.
- The world's rarest land mammal is the Javan rhinoceros. Only about 50 of these rhinos still survive.
- One in 8 bird species, 1 in 4 mammal species, and 1 in 3 amphibian species are believed to be currently at risk of extinction.

# WHAT'S BEING DONE?

Around the world, national parks and wildlife reserves help animals by protecting their natural habitats. Breeding rare animals in captivity and releasing them into the wild has also had some success. Animals are further protected by international laws, such as those that place limits on hunting and make it illegal to trade in rare species.

▶ BREEDING
*The golden lion tamarin is one of the world's rarest monkeys. Zoo-bred tamarins successfully released into the wild have helped to boost numbers.*

▶ PLANNING
*American bison, once counted in millions, were hunted almost to extinction. Under a protection plan, small herds are now thriving.*

▶ RELOCATION
*New Zealand's rare flightless parrot, the kakapo, has been moved to a safer location. This may save the species from being wiped out by predators.*

▶ HEALTHCARE
*To protect the last few hundred Ethiopian wolves, domestic dogs in nearby areas are vaccinated to prevent the spread of canine diseases.*

▶ LUCK
*The endangered American crocodile found safe refuge when it moved into the water channels built to supply a nuclear power plant.*

# MAMMALS

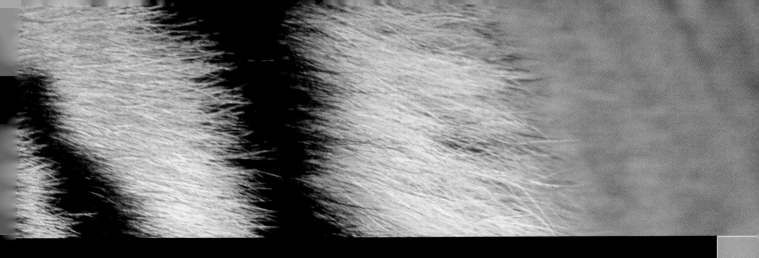

*Definition:* **Mammals** are warm-blooded creatures like you and me. They drink milk from their mother when they're first born, and most grow hair and give birth to live young.

# What is a MAMMAL?

Mammals are vertebrates that feed their young from the female's mammary glands – these glands give the class its name. Mammals also maintain a constant internal body temperature.

## BORN ALIVE

Most mammals give birth to live young – only a few lay eggs. The young of most placental mammals are born fully developed. Newborn marsupials (such as kangaroos) develop further in their mother's pouch.

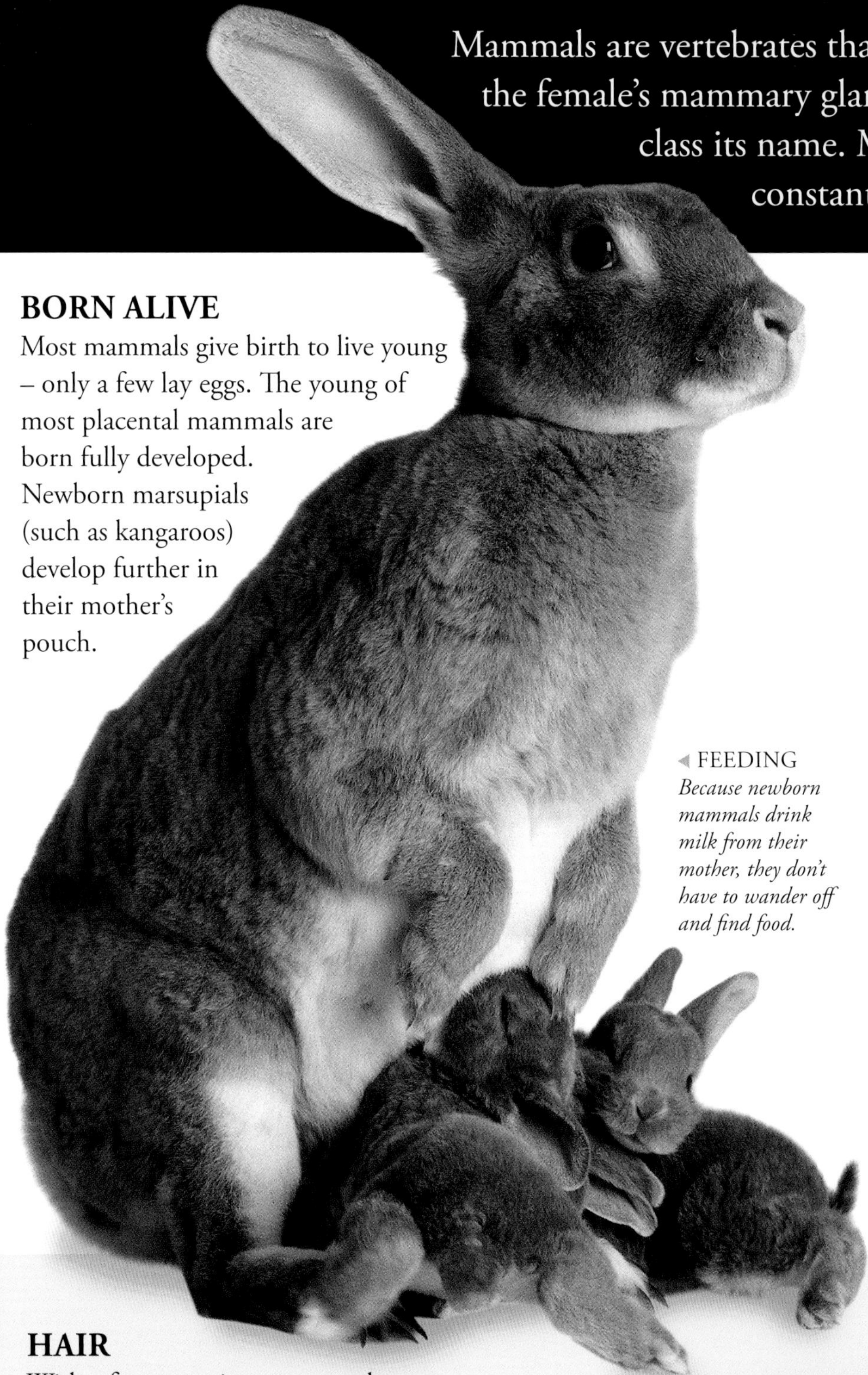

◀ FEEDING
*Because newborn mammals drink milk from their mother, they don't have to wander off and find food.*

### FACTFILE

There are about 4,800 species of mammals, which are grouped into different families and orders including:

- **Marsupials**, which give birth to embryos early in their development. The tiny creatures crawl up to the mother's pouch, and continue growing there.
- **Insectivores**, small mammals that eat insects, spiders, and worms.
- **Bats**, the only mammals that have true wings and are able to fly.
- **Rodents**, small mammals with four legs, a long tail, clawed feet, long whiskers, and teeth. There are more species of rodent than any other mammal.
- **Cetaceans,** such as whales, dolphins, and porpoises. These are aquatic mammals that breathe through lungs.
- **Carnivores**, animals with long, sharp canine teeth. Most carnivores are meat-eaters, but some plant-eaters, such as pandas, are also carnivores.
- **Hoofed mammals**, which are known for their speed and strength. Hoofed mammals have long muzzles, grinding teeth, and barrel-shaped bodies.

## HAIR

With a few exceptions, mammals have a covering of hair or fur on their body. (Whales and dolphins have no fur.) This helps to keep them warm. In cold conditions, each hair will be pulled upright by a tiny erector muscle, trapping a layer of warming air.

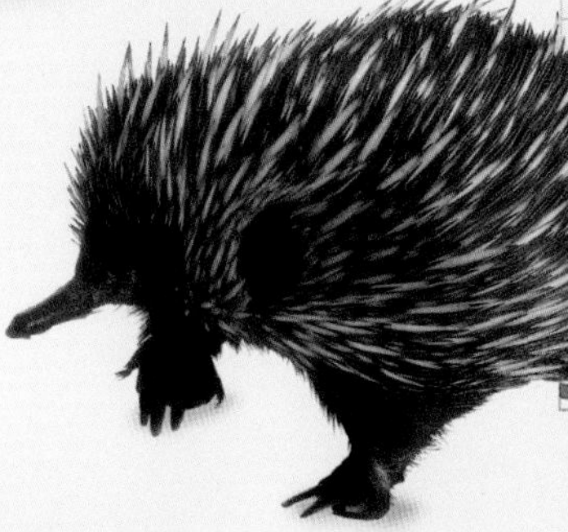

▶ SPINY BEAST
*The short-nosed echidna is a rare, egg-laying mammal. It has both spines and fur.*

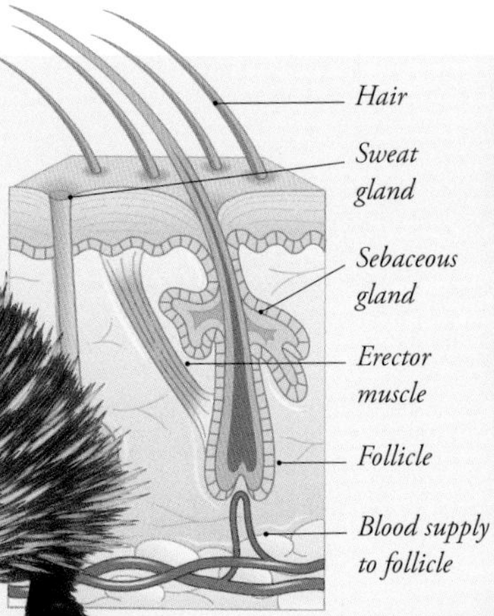
Hair
Sweat gland
Sebaceous gland
Erector muscle
Follicle
Blood supply to follicle

# BONE STRUCTURE

Mammal sketetons differ from those of other vertebrates in that the jaw is hinged directly to the skull. Also, the lower jaw consists of a single bone. Together, these factors make the jaw extremely efficient at cutting and then chewing food.

*Skull*

*Rib cage*

*Jaw*

*Humerus*

*Radius*

*Carpal*

*Spine*

*Hip bone*

**Hare skeleton** Like most mammals, hares have a backbone that curves up to help resist the downward pull of their body weight. The vertebrae are bigger towards the bottom, or lumbar, end of the spine, where there is most stress.

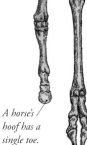

MONKEY SKULL
*Like human jaws, monkeys' jaws are designed to chew rather than tear, since monkeys gather food with their hands.*

ELEPHANT SKULL
*To grind tough plant fibre, elephants' jaws can move from side to side as well as up and down.*

TIGER SKULL
*A tiger's jaws anchor huge, sharp teeth for tearing chunks of meat.*

▲ JAW ADAPTATIONS
*Mammal jaws, like those of all animals, are shaped and constructed to suit the food they eat. Long, thin jaws, for example, are good for probing and nibbling, while short, broad jaws are ideal for grinding plants or cracking bones.*

*An elephant's foot bones are surrounded by a thick pad to spread the animal's weight.*

*A seal's foot has long "fingers".*

*A horse's hoof has a single toe.*

*A gazelle's hoof is divided into two toes.*

*A badger has wide claws for digging.*

### Feet and toes
Mammals' feet are individually adapted to suit their lifestyle and habitat. Some have hooves with one or more "toes", while some have footpads, with or without claws, and others have flippers.

| | Arm bones |
| | Wrist bones |
| | Palm bones |
| | Finger bones |

**Amazing variety**
Mammals, which originally developed from prehistoric reptiles, come in all shapes and sizes. They live mostly on land, but they can live in water, too. Some mammals are widely familiar, but other, rarer, species are not as well known.

▲ SLOTHS *live in the rainforest trees of South America. They move slowly, and come down only occasionally to leave droppings.*

▲ ARMADILLOS *are native to South and Central America. They have bony bands around their middle and skin like leather.*

▲ THE DUCK-BILLED PLATYPUS *has a furry body, but it lives in water and walks like a reptile. It lays eggs, but its young feed on their mother's milk.*

▶ BOWHEAD WHALES *have no teeth; they feed on the plankton in sea water. Vast quantities of this water are filtered through a tough fringe called baleen, which dangles inside the whale's mouth.*

# Marsupials

All marsupials give birth to live young, but these are poorly developed. Most complete their development in a pouch containing teats, from which they drink milk. There are about 250 species of marsupial. Most live in Australia and New Guinea. Some live in the Americas.

## LIFE IN A POUCH

When a marsupial is born it makes its way to its mother's pouch where it attaches itself to a teat. It remains firmly attached until it is fully formed and can explore the outside world. Some pouches face up, as in kangaroos, and some face down, as in koalas. Some pouches can hold several babies, but others are a simple flap and the young have to cling tight to their mother's fur.

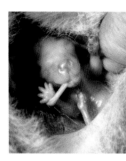

◄ PARMA WALLABY (Macropus parma) *The tiny new-born wallaby, called a joey, develops in its mother's pouch. It can leave the pouch after about 30 weeks, but is not independent until it is about 40 weeks old.*

## Eastern grey kangaroo
*Macropus giganteus*

**19**

- **Length** 1.5–1.8 m (5–6 ft)
- **Weight** 32–60 kg (70–132 lb)
- **Speed** 55 kph (34 mph)
- **Location** Eastern Australia, Tasmania

The eastern grey kangaroo is a steely grey colour with white underparts, legs, and underside of the tail. Its tail is strong and is **used for balance** while jumping and leaping, and as a prop while standing upright. Females are much smaller than males.

# Red kangaroo
*Macropus rufus*

**Length** 1.6 m (5 ft)
**Weight** 90 kg (200 lb)
**Speed** 50 kph (30 mph)
**Location** Australia

The red kangaroo is the **largest marsupial**. Males are orange-red in colour while the smaller females are blue-grey. Like grey kangaroos, the red kangaroo **bounds along** on its hind legs. It eats grass shoots, herbs, and leaves.

# Doria's tree kangaroo
*Dendrolagus dorianus*

■ **Length** 78 cm (31 in)
■ **Weight** 14.5 kg (32 lb)
■ **Location** New Guinea

Tree kangaroos have **short, broad feet** with long claws, which are useful for gripping as they climb through the trees. They use their long tails to help them **balance on the branches**. Doria's tree kangaroo has dense brown fur, black ears, and a pale brown or cream tail.

# Koala
*Phascolarctos cinereus*

■ **Length** 82 cm (32 in)
■ **Weight** 15 kg (33 lb)
■ **Location** Eastern Australia

Although it is often called a koala bear, the koala is not at all related to the bear. It lives in **eucalyptus trees** and its only food is eucalyptus leaves. It feeds at night and spends all day asleep in a tree. Female koalas have one baby at a time. This spends more than six months in its mother's pouch then climbs out and **rides on her back**.

# Northern quoll
*Dasyurus hallucatus*

■ **Length** 30 cm (12 in)
■ **Weight** 900 g (2 lb)
■ **Location** Australia

Quolls are **carnivorous** marsupials and have many sharp teeth for killing their prey. Northern quolls eat mainly insects, worms, small mammals, and reptiles, but they also like a bit of **honey** and fruit. They are active mostly at night, preferring to sleep during the heat of the day.

---

## MONOTREME FACTFILE

**Monotremes** are the only egg-laying mammals. There are three living species: one platypus and two echidnas. They have a beak-like mouth and the females produce milk in mammary glands over the skin.

■ **Duck-billed platypus** (*Ornithorhynchus anatinus*) live in bank-side burrows in lakes and rivers in Australia. They have a duck-like beak covered with sensitive skin, which they use to find crustaceans and insect larvae on the river bed.

Duck-billed platypus skull

■ **Echidnas** have fur and spines and a long, cylindrical beak. The long-beaked echidna (*Zaglossus bruijni*) lives only in New Guinea. The short-beaked echidna (*Tachyglossus aculeatus*) lives in Australia. They eat ants and termites, which they collect with a long sticky tongue.

Long-nosed echidna skull

### Duck-billed platypus
*Ornithorhynchus anatinus*

■ **Length** 60 cm (24 in)   ■ **Weight** 2.5 kg (5½ lb)
■ **Location** Eastern Australia and Tasmania

The platypus is well equipped for an **aquatic life**. It has waterproof fur to keep it dry, and dense underfur to keep it warm. It also has webbed feet, which it uses like flippers to propel itself through the water.

## WHY DO THEY GLIDE?

Gliding is a useful method of escaping from predators as well as a quick way to get from tree to tree to find better food. Not many mammals can glide. They include the sugar glider, shown on the right, and the flying lemurs.

**Flying lemurs**, or colugos, are the world's largest gliding mammals – they are about the size of a domestic cat. Their name is a bit misleading, as they are not actually lemurs and they glide instead of fly! There are two species and they both live in the forests of Southeast Asia. They feed on leaves, flowers, and fruit.

**Sunda flying lemur**
*Galeopterus variegates*

### Southern flying squirrel
*Glaucomys volans*

*The southern flying squirrel lives in hollow trees, deserted woodpecker holes, and even in bird boxes. It builds a nest out of soft materials such as moss and fur.*

**Southern flying squirrels** live in North and Central America. They look very like the sugar glider but they are rodents. Flying squirrels eat lots of different kinds of food including nuts, seeds, fruit, fungi, insects, young birds, and mice. Like other squirrels, they collect and store food for the winter.

# Flying *mammals*

A few mammals can glide through the trees, but they do not actually fly (like birds and bats). They have a membrane of skin on either side of their body, attached between their fore and hindlimbs. This skin acts like a sail, allowing the animals to glide down through the air.

## Sugar glider
*Petaurus breviceps*

- **Length** 30 cm (12 in)
- **Tail** 44 cm (17½ in)
- **Weight** 150 g (5 oz)
- **Diet** Eucalyptus leaves, pollen, nectar, insects
  - **Location** Australia, New Guinea, Indonesia

This animal is a possum and therefore a marsupial, and the female has a pouch. One or two young are born and will remain in the pouch for the first **70 days of life**, before venturing out to explore their world.

PLANNING A PERFECT FLIGHT
*A sugar glider is able to make "flights" through the trees of more than 50 m (165 ft)! Its long, flat, furry tail is used just like a rudder, to guide it through the air.*

## Look out! I'm **coming** down.

The piece of skin that a glider uses to float through the air is called a patagium. When the animal is gliding, this is stretched taut. When the animal is walking, running, or sitting, the patagium is loose and folded out of the way.

MAMMALS

# Insect *eaters*

Many different animals eat insects. Six related families, including moles, hedgehogs, and shrews, are called insectivores because they eat mainly insects. Aardvarks and anteaters specialize in eating ants and termites. They both have long sticky tongues for sweeping up their prey and powerful claws for digging out the insects' nests.

◄ RUSSIAN DESMAN (Desmana moschata) *A member of the mole family, the desman uses its long, whiskered snout and strong sense of smell to investigate.*

► AARDVARK (Orycteropus afer) *The "earth pig" spends the day in burrows underground. It comes out at night to find ants and termites.*

## WELL-DEVELOPED NOSES

Most insectivores, such as desmans, have poor eyesight but a good sense of smell, with snouts ideal for sniffing out insects. Aardvarks also have a good sense of smell. They have a pig-like snout and nostrils surrounded with hair to filter out dust.

### Out of the way. I'm **coming out!**

The aardvark has large upright ears. When it is underground, it folds its ears out of the way. It surfaces at night, and always comes out of its burrow head first.

---

### FACTFILE

MOLES

■ **Moles** live in most parts of the world except Australia and New Zealand. They live in underground tunnels that they dig with their powerful front legs. They have an acute sense of smell.

HEDGEHOGS

■ **Hedgehogs** live only in Europe, Africa, and Asia. They live in many different habitats. Hedgehogs have spines and curl up into prickly balls when danger threatens. They have good hearing.

SHREWS

■ **Shrews** live across most parts of the world except Australia and New Zealand and parts of South America. Most have tiny eyes and ears and a long, pointed snout. They have poor vision but good hearing.

◄ ANTEATER *The giant anteater* (Myrmecophaga tridactyla) *is related to sloths and armadillos. It rips open ant and termite nests with its large claws and collects the ants with its long tongue. It eats up to 30,000 ants in a single day.*

## Long-eared hedgehog
*Hemiechinus auritus aegyptius*

- **Length** 27 cm (10½ in)
- **Weight** 280 g (10 oz)
- **Location** Asia and northern Africa

This hedgehog is found in **dry areas** such as deserts. It is nocturnal and burrows under small bushes during the day, or rests under rocks or in hollows in the ground. It feeds mainly on small invertebrates and insects, which it finds using its **acute senses** of hearing and smell.

## Eurasian water shrew
*Neomys fodiens*

- **Length** 9.5 cm (3¾ in)
- **Weight** 14 g (½ oz)
- **Location** Europe, northern Asia

This shrew has water-repellent fur so it can keep dry. Its tail has a row of bristles, which may help with swimming. The shrew hunts for food under water, killing insects, small fish, and frogs with a **poisonous bite**. It also feeds on land, where it preys on worms, beetles, and grubs.

## Streaked tenrec
*Hemicentetes semispinosus*

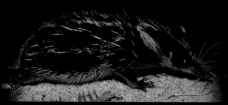

- **Length** 15 cm (6 in)
- **Weight** 280 g (10 oz)
- **Location** Madagascar

Tenrecs look a bit like a cross between a shrew and a hedgehog because they have **sharp spines** as well as fur. Their main diet consists of worms and grubs, which they find in grasses or under leaves on the rainforest floor.

## European mole
*Talpa europaea*

- **Length** 16 cm (6½ in)
- **Weight** 125 g (4½ oz)
- **Location** Europe, northern Asia

This mole has fur that can lie at any angle, which means it can go forwards and backwards in its **tunnels**. As it digs, it pushes up piles of soil as molehills. The mole eats worms and other soil animals that fall into the tunnels, often biting off the head and **storing them** for later.

## Russian desman
*Desmana moschata*

- **Length** 21 cm (8½ in)
- **Weight** 220 g (7¾ oz)
- **Location** Eastern Europe to central Asia

A desman has a **long tail** – as long as its head and body put together. The tail is flattened from side to side, and the desman uses it as a paddle and **a rudder** to move and steer through water.

## Giant anteater
*Myrmecophaga tridactyla*

- **Length** 120 cm (4 ft)
- **Weight** 39 kg (86 lb)
- **Location** Central and South America

The giant anteater is mainly grey with black and white markings. It has coarse, long fur and a very **bushy tail**. The anteater walks on the knuckles of its front feet so that its **long claws** are kept out of the way. It wanders around its home range like this looking for food and is active day and night.

*Furry epaulettes*

◄ IN FLIGHT *Bats* ... *like birds, by flappi... their wings up and dow... They are good fliers ar... can easily chase aft... flying insects and ... around obstacle...*

**Franquet's epauletted fruit bat**
*Epomops franqueti*

## Can you see my **epaulettes**?

Male epauletted bats have patches of different fur on their shoulders, which is how they got their name. (An epaulette is an ornament on the shoulder of a soldier's uniform.)

▼ SKELETON
*This bat's skeleton shows how its arms, legs, and long fingers provide a frame for the wings.*

# Bats

There are two groups of bats called megabats and microbats. Megabats eat fruit and are often called fruit bats. Most microbats eat insects. Bats usually go looking for food at night. During the day they find somewhere to sleep, or roost, hanging upside down and clinging on with their toes.

## BAT WINGS

Bats are the only mammals that can truly fly, not just glide. Their wings are formed from a double layer of skin stretched between the side of the body and the four long fingers on each hand. The Latin name for bats, *Chiroptera*, means "hand wings".

---

### FACTFILE

■ **Megabats** These bats use their eyes and noses to find their food. They have large eyes so they can see in the dark. Many megabats are found in tropical areas where there are lots of different fruits to eat. They often feed in groups and fly long distances in search of food.

■ **Microbats** Most microbats eat insects, but some prey on lizards, frogs, or fish. Vampire bats drink fresh blood from animals. Microbats have poor eyesight and find food using echolocation (see page 34). They live in both temperate and tropical areas.

▶ BIGGEST *The Malaysian flying fox (Pteropus vampyrus) has a wingspan of about 1.5 m (5 ft), bigger than any other bat.*

◄ SMALLEST *Kitti's hog-nosed bat (Craseonycteris thonglongyai) is the smallest bat in the world. It weighs about 2 g (1/16 oz) and is only 3 cm (1¼ in) long.*

**Size comparison**

Malaysian flying fox

Kitti's hog-nosed bat

# Straw-coloured fruit bat
*Eidolon helvum*

**21**

- **Length** 18 cm (7 in)
- **Weight** 280 g (10 oz)
- **Wingspan** 76 cm (30 in)
- **Location** Africa

This is one of the **larger species** of fruit bat. It roosts in large colonies of between 100,000 and 1,000,000 individuals. The bats go out at night in small groups to search for food. They **eat mainly fruit** but they do not eat the whole fruit. Instead they suck the juice and spit out the pulp.

◀ COLOUR
*The straw-coloured fruit bat gets its name from the colour of its neck and back. Its underside is brown or grey.*

# Comoro black flying fox
*Pteropus livingstonii*

**10**

- **Length** 30 cm (11¾ in)
- **Weight** 600 g (21 oz)
- **Wingspan** 1.5 m (5 ft)
- **Location** Comoros islands

Fruit bats are sometimes called **flying foxes**. The Comoro black flying fox is found only on two islands in the Comoros island chain, off the east coast of Africa. It is **critically endangered** and it is estimated that only about 400 individuals exist. They roost in small groups called harems and stick together in groups when they go out to look for food.

# Hammer-headed fruit bat
*Hypsignathus monstrosus*

**30**

- **Length** 20–30 cm (8–12 in)
- **Weight** 326 g (11½ oz)
- **Wingspan** 90 cm (35 in)
- **Location** Central Africa

This is the largest bat found in Africa. It roosts high in the trees in **tropical forests** to avoid enemies on the ground. It is sometimes known as the **big-lipped bat** because males have huge lips. They may use these to make their loud honking noises, which can be heard in the forest at night at certain times of the year. The noises attract females to come and hang beside the males on their branch.

# Franquet's epauletted fruit bat
*Epomops franqueti*

**7**

- **Length** 15 cm (6 in)
- **Weight** 100 g (3½ oz)
- **Wingspan** 60 cm (24 in)
- **Location** West and central Africa

Like the hammer-headed fruit bat, the male of this species makes high-pitched whistling calls at night to attract females. The bats' **favourite food** is figs, but they also eat guavas, bananas, and other tropical fruits.

# Jamaican fruit bat
*Artibeus jamaicensis*

**10**

- **Length** 9 cm (3½ in)
- **Weight** 46 g (1½ oz)
- **Wingspan** 45 cm (18 in)
- **Location** Mexico to Bolivia and Brazil

This fruit bat roosts in caves and buildings but also **makes "tents"** from leaves. It bites through the mid rib of a leaf so that it collapses to form a roof to sleep under. Unlike many other bats, this fruit bat feeds alone.

# Listening bats

Most of the bats in the world are microbats. They are smaller than megabats and live on every continent except the Arctic and the Antarctic. Sometimes known as insect-eating bats, they have good hearing that enables them to sense insects flying by. They also use it to avoid obstacles in the dark.

**Grey long-eared bat**
*Plecotus austriacus*

## SPECIAL FEATURES

Microbats hunt in the dark, finding insects using a technique called echolocation. Many of these bats have special features to help them. Some have long ears for hearing. Some have a growth on their nose, called a nose-leaf, which focuses sounds.

**Echolocation** To find insects in the dark, microbats make a series of clicks (shown here by red bars). The sound bounces off objects like an echo and the bat can pinpoint a moth's position by listening to the echoes. These get closer together as the bat approaches its prey.

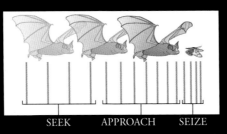

SEEK    APPROACH    SEIZE

## Grey long-eared bat
*Plecotus austriacus*

- **Length** 5 cm (2 in)
- **Weight** 14 g (½ oz)
- **Wingspan** 30 cm (12 in)
- **Location** Central and southern Europe, northern Africa, southwest Asia

These long-eared bats like to live **near human** settlements, where they can roost in buildings. When they come out to feed, they hunt for moths, flies, and beetles and use their long ears to **listen** for their prey.

## Common pipistrelle
*Pipistrellus pipistrellus*

- **Length** 3.5–4.5 cm (1½–2 in)
- **Weight** 5–8 g (¼–⅛ oz)
- **Wingspan** 19–25 cm (7½–10 in)
- **Location** Europe

These bats are found in a wide range of habitats, from **farms and forests to city buildings**, and are among the smallest and most widespread of all bats. They come out to **feed early** (sometimes before sunset) and hunt for moths, gnats, and other small insects – a single bat can eat up to 3,000 insects in one night. The young are born in early summer and leave the roost in August

## Townsend's big-eared bat
*Corynorhinus townsendii*

- **Length** 7 cm (2¾ in)
- **Weight** 20 g (⅗ oz)
- **Wingspan** 30 cm (12½ in)
- **Location** North America

As their name suggests, these bats have **enormous ears**, which reach to the middle of their body when they are laid flat. The bats go out hunting late in the evening and feed almost entirely on moths. Male Townsend's big-eared bats live on their own, but females form groups when they have their young. These groups, called **nurseries**, contain several hundred animals. They live together for protection.

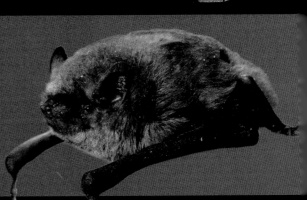

## Got it! This **moth** will do nicely for supper.

The grey long-eared bat has ears almost as long as its head and body put together. These are useful for picking up sounds for echolocation.

◀ FOLDED AWAY *When this long-eared bat hibernates, it folds its ears and tucks them under its wings.*



## Proboscis bat

*Rhynchonycteris naso*

- **Length** 5 cm (1⅗ in)
- **Weight** 5 g (⅕ oz)
- **Wingspan** 24 cm (9⅖ in)
- **Location** Central America

This species is named for its **long pointed nose.** (A "proboscis" is a long nose.) The bats like to roost head down against the trunks or branches of trees. They are well camouflaged here because their grey-brown speckled fur and small size makes them look a bit like lichen growing on the tree. Small groups of proboscis bats roost together, sometimes spaced out evenly in a vertical line down a tree trunk.

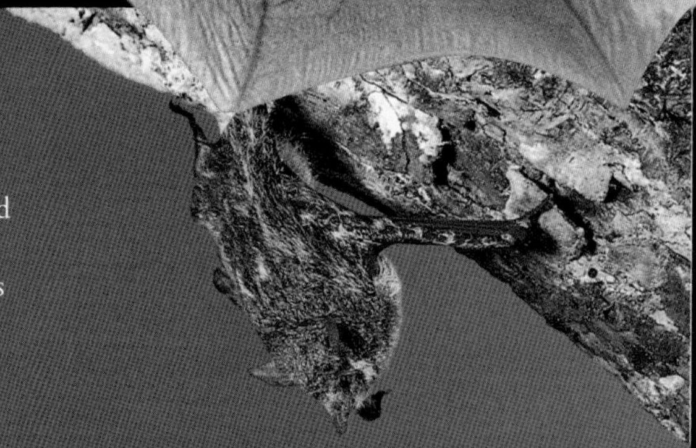

## Lesser horseshoe bat

*Rhinolophus hipposideros*

- **Length** 4 cm (1½ in)
- **Weight** 4–10 g (⅛–⅖ oz)
- **Wingspan** 23 cm (9 in)
- **Location** Europe, northern Africa to west Asia

There are many species of horseshoe bat and the lesser horseshoe bat is one of the **smallest**. Its body is smaller than a human thumb. Horseshoe bats have a **horseshoe-shaped nose leaf**, which is formed of bare, folded skin. During the day these bats roost in tree holes, chimneys, and caves. They come out at night to hunt for flying insects. In the winter they hibernate in groups of up to 500 animals.

## Vampire bat

*Desmodus rotundus*

- **Length** 9 cm (3½ in)
- **Weight** 50 g (1¾ oz)
- **Wingspan** 20 cm (8 in)
- **Location** Mexico to South America

The vampire bat is a strong flyer but can also **scuttle along the ground** using its wings as front legs. It is well known for its eating habits. It lands on the ground and moves towards its prey, such as a horse or a cow. It bites away any fur, cuts into the skin, then **licks up the fresh blood**. Its teeth are so sharp that they can cut into the skin easily and the victim hardly notices.

# Primates

Humans are primates, as are our closest relatives, the great apes and gibbons. The group also includes all types of monkey and many less familiar species, including the diverse lemurs of Madagascar and the nocturnal lorises, galagos, and pottos.

## PRIMATE FEATURES

All primates are good climbers and some spend almost their whole life in trees. They have strong arms and legs and long, grasping fingers and toes for hanging on to branches. Their forward-facing eyes allow them to judge distances accurately – a useful skill when leaping from branch to branch.

FAST LEARNERS *Youn... chimpanzees pick up skills ... watching adults, but also ... trial and error. It takes a l... of practice to fine-tune me... such as fishing for termites...*

### I'm ready to go **fishing!**

Chimpanzees eat many different kinds of food. Ants and termites make a good snack because they contain a lot of protein. To catch them, chimps use stripped twigs or plant stems, which they poke into holes in the termite nest or mound. Only the smartest animals have the ability to make and use tools in this way.

### FACTFILE

■ The aye-aye's long skinny fingers are perfect for picking insect grubs out of small crevices in tree bark.

■ The pads on a tarsier's fingers, toes, palms, and soles provide excellent grip on smooth trunks and branches.

■ Chimpanzees are as comfortable moving on the ground as in the trees. Their feet have large flat soles for walking on.

# ygmy mouse lemur

*acrocebus myoxinus*

**Length** 18–22 cm (7–8½ in)
**Weight** 24–38 g (¾–1¼ oz)
**Location** Madagascar only

his is the world's **smallest primate.** It lives forests and is active mainly at night, when scrambles nimbly through the trees, raging for fruit, insects, spiders, frogs, and her small animals. The long tail is used for lance when climbing. By day, mouse lemurs eep in a spherical nest of leaves, which they metimes share with several others.

# Hamadryas baboon

*Papio hamadryas*

- **Length** 60–75 cm (24–30 in)
- **Height (on four legs)** 70 cm (28 in)
- **Weight** 10–20 kg (22–44 lb)
- **Location** Eastern Africa including Egypt, Ethiopia, Sudan and Somalia, also in Arabia

Hamadryas baboons spend most of their time at ground level, eating grass and any other plant or animal food they can find. They live in **large groups** called troops. A troop can contain several smaller bands, each led by a large, experienced male. Members of the band show their loyalty by grooming one another's fur.

# Red howler monkey

*Alouatta seniculus*

- **Length** 60–90 cm (24–36 in)
- **Weight** 5–10 kg (11–22 lb)
- **Location** Northern and central South America

An acrobatic **tree-dwelling** monkey, which lives in groups and eats mainly fruit and leaves. Howlers are famous for having one of the **loudest calls** of any animal. They gather each morning for a deafening chorus that lets other groups know their position. Their throaty howls can be heard from an incredible 3–5 km (1¾–3 miles) away.

MAMMALS

---

## CONSERVATION

Many species of primate are endangered in the wild. Their habitat is disappearing and some species are illegally hunted for meat. Some young primates are taken from the forests to be sold as pets, and primates are still widely used for medical research.

# Bonobo

*Pan paniscus*

- **Height** 70–83 cm (28–32 in)
- **Weight** 30–60 kg (66–132 lb)
- **Location** Central Africa

These **highly intelligent and social** apes are told apart from chimpanzees by their dark skin and habit of often **walking upright**. Bonobos live in organized groups and are active mainly by day, when they forage for fruits, leaves and small animals. A large amount of time is spent in social activities such as grooming, cuddling, and mating.

◀ MACAQUE SOCIETY *Most primates live in social groups. Members of the group often groom each other to strengthen the bonds between them and to earn favours.*

# New World, Old World

Monkeys can be either New World monkeys or Old World monkeys. New World monkeys include spider monkeys, squirrel monkeys, and marmosets. Old World monkeys include baboons, macaques, and mandrills. They all live in forests and are good climbers.

## NOSES AND TAILS

New World monkeys have flat nose and their nostrils are directed outward. The nostrils of Old World monkeys are close together and directed downward. New World monkeys have a fully prehensile tail but Old World monkeys never do. Old World monkeys are more close related to apes than the New World monkeys.

◄ ACROBATS *Li all spider monkeys, the black spider monkey (Ateles chamek) can swing through the forest canopy incredibly quickly. It uses its long, prehensile tail as a "fifth limb".*

## Japanese macaque
*Macaca fuscata*

- **Length** 95 cm (37 in)
- **Tail** 10 cm (4 in)
- **Weight** 14 kg (31 lb)
- **Location** Japan

Japanese macaques **live in groups**, with females usually outnumbering males by about 3 to 1. Females stay in a group for life and daughters inherit their mother's rank, or position, in the pecking order.

▼ NORTHERN SOULS *Japanese macaques live further north than any other primate (not counting humans). They grow a thick coat to help them cope with the cold winters. Sometimes the monkeys bathe in hot springs to keep warm.*

### FACTFILE

- New World monkeys are found from Mexico down through Central America to Argentina.
- Old World monkeys can be found in most of Africa and southern and eastern Asia.

The numbers show where the featured monkeys are found.

# Chacma baboon

*...pio ursinus*

- **Length** 82 cm (32 in)
- **Tail** 84 cm (33 in)
- **Weight** 30 kg (66 lb)
- **Location** Southern Africa

This is the **largest baboon** and it spends most of its time on the ground. Males are twice as big as females and have two large canine teeth. The baboons eat a variety of food – fruit, nuts, grass, roots, insects, and other small animals. At night, they **sleep in a tree** or on a cliff, using one of several chosen spots in their territory.

# Mona monkey

*Cercopithecus mona*

- **Length** 63 cm (25 in)
- **Tail** 88 cm (34½ in)
- **Weight** 5.3 kg (12 lb)
- **Location** Western Africa

This small monkey spends its time in trees, where it feeds on fruit, leaves, shoots and insects. It has **pouches in its cheeks** where it can carry food while it is looking for more. It lives in groups of up to 30 animals, which contain one adult male and several females.

# Common marmoset

*Callithrix jacchus*

- **Length** 25 cm (10 in)
- **Tail** 35 cm (14 in)
- **Weight** 350 g (12 oz)
- **Location** Brazil

Common marmosets are unusual among primates because they have **claw-like nails** instead of true nails. They use these to help them cling vertically to tree trunks and run on all fours along branches. These marmosets **eat tree sap** as well as fruit and insects.

# Common squirrel monkey

*Saimiri sciureus*

- **Length** 32 cm (12½ in)
- **Tail** 42 cm (16½ in)
- **Weight** 950 g (34 oz)
- **Location** Western to central South America

Squirrel monkeys **form large troops**, sometimes containing more than 200 individuals. They eat a wide range of food including fruit, nuts, berries, leaves, seeds, flowers, insects, and small animals.

# Brown capuchin

*Cebus apella*

- **Length** 42 cm (17 in)
- **Tail** 49 cm (19 in)
- **Weight** 4.5 kg (10 lb)
- **Location** Northern, central and eastern South America

These intelligent monkeys eat mostly fruit, but they also eat nuts, eggs, insects, and other small animals. They are known to **use tools**, such as stones, to crack open hard nuts. Groups of up to 20 animals **leap and climb** through the trees, and the young often come down to the ground to play.

**MAMMALS**

# Golden lion tamarin

*Leontopithecus rosalia*

- **Length** 25 cm (10 in)
- **Tail** 37 cm (14½ in)
- **Weight** 800 g (28 oz)
- **Location** Eastern South America

These monkeys are **rare** because their habitat has almost vanished and many of them are captured and sold as pets. Tamarins live in small troops in which only one dominant pair breed. They look for food during the day, using their **long, thin fingers** to find grubs in crevices and tree bark. At night, they often sleep in a hole in a tree.

# Mandrill

*Mandrillus sphinx*

- **Length** 81 cm (32 in)
- **Tail** 9 cm (3½ in)
- **Weight** 37 kg (82 lb)
- **Location** Western central Africa

Mandrills are easily recognized by the **bright red and blue nose**. Males are much larger than females and are the largest monkeys in the world. These monkeys **live in mixed groups** containing one dominant male, and can form troops of up to 250 animals. They spend most of their time on the ground looking for fruits, seeds, eggs, and small mammals.

**MUM AND BABY** *A female gelada's main job is to care for her young. She carries, grooms, nurses, and protects her offspring until they are independent enough to find their own food, usually when they are around 12 to 18 months old.*

# The *unique* gelada

The gelada's ancestors roamed over the whole of Africa, but the modern-day gelada is found only in the grassy highlands of Ethiopia and is the only grass-eating primate. Geladas nibble away at blades of grass, as well as stems, seeds, and roots. All this munching can take up a lot of time: these monkeys spend up to 60 per cent of their day eating – longer than any other monkey.

# Gelada
*Theropithecus gelada*

19

- **Length** 70–74 cm (28–29 in)
- **Tail** 70–80 cm (28–31 in)
- **Weight** 20 kg (44 lb)
- **Location** Ethiopia, Africa

The gelada is a close cousin of the baboon and is sometimes known as a gelada baboon. **Both males and females have a triangular shaped patch of bright pink skin** on their chest, outlined with white hairs. This is why this species of monkey is sometimes called the pink-chested gelada. The male has a thick mane that hangs halfway down his back and a very long tail with a dense tuft of hairs at the tip.

MAMMALS

## COMING TO BLOWS

Gelada males rarely fight, but when they do they can be quite vicious, tearing at each other's flesh with their long, pointed canine teeth. Fortunately, most conflicts are resolved long before this happens. Angry stares and slapping the ground to warn off an aggressor are usually all it takes to restore peace.

**Safety in numbers** Geladas are not very territorial, so separate families often graze together. Troops of up to 400 individuals are common. Each family in the troop is made up of an adult male, his "harem" of three to five females and their young. Grooming each other helps the adults to bond, but it is the close friendships of the females that hold the family together.

## My baby likes to ride **on my back**.

From about three months old, young geladas ride on their mother's back just like a jockey rides a horse. Females usually have one baby at a time and only four or five in a lifetime. But they spend a lot of time and energy looking after them.

# Apes

An ape is not a monkey! Apes do not have a tail, but most monkeys do. Apes are able to swing from branches from their hands and feet, but monkeys cannot. There are two families of apes – the lesser apes (gibbons) and the great apes (orang-utans, gorillas, and chimpanzees).

## LIVING IN THE TREES

Apes are found mainly in tropical forests and are largely vegetarian. Like most primates, they are good climbers and their long arms and grasping hands are ideal for swinging through the trees. All great apes are on the endangered list of species because their forest homes are being cut down.

### We can **stay** up here all day.

Orang-utans spend most of their time in the trees. They have longer arms and more flexible joints than other great apes, so they can swing through the branches with ease.

## FACTFILE

■ **Great apes** There are five species of great ape. They are the orang-utan, two species of gorilla, the chimpanzee, and the bonobo, or pygmy chimpanzee. They are known for their intelligence and the ability to hold things in their hands.

■ **Lesser apes** There are 14 species of lesser ape, or gibbon. They have long arms and use their hands like hooks to swing from branch to branch. This way of moving is called brachiation. The apes can travel through the trees at about 15 kph (9 mph).

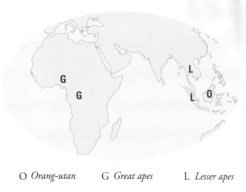

O *Orang-utan*    G *Great apes*    L *Lesser apes*

■ **Distribution** The orang-utan lives in forests only on the islands of Sumatra and Borneo in Indonesia and Malaysia. Other great apes live in forests in western and central Africa. Lesser apes live in southern and Southeast Asia.

▲ INFANT APE *Female orang-utans give birth in a treetop. The young ape clings to its mother as she clambers around and stays with her until it is about eight years old.*

▶ GRASPING HANDS *All apes can move their thumbs around to touch their fingers, like humans. They are called opposable thumbs. This means they can pick up and hold things.*

# Western gorilla
*Gorilla gorilla*

- **Height** 1.8 m (6¼ ft)
- **Weight** 180 kg (397 lb)
- **Location** Central Africa

Gorillas are the **largest** great ape. They may look fierce, but they are shy and peaceful unless threatened. Males are more agressive than females and show off their strength by standing up and **beating their chests** with their fists. Gorillas walk on all fours with their hands curled over so that their knuckles touch the ground. The animals live in small groups in forests, where they eat mainly plant stems, leaves, and berries.

# Bornean orang-utan
*Pongo pygmaeus*

- **Height** 1.4 m (4½ ft)
- **Weight** 80 kg (175 lb)
- **Location** Borneo, Malaysia

The orang-utan's **bright red** fur makes it easy to recognize. The name orang-utan is a Malay word meaning "**man of the forest**", and this great ape spends most of its time on its own in the treetops. During the day, it looks for food, such as fruits, leaves, and honey, or sometimes small lizards and baby birds. At night, it sleeps on a platform, which it makes by weaving branches together.

MAMMALS

# Siamang gibbon
*Symphalangus syndactylus*

- **Height** 90 cm (35 in)
- **Weight** 15 kg (33 lb)
- **Location** Southeast Asia

The siamang is the largest gibbon and it has an amazingly **loud voice**. Males and females sometimes "sing" together. The female's voice is like a bark but the male's voice is more like a **scream**. Their duet can be heard more than 1 km (0.6 miles) away.

# White-handed gibbon
*Hylobates lar*

- **Height** 65 cm (25 in)
- **Weight** 5.5 kg (12 lb)
- **Location** South and southeast Asia

This gibbon hardly ever comes down to the forest floor. It stays up in the trees, moving through its territory in the forest by **swinging** from branch to branch. A male and female usually **stay together** for their whole lives. They live with their young, which leave the family to find partners when they are ready.

# Chimpanzee
*Pan troglodytes*

- **Height** 1 m (3 ft)
- **Weight** 60 kg (130 lb)
- **Location** West to central Africa

The chimpanzee is one of the **most intelligent** of all animals. It is one of very few animals to use **tools**, using stones to crack nuts and sticks to get ants and termites out of their nests. It does this by stripping off the bark with its teeth, then poking the stick into the ants' nests to make them swarm out. Then it eats them. Chimps live in close-knit groups of up to 120 animals, and a young chimp will stay and travel with its mother for up to 10 years.

# Crested gibbon
*Nomascus concolor*

- **Height** 64 cm (25 in)
- **Weight** 9 kg (20 lb)
- **Location** Southeast Asia

Young crested gibbons are born with yellow fur, but they gradually **change colour** as they grow older. Males become black with white cheeks, while females turn brown or grey. Crested gibbons live in **family groups**, but they may join other families to feed at a good spot. They eat buds, young leaves, and fruit. The fruit must be ripe and juicy!

43

# Prosimian *primates*

What is a prosimian? The word means "before monkeys", and this group of animals are the most primitive of all primates. Like monkeys and apes, they are adapted for life in trees, with grasping hands and feet. They include lemurs, bushbabies, and lorises.

MAMMALS

## I like to dance **and leap.**

Verreaux's sifaka (*Propithecus verreauxi*) is a species of lemur that spends lots of time on the ground as well as in trees. It takes great strides and springs through the air at speed as if it were dancing. Babies have to hold on tight!

▲ LONG FINGER *The aye-aye* (Daubentonia madagascariensis) *lives in Madagascar. It taps on trees with its long middle finger then listens for insects moving under the bark. If anything is there, it rips off the bark with its teeth and hooks out the victims with its finger.*

HITCHING A RIDE *When they are old enough, young Verreaux's sifakas ride piggy-back style on their mother's back. Younger infants cling to their mother's belly where they are safer.*

### FACTFILE

■ **Lemurs,** such as this black lemur (*Eulemur macaco*), live in Madagascar and the Comoro Islands. Most are larger than other prosimians, with long limbs and long snouts.

■ **Bushbabies** (or galagos), such as this lesser bushbaby (*Galago senegalensis*), live south of the Sahara in Africa and on nearby islands. They have a bushy tail and a child-like cry.

■ **Lorises,** such as this slender loris (*Loris tardigradus*), are found in southeastern and southern Asia. The related pottos live in central and western Africa. They move hand-over-hand, always gripping a branch, never leaping.

## hick-tailed bushbaby
*olemur crassicaudatus*

| | **15** | ⚠ | |

- **Length** 40 cm (16 in)
- **Tail** 49 cm (19 in)
- **Weight** 2 kg (4½ lb)
- **Location** Central, eastern, and southern Africa

his is the **largest bushbaby**. It is nocturnal nd has huge ears and eyes to help it find nsects in the dark. It catches its prey by hand n a split second. It also scrapes up gum nd sap with s teeth.

## Ring-tailed lemur
*Lemur catta*

| | **25** | ⚠ | |

- **Length** 46 cm (18 in)
- **Tail** 62 cm (24 in)
- **Weight** 3.5 kg (7¾ lb)
- **Location** Southern Madagascar

Unlike most lemurs, ring-tailed lemurs are **active during the day** and feed on the ground. They gather flowers, fruits, and leaves with their hands. They are **sociable** and form groups of up to 25 animals with the females in charge.

## Lesser bushbaby
*Galago senegalensis*

| | **10** | ⚠ | |

- **Length** 16 cm (6 in)
- **Tail** 23 cm (9 in)
- **Weight** 250 g (9 oz)
- **Location** Western Africa

With its large ears and eyes, and bushy tail, this animal is a perfect example of a bushbaby. It can leap as far as 5 m (16½ ft) using its **long back legs**. As well as having good senses of smell, hearing, and sight, the lesser bushbaby has a **good sense of touch**. It can even catch flying insects in its hands!

MAMMALS

## Angwantibo
*Arctocebus calabarensis*

| | **13** | ⚠ | |

- **Length** 30 cm (12 in)
- **Tail** 1 cm (½ in)
- **Weight** 475 g (17 oz)
- **Location** Western Africa

The angwantibo is nocturnal and largely solitary. It has **unusual hands** with two long fingers and two shorter fingers (one is hardly more than a fleshy pad). It is a **good climber**, moving slowly through the trees looking for insects to eat, and picking them off twigs and leaves with its hands. It also eats fruit.

## White-footed sportive lemur
*Lepilemur leucopus*

| | **7** | ⚠ | |

- **Length** 30 cm (12 in)
- **Tail** 25 cm (10 in)
- **Weight** 600 g (21 oz)
- **Location** Southern Madagascar

This species of lemur **eats mostly leaves**. It moves through the forest by leaping between tree trunks rather than from branch to branch, and has large pads on its fingers and toes to help it cling on tight. A female and her young form small groups, while **males live alone**. The males have a territory where one or two females live, and they defend it fiercely.

LIFE IN TREES
*The white-footed sportive lemur spends most of its time in trees and looks for food at night.*

# Rodents

Rodents are found worldwide, except Antarctica, and can be divided into three groups – squirrel-like rodents, cavy-like rodents, and mouse-like rodents. They get their name from the Latin word *rodere*, which means "to gnaw". All rodents gnaw food and other things with their long front teeth.

▲ BABIES *The world's largest rodent, the capybara, usually has one litter a year, with five young. Most smaller rodents have more offspring. A house mouse can have up to 120 babies a year (in separate litters!).*

## FACTFILE

■ **Squirrel-like rodents** have long whiskers and a furry tail. There are a variety of squirrel-like species with different lifestyles, living in lots of different habitats worldwide.

■ **Cavy-like rodents** are found in Africa, the Americas, and Asia. Most species have a large head, sturdy body, short tail, and slender legs. The cavy is the ancestor of the guinea pig.

■ **Mouse-like rodents** have a pointed face and long whiskers. Most species are small and nocturnal. They are found worldwide.

HUGE INCISORS  *All rodents have four large front teeth called incisors, which never stop growing and always stay sharp. This is the skull of a paca (*Agouti paca*), a cavy-like rodent from South America.*

## GOOD SENSES

Most rodents have excellent senses of smell and hearing. They also have sensitive whiskers. They use their senses to find their way around, find food, and also to be alert to predators. Nocturnal species, such as the dormouse, have large eyes for seeing in the dark.

### I **need to** put on weight.

The dormouse hibernates from October through to April. Before it curls up in its nest, it eats enough almost to double its weight. It then has enough body fat to live on during the winter.

TREE DWELLER *The dormouse* (Muscardinus avellanarius) *lives in trees. It sleeps during the day in a nest made from grasses and strips of bark woven together. It comes out at night to feed, mainly on flowers, fruits, and nuts.*

# rown rat
*atus norvegicus*

- **Length** 28 cm (11 in)
- **Weight** 575 g (20 oz)
- **Location** Worldwide, except polar regions

his **intelligent** mammal eats almost
nything, and can survive
almost any habitat. It
ves in huge groups near
umans because food
easy to find there.
ild brown rats are
ot liked** by humans
ecause they spread
isease and eat
ood stores.

# Wood mouse
*Apodemus sylvaticus*

- **Length** 11 cm (4 in)
- **Weight** 30 g (1 oz)
- **Location** Western
Europe to western and
central Asia

The wood mouse is
a fast and agile mouse. It lives mainly in
woods and fields, but can be found in **most
habitats** that are not too wet. Its food changes
with the seasons – seeds in winter, buds in
spring, caterpillars and grubs in summer, and
fruit and fungi in autumn. Most wood
mice live in an **underground burrow**, which
gets passed on from generation to generation.

# Long-tailed chinchilla
*Chinchilla lanigera*

- **Length** 38 cm (15 in)
- **Weight** 800 g (28 oz)
- **Location** Southwest South America

The chinchilla is often kept as a **pet**, but
some wild chinchillas still live in the Andes
mountains. Chinchillas have **thick, soft
fur**, which keeps them warm
during the cold nights.
They are very active at
twilight and at night.

MAMMALS

# astern chipmunk
*amias striatus*

- **Length** 16.5 cm (6.5 in)
- **Weight** 125 g (4 oz)
- **Location** Southeastern Canada
central and eastern USA

his **bold**, inquisitive animal is a popular
isitor to picnic sites in the areas
where it lives, and is not afraid
f people. It normally
ats **seeds, berries,
nd nuts** but this
heeky creature also
ikes sandwiches!

# Mongolian gerbil
*Meriones unguiculatus*

- **Length** 12.5 cm (5 in)
- **Weight** 60 g (2 oz)
- **Location** Eastern Asia

Wild gerbils live in hot,
**dry places**
and eat mainly
seeds. They get most
of the water they
need from their
food. Like many other desert mammals,
gerbils have **furry feet** to keep them cool
on the hot ground. They have a burrow
underground where they shelter from the hot
sun, store food, and have their young.

# Cape porcupine
*Hystrix africaeaustralis*

- **Length** 80 cm (31 in)
- **Weight** 20 kg (44 lb)
- **Location** Central to sourthern Africa

The most noticeable thing about this rodent
is the **long spines** that grow in its fur. The
spines, called quills, cover the porcupine's back
and sides. Shorter ones
grow on its tail.
They come out
easily, and if a
predator gets
one stuck
in its nose,
it hurts!

# Southern viscacha
*Lagidium viscacia*

- **Length** 40 cm (16 in)
- **Weight** 3 kg (6½ lbs)
- **Location** Western South America

With its soft, **woolly coat** and
large ears, the viscacha looks a
bit like a rabbit, but it is related
to the chinchilla. It lives in
groups of about 50 animals
among rocks in the Andes
mountains. Males do **sentry-
duty** at the entrance to the
burrow and warn the others
if danger threatens.

# A *world* of rodents

Rodentia is the largest group of mammals, with more than 1,800 species. Because of their huge numbers, rodents are of great significance to humans. Several make good pets, others help to shape the environment, but others cause damage and spread disease.

**Common vole**
*Microtus arvalis*

**Northeast African spiny mouse**
*Acomys cahirinus*

**Naked mole rat**
*Heterocephalus glaber*

**Long-tailed field mouse**
*Apodemus sylvaticus*

**Malagasy giant rat**
*Hypogeomys antimena*

**House mouse**
*Mus musculus*

**Eastern grey squirrel**
*Sciurus carolinensis*

**Golden hamster**
*Mesocricetus auratus*

**Domestic guinea pig**
*Cavia porcellus*

**Flying squirrel**
*Glaucomys sabrinus*

**Brown rat**
*Rattus norvegicus*

**Bank vole**
*Myodes glareolus*

**Yellow-necked field mouse**
*Apodemus flavicollis*

**Black rat**
*Rattus rattus*

**Striped desert hamster**
*Phodopus sungorus*

**Mongolian gerbil**
*Meriones unguiculatus*

**Pale gerbil**
*Gerbillus perpallidus*

**Long-tailed chinchilla**
*Chinchilla lanigera*

**Eastern chipmunk**
*Tamias striatus*

The capybara is **up to 130 cm (4¼ ft)** in length. Roborovski's hamster (one of the smallest rodents) is only 4 cm (1½ in) long.

**BIGGEST RODENT**
Capybara
*Hydrochaeris hydrochaeris*

**Roborovski's desert hamster**
*Phodopus roborovskii*

# Beaver *engineers*

An American beaver can fell a tree by gnawing through the trunk! Once it has felled enough trees, branches are dragged to dam a stream. Why? The dam creates a lake, in the middle of which a beaver family build their home: a lodge. Underwater entrances provide protection from land predators. It's a fantastic piece of engineering.

## I've just got to **finish** this bit.

Beavers start to build a dam in the summer. Families work together to push branches into position, before covering them with mud and stones. The task must be done before winter, when they retreat into the dark protection of the lodge.

# American beaver
*Castor canadensis*

- **Length** 88 cm (35 in)
- **Weight** 26 kg (57 lb)
- **Location** Canada and USA

Beavers eat leaves, twigs, and bark. In the autumn, they fell small trees, cut them into logs, and store them near their lodge so they have a **supply of bark**. They live in family groups, with males and females pairing up for life.

▲ BUILT TO LAST *Beaver dams and lodges are strong and last for several years. In fact they are usually abandoned only because the beavers have exhausted local supplies of food. After a few years, a new family may move in and repair an old dam and lodge, giving it a new lease of life.*

▲ FEAT OF ENGINEERING *Beaver dams are about 3 m (10 ft) high. They can be more than 500 m (1,640 ft) long, depending on the size of the stream the beavers are trying to block. They alter the landscape in a big way.*

## BEAVER TEETH

Beavers have strong, upper incisors for gnawing wood. These teeth are orange. They are about 5 mm (⅕ in) wide and up to 25 mm (1 in) long. As with all rodents, these teeth never stop growing, so the beaver can go on cutting down trees as long as necessary.

FIT FOR LIFE *The beaver is well adapted for its water-based life. It has thick, waterproof fur, a large flat tail that can act as a propeller and a rudder, and large, webbed hindfeet.*

## My **body** is about as warm as yours.

Like all mammals, whales and dolphins are warm-blooded, which means their blood is kept at a certain temperature by their own body heat. In contrast, fish are cold-blooded.

# Whales and dolphins

Whales and dolphins look like big fish; most adults have no hair, and they have flippers instead of arms or legs, yet they are mammals. They breathe air with their lungs and suckle their young with milk. They even have belly-buttons!

◄ *Whales close their blowhole when under water. As they surface they release a spout of air – a blow – before taking another breath.*

**Bottlenose dolphin**
*Tursiops truncatus*

## BLOWHOLES

No whale, dolphin, or porpoise can breathe under water. They breathe air – but not through a nose and not through their mouth. They use a hole (or two holes) on the top of their heads called a "blowhole".

▶ *Whales and dolphins choose when they want to take a breath. This means they cannot go to sleep. Instead, they shut down half their brain at a time, resting one half, then the other.*

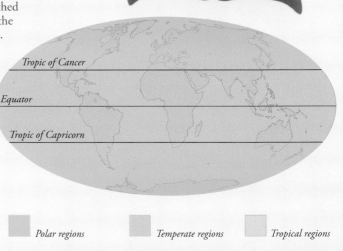

## FACTFILE

**Size comparison**

**Toothed whale**

**Baleen whale**

■ **Number of species:** 84, of which 71 are toothed whales and 13 are baleen whales. The largest is the blue whale; the smallest is the harbour porpoise.

■ **Toothed whales** include dolphins and porpoises, as well as the killer whale and the sperm whale. They have sharp teeth for catching slippery prey, such as fish or squid. Toothed whales have one blowhole.

■ **Baleen whales** filter feed by straining mouthfuls of water through fringed plates of flexible baleen that hang from the upper jaw. Baleen whales have two blowholes.

■ **Distribution** One type of whale lives in every ocean. Many species are wide-ranging, living in both tropical and temperate waters.

*Tropic of Cancer*

*Equator*

*Tropic of Capricorn*

■ *Polar regions*   ■ *Temperate regions*   ■ *Tropical regions*

# Blue whale
*Balaenoptera musculus*

- **Length** 20–30 m (66–98 ft)
- **Weight** 100,000–160,000 kg (220,500–352,730 lb)
- **Diet** Krill
- **Location** Worldwide (except Mediterranean, Baltic, Red Sea, Arabian Gulf)

The blue whale is Earth's **biggest animal**, and can weigh as much as 35 elephants. It can swallow thousands of krill (a shrimp-like animal) in one enormous gulp, and its song is the loudest noise made by any animal.

# Northern right whale
*Lissodelphis borealis*

- **Length** 13–17 m (43–56 ft)
- **Weight** 90,000 kg (198,400 lb)
- **Diet** Plankton
- **Location** Temperate and near-polar waters worldwide

One of the **most endangered** of all the big whales, this ocean cruiser feeds on plankton near the surface and doesn't tend to dive down. This can result in potentially fatal collisions with ships.

# Gray whale
*Eschrichtius robustus*

- **Length** 13–15 m (43–49 ft)
- **Weight** 14,000–35,000 kg (30,000–77.000 lb)
- **Diet** Marine invertebrates
- **Location** North Pacific (temperate and tropical)

The gray whale has an unusual feeding habit (in addition to filter feeding). It scoops up huge mouthfuls of mud and filters out seastars, crabs, and worms to eat. It **travels the furthest** of any mammal – migrating from the Arctic to Mexico in winter.

# Common dolphin
*Delphinus delphis*

- **Length** 2.3–2.6 m (7½–8½ ft)
- **Weight** 80 kg (175 lb)
- **Diet** Fish and squid
- **Location** Temperate and tropical waters worldwide

Common dolphins are both **social** and chatty. Their whistles and squeaks as they leap, tumble, and ride the waves can be heard from nearby boats. They travel in big groups, sometimes with thousands of members.

# Bottlenose dolphin
*Tursiops truncatus*

- **Length** 1.9–4 m (6¼–13 ft)
- **Weight** 500 kg (1,100 lb)
- **Diet** Fish, molluscs, and crustaceans
- **Location** Worldwide (except polar regions)

The bottlenose is **found everywhere** except the chilly waters around the poles. It can leap high out of the water – up to 5 metres (16 feet) – landing with a spectacular splash. It eats a wide variety of foods, from soft squid to crunchy crabs.

# Amazon river dolphin
*Inia geoffrensis*

- **Length** 2–2.6 m (6½–8½ ft)
- **Weight** 100–160 kg (220–350 lb)
- **Diet** Fish, crabs, river turtles
- **Location** South America (Amazon and Orinoco basins)

This slow-moving, **small-eyed** river dolphin uses its long beak to poke around the river bed for fish and crabs that may be hiding in the mud. It makes short dives lasting just one or two minutes. They usually live alone or in pairs.

# Narwhal
*Monodon monoceros*

- **Length** 4–4.5 m (13–15 ft)
- **Weight** 800–1,600 kg (1,750 –3,500 lb)
- **Diet** Fish, molluscs, and crustaceans
- **Location** Arctic Ocean

The narwhal **lives further north** than any other mammal, among ice-floes in Arctic waters. Only the male grows a long tusk, which it uses like a sword to fence with rival males. Their powerful lips and tongues are used to "suck" prey into their mouths.

# Dall's porpoise
*Phocoenoides dalli*

- **Length** 2.2–2.4 m (7¼–7¾ ft)
- **Weight** 170–200 kg (380–440 lb)
- **Diet** Fish and squid
- **Location** North Pacific (temperate and tropical)

A friendly and curious porpoise, Dall's porpoise is known to surface close to boats and playfully "bow ride" at high speeds. And they can really move! They zip along at 55 kph (34 mph) making them the **fastest** of all the whales, dolphins, and porpoises.

# Killer whale
*Orcinus orca*

- **Length** Up to 9 m (30 ft)
- **Weight** Up to 10,000 kg (22,000 lb)
- **Diet** Varied, but can include fish, marine mammals, turtles, and birds
- **Location** Worldwide

These intelligent and sociable whales are **built for hunting**. They are stocky, powerful, fast, and have an awesome set of teeth. They eat a wide assortment of prey, including other whales.

## Hector's beaked whale

*Mesoplodon hectori*

- **Length** 4 m (13 ft)
- **Weight** 1,000 kg (2,200 lb)
- **Location** Temperate waters in the southern hemisphere, North Pacific Ocean

This is **one of the smallest** of the beaked whales and has a relatively short beak. This species lives in deep waters and is **rarely seen**. It feeds on deep-water squid and fish, which it catches by sucking them in with sea water.

## Bowhead whale

*Balaena mysticetus*

- **Length** 19.8 m (65 ft)
- **Weight** 100,000 kg (220,460 lb)
- **Location** Arctic and sub-Arctic

The bowhead whale gets its name from its strongly curved, or "bowed", upper jaws. Its **huge head** accounts for about one-third of its total weight and it has the longest baleen of any whale. The plates can reach 4.6 m (15 ft) long. This whale has a layer of blubber under its skin, which can be 25–50 cm (10–20 in) thick. This keeps it warm in the **icy cold** waters of the Arctic Ocean.

## Sperm whale

*Physeter macrocephalus*

- **Length** 20 m (66 ft)
- **Weight** 57,000 kg (125,600 lb)
- **Location** Worldwide

This is the largest toothed whale and the world's **largest carnivore**. Bulls, or males, are twice as big as the cows, or females. Cows form mixed groups with their young. Young bulls often form groups, but become **more solitary** as adults.

## We have been **hunted** by humans for our **oil**.

Sperm whales have waxy oil in their head. This helps them to control their buoyancy and may focus sound when they are using echolocation. The sperm whale has been hunted by humans for its oil and other body parts and it is a threatened species.

## DEEP DIVERS

The sperm whale can stay under water for nearly two hours. It is probably the deepest diver of all whales and may travel 3,000 m (9,800 ft) below the surface. When whales go under water, their heart rate slows, while blood flow to the skin is stopped so that it can flow to the vital organs for longer.

# Humpback whale
*Megaptera novaeangliae*

■ **Length** 14 m (46 ft)
■ **Weight** 30,000 kg (66,140 lb)
■ **Location** Worldwide except Mediterranean, Baltic, Red Sea, Arabian Gulf

This baleen whale is **extremely vocal**. The male "sings" using a variety of sounds. The song can last up to 30 minutes and may be to attract females, warn off other males, or be a form of sonar to detect other whales. This whale has the **longest flippers** of any whale. It uses these like wings to swim through the water.

# Harbour porpoise
*Phocoena phocoena*

■ **Length** 1.83 m (6 ft)
■ **Weight** 90 kg (200 lb)
■ **Location** North Pacific, North Atlantic, Black Sea

Also known as the **common porpoise**, this porpoise is numerous in the areas where it lives. It likes shallow seas and stays near the coast for most of the time. Sometimes it **swims into harbours**, which is how it gets its name. It feeds on fish and shellfish on the sea bed, gripping its prey in its teeth.

# Sei whale
*Balaenoptera borealis*

■ **Length** 16 m (52 ft)
■ **Weight** 40,000 kg (88,185 lb)
■ **Location** Worldwide except Mediterranean, Baltic, Red Sea, Arabian Gulf

The sei whale is a **baleen whale**. It eats a variety of food, from plankton to small squid and fish. These whales usually swim in groups of up to **five animals**. They do not dive more than 300 m (1,000 ft) and stay under water for no more than 20 minutes.

MAMMALS

TAIL SPIN *The sperm whale lifts its tail high into the air before taking a dive. This helps it to get into position. The powerful tail then propels the whale through the water.*

# A *world* of whales

There are more than 100 different types of whales and dolphins. These range in size from Hector's dolphin, which can reach 1.3 m (4 ft) in length, to the world's largest animal – the blue whale. This enormous creature can grow to 30 m (98 ft) long. It is so heavy that on land its internal organs would be crushed by its great weight.

**Indus river dolphin**
*Platanista minor*

**Hector's beaked whale**
*Mesoplodon hectori*

**Cuvier's beaked whale**
*Ziphius cavirostris*

**Sei whale**
*Balaenoptera borealis*

*A fully grown blue whale is about as long as 19 divers swimming head to foot.*

**Blue whale**
*Balaenoptera musculus*

**Pygmy killer whale**
*Feresa attenuata*

**Short-finned pilot whale**
*Globicephala macrorhynchus*

**Northern right whale**
*Lissodelphis borealis*

**False killer whale**
*Pseudorca crassidens*

Northern right-whale dolphin
*Lissodelphis borealis*

Beluga
*Delphinapterus leucas*

Atlantic spotted dolphin
*Stenella frontalis*

Chilean dolphin
*Cephalorhynchus eutropia*

Harbour porpoise
*Phocoena phocoena*

Bottlenose dolphin
*Tursiops truncatus*

Killer whale
*Orcinus orca*

Gray whale
*Eschrichtius robustus*

Humpback whale
*Megaptera novaeangliae*

Sperm whale
*Physeter macrocephalus*

Hector's dolphin
*Cephalorhynchus hectori*

This dolphin is found off the coast of New Zealand. It is incredibly rare.

Common dolphin
*Delphinus delphis*

Dall's porpoise
*Phocoenoides dalli*

Spinner dolphin
*Stenella longirostris*

Shepherd's beaked whale
*Tasmacetus shepherdi*

Narwhal
*Monodon monoceros*

57

# Mother and calf

A humpback female usually gives birth to a single calf, and will feed and protect it for the first year. The calf suckles its mother's milk until it is about six months old, when it can begin to catch fish itself. It grows rapidly, doubling its length in the first year.

# Humpback whale

*Megaptera novaeangliae*

- **Length** 14 m (14 ft)
- **Weight** 66,000 lb (30,000 kg)
- **Diet** Small fish, krill
- **Location** Worldwide except Mediterranean, Baltic, Red Sea, Arabian Gulf

This whale's enormous flippers can be up to one-third the length of its body. It is a **baleen whale**, and feeds by filtering fish from the water through long baleen plates.

## SINGING

Humpbacks are noisy whales, and male humpback whales actually sing. It's not known why they sing, but it may be to attract a female and warn off a rival male. It also may help them to detect other whales. Each song can last for about 30 minutes.

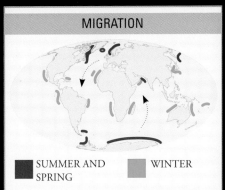

▲ FISHING *Small groups of humpbacks join together to encircle fish, trapping them in blown "nets" of bubbles. It's an effective technique.*

### MIGRATION

■ SUMMER AND SPRING    ■ WINTER

- Humpback whales undergo long migrations, from cold summer waters near the poles, which are rich feeding grounds, to warmer tropical or sub-tropical waters in the winter, where females calve and males seek mates.

MAMMALS

# Dolphin *communication*

Dolphins are sociable animals and live together in groups called pods. Pods vary in size from just a few dolphins to more than one thousand. The dolphins communicate with each other in a "language" of whistles, clicks, and cries. This enables them to recognize, locate, and help each other.

# Quick! Someone's in **trouble**.

When dolphins recognize a distress call they will follow it in search of a lost friend or relative. If a dolphin is sick, others will help push it to the surface so it can breathe.

TEAMWORK *Pods, like this one of common dolphins* (Delphinus delphis), *are larger where there are lots of fish. Dolphins co-operate with each other to catch the fish.*

## DOLPHIN COMMUNICATION

## DOLPHIN SPEAK

Communication in dolphins is still being investigated, but scientists think that dolphins have a complex system of language. They respond to each other's whistles and clicks, and make noises when playing, hunting, or when predators are near. They make lots of different sounds.

**Look at me** Bottlenose dolphins (*Tursiops truncatus*) are probably the most friendly dolphins. They even communicate with humans, sometimes coming inshore to ask for food. They often swim near boats and swimmers.

*The dolphin listens to the sounds bouncing off prey. The nearer the prey, the more quickly the echoes come back.*

▲ FINDING PREY *Dolphins find their food using a technique called echolocation. They send out sounds, which bounce back off their prey and tell them exactly where their victim is.*

MAMMALS

⚠ **CONSERVATION**

Some dolphins are hunted by humans for their flesh and many are eaten by killer whales and big sharks. Thousands more are caught in commercial fishing nets, which is greatly reducing dolphin numbers. Some nets are now designed to be "dolphin friendly".

61

# Dogs

Dogs and foxes belong to the group of meat-eating mammals called carnivores. They are well designed for hunting, with excellent senses for tracking prey, strong legs for running, and sharp teeth for biting.

Red fox
*Vulpes vulpes*

**Pet dogs** are descended from the grey wolf – even small dogs such as terriers and chihuahuas. Dogs were first domesticated about 12,000 years ago. They were bred to protect and herd livestock, such as sheep, from as early as 1,000 BCE. They reached Australia about 4,000 years ago. The Australian dingo (*above*) is descended from these, but now lives in the wild.

## African wild dog

*Lycaon pictus*

| 10 | ⚠ |
|----|---|

- **Length** 76–112 cm (2½–3½ ft)
- **Tail** 30–45 cm (12–18 in)
- **Weight** 15–35 kg (33–77 lb)
- **Location** Africa

The Latin name for this dog means "painted wolf" and comes from its striking **patterned coat.** The African wild dog lives in packs of about 10 individuals. All the adults help to look after the young, but only one pair breed. The pack **hunt together** and bring down animals as large as wildebeest and zebra. This dog is endangered because of disease and is also hunted.

## Arctic fox

*Vulpes lagopus*

| 10 | ⚠ |
|----|---|

- **Length** 46–67 cm (1½–2 ft)
- **Tail** 25–43 cm (10–17 in)
- **Weight** 2–9 kg (4½–20 lb)
- **Location** Arctic

This small fox is perfectly suited to its freezing home. The Arctic fox has a thick fur coat, **the warmest fur of any mammal.** This snugness is helped by its clever body-temperature control and layers of insulating fat. These predators prey on smaller mammals, such as lemmings and Arctic hares. Arctic fox males and females both look after their litter of kits, usually in a den that can house several generations of foxes.

▶ SUMMER COAT
*An Arctic fox has a darker, thinner coat in the summer to prevent overheating.*

◀ WILD PACK
*Male African wild dogs will stay with their family pack. This is unusual for social pack mammals.*

# We are **red fox cubs**.

The red fox can have up to 12 cubs in a litter. They are born underground in a den and don't leave there until they are about four or five weeks old. Both parents help to look after the cubs.

▼ GOOD PRACTICE
*When fox cubs come out of their den, they tumble around together and play-fight. This helps them to learn the skills they will need for hunting when they are adults.*

## Coyote
*Canis latrans*

15

- ■ **Length** 75–100 cm (2½–3 ft)
- ■ **Tail** 25–40 cm (10–15½ in)
- ■ **Weight** 7–21 kg (15–46 lb)
- ■ **Location** North America to northern central America

he coyote is well-known for **its howl**, which can be heard at ight, echoing across the landscape. Coyotes howl to tell eighbouring coyotes where they are and where their territory is. hese dogs usually go looking for food on their own. They **eat lmost anything** – snakes, mice, fruit, and dead animals. They ill also search through rubbish to find something tasty to eat. he female gives birth to her puppies in the safety of a burrow nd the male brings them food.

## Grey wolf
*Canis lupus*

16

- ■ **Length** 150–200 cm (4¼–6½ ft)
- ■ **Tail** 35–56 cm (14–22 in)
- ■ **Weight** 20–60 kg (44–130 lb)
- ■ **Location** North America, eastern Europe, Asia

The **largest member of the dog family**, the grey wolf used to live all over the northern hemisphere. Now it is only found in remote areas. Wolves **live in packs** containing a pair of adults and several generations of their young. The pack has a strict order of seniority and all the wolves know where they stand in the pecking order.

## Golden jackal
*Canis aureus*

10

- ■ **Height** 70–105 cm (2¼–3⅓ ft)
- ■ **Tail** 20–30 cm (8–12 in)
- ■ **Weight** 7–15 kg (15–33 lb)
- ■ **Location** North and eastern Africa o southeastern Europe and Asia

pair of golden jackals ive together **for life** and hare the task of looking after their puppies. When the puppies grow up, one or wo will usually stay with their parents for a year to help look after the next litter. They hunt small animals, as well as scavenging for carcasses, such as a lion's eftovers. Sometimes, they **bury pieces of meat** to hide them from other animals.

# Born for the cold!

It's a strange fact, but one of a polar bear's biggest problems can be keeping cool. Although they have the most northerly range of any bear, and so live surrounded by ice and snow, these enormous bears can overheat. Hollow hairs, black skin, and a thick layer of blubber all contribute to storing the Sun's heat. It's an efficient system.

POLAR BEARS *roll in the snow to cool down. Their fur acts as a natural insulator, but they can overheat at temperatures above 10°C (50°F).*

## I'm safer with mum.

Young polar bears are born in snow dens. After emerging, they stay with their mother for the first 2½ years.

# Polar bear
*Ursus maritimus*

- **Height** 2–3.4 m (7–11 ft)
- **Weight** 400–680 kg (880–1500 lb)
- **Speed** 10 kph (6 mph) swimming speed
- **Location** Arctic, N. Canada

The male polar bear is the **world's largest marine predator**, though at birth a cub weighs little more than a small bag of sugar. Their main food source is from ringed seals, but they will also prey on walruses, belugas, and narwhals, as well as seabirds. They will eat carrion, too.

⚠ **CONSERVATION** 🐾

The polar bear population, estimated at just over 20,000, is under threat because of global warming. In Northern Canada, more and more ice melts each spring, and polar bears are being forced further inland before they have built up their fat stores by eating seal pups.

MAMMALS 🐾

## AT HOME ON THE ICE

Polar bears live in the Arctic at the edge of the ice shelf. Non-retractable claws help them to grip the ice, digging in like ice picks as the animal walks (it's a bit like having built-in snowshoes!).

▲ PAW PADDLES *Polar bears are superb swimmers. They use their front paws to paddle through water, and they can hold their breath for up to two minutes to dive. However, as the Arctic ice melts due to climate change, bears are having to swim greater distances between ice floes. Sometimes they become exhausted and drown.*

65

## I'm just **playing**.

Bear cubs are born helpless and without fur. They stay with their mother for two or three years until they can fend for themselves. Their mother protects them fiercely and teaches them how to survive.

# Bears

There are seven species of bear. (Some scientists say that the giant panda is a bear, making eight.) Bears are large meat-eaters, but eat lots of other things too. They can move fast if they have to and can stand upright, making themselves look even bigger.

## DON'T SURPRISE A BEAR

Bears have a good sense of smell but not such good eyesight and hearing. This means that they can be taken by surprise, and then they can be dangerous. They have large, strong paws with long claws, and can kill another animal with one blow.

◀ WINTER SLEEP *Bears that live where it gets cold go to sleep through the winter in a cave, hollow tree, or a den they dig themselves. Cubs are born in late winter and come out of their den in the spring.*

**Brown bear cub**

◀ CANINE TOOTH *Bears have powerful jaws and teeth for eating different kinds of food. Canines, such as this brown bear's tooth, tear into meat, but bears also have teeth for grinding plant material.*

### ⚠ CONSERVATION

Most species of bear are endangered. They are hunted for their gall bladders, which are used in traditional Chinese medicine. Their habitat is also being destroyed as people cut down the trees to make room for their own homes and farms, or for logging.

### FACTFILE

■ Bears can be found in Europe, Asia, North America, and parts of north Africa and South America. They live in all sorts of habitat, from ice floes in the Arctic (*see page 64 for the polar bear*) to grasslands, deserts, and mountains – but most of them live in forests in the northern hemisphere. They all like to be within easy reach of water, for drinking and for food (such as fish).

The numbers show where the featured bears are found.

## merican black bear
*sus americanus*

- **Length** 1.8 m (6 ft)
- **Weight** 300 kg (660 lb)
- **Location** North America

e American black bear is the **smallest**
orth American bear and the most
mmon. It is an **excellent climber** and will
mb up a tree if it is scared. Mother black
ars teach their cubs to climb at an early
e. Black bears are intelligent animals and
ve learnt to live in a variety of habitats.
ost of them hibernate during the winter,
pending on what the weather is like in
eir area and how much food is available.

## Spectacled bear
*Tremarctos ornatus*

- **Length** 2 m (6½ ft)
- **Weight** 175 kg (390 lb)
- **Location** Western South America

The **pale fur** around this
bear's eyes give it its name.
This is the only bear that
lives in South America.
It spends most of its
time in trees, **sleeping
or eating**. It bends
branches down so it
can reach the fruit
more easily.

## Sun bear
*Helarctos malayanus*

- **Length** 1.4 m (4½ ft)
- **Weight** 65 kg (145 lb)
- **Location** Southeast Asia

This bear has a **long
tongue** for licking grubs
and honey from holes. It
also lets ants crawl over
its paws then licks
them off. The bear has
unusually **loose skin**.
If it is grabbed by a
tiger, it can turn
around in its skin
and bite back!

## Sloth bear
*Melursus ursinus*

- **Length** 1.8 m (6 ft)
- **Weight** 145 kg (320 lb)
- **Location** Southern Asia

A sloth bear loves to eat
ants and termites. It tears
open their nests then
forms its mouth into a
tube and **sucks up** the
insects – very noisily!
It can even **close its
nostrils** to stop ants
from crawling
up its nose.

## Asiatic black bear
*Ursus thibetanus*

- **Length** 1.8 m (6 ft)
- **Weight** 200 kg (440 lb)
- **Location** Eastern, southern and
Southeast Asia.

The Asiatic black bear is often
called the **moon bear** because
of the white crescent of fur on
its chest. It is a good climber
and spends a lot of time in trees
where it eats fruits and nuts.
It also takes **honey** from bees'
nests. This bear feeds mostly at
night but will come out during
the day if there is no danger.

## Brown bear
*Ursus arctos*

- **Length** 3 m (10 ft)
- **Weight** 780 kg (1,720 lb)
- **Location** Northern North America,
Northern Europe and northern Asia

There are several different kinds of brown
bear, which live in different places. The
**Kodiak bear** is the largest. It lives on Kodiak
Island in Alaska. The grizzly bear lives in
North America. It is called the **grizzly bear**
because its fur is tipped with paler fur which
makes it look "grizzled" or as if it is going
grey. Brown bears are not good climbers and
prefer to stay on the ground. They eat almost
anything (including other bears) and often
catch salmon as the fish migrate up rivers.

# Saving *giant* pandas

The giant panda is one of the world's rarest animals. There are probably only about 1,600 left in the wild. Pandas eat little else but bamboo, but more than half the bamboo forests where they live, in central and western China, have disappeared since 1974.

# We were bred in captivity.

Around 150 pandas live in zoos or nature reserves, but only about a third of the cubs that are born in captivity survive more than six months.

MOTHER LOVE *By the time a giant panda cub is four months old, it is really energetic, running along behind its mother and climbing trees. Mother pandas often wrestle and roll around with their playful infants.*

## Giant panda
*Ailuropoda melanoleuca*

27

- **Length** 1.5–2 m (5¼–6¾ ft)
- **Weight** 70–160 kg (155–350 lb)
- **Location** Central China

The giant panda's **black and white coat pattern** does not appear until it is a few weeks old. At birth, the cub is a tiny pink creature, barely 8 cm (3 in) long, covered in white hairs. It will develop a thick, oily fur coat to keep it warm in the sub-zero winters of central China. Adults have strong jaws and teeth, essential for chewing the 38 kg (84 lb) of bamboo they need to eat daily to stay healthy.

▲ SPECIAL "THUMB" *Pandas have a bony lump on each front paw. They can move these false "thumbs", and use them with their toes to help them get a firm grip on a bamboo stem, while they nibble away at the juicy green shoots.*

▶ FEMALE PANDAS *usually give birth to one or two blind, helpless cubs, but often only one will survive as they need so much care from the mother. A cub stays with its mother for up to three years.*

### ⚠ CONSERVATION

Bamboo forests in China are being cleared by farmers, destroying the panda's main source of food. Poachers also kill pandas for their fur. To save these special bears from extinction, the Chinese government has set up more than 50 special panda reservations.

# Cats

All cats are carnivores and most of them eat only meat. Helped by their acute senses of hearing and sight, supple muscles, and sharp teeth and claws, they are all excellent hunters. Each cat hunts according to its size, strength, speed, and stamina.

## CUDDLY CATS

Although they are expert hunters and killers, cats are some of the most loved animals. Their round faces, bright eyes, and beautiful soft fur make them look cute and cuddly. Unfortunately their beauty has come at a cost, because many cats are hunted for their fur.

▲ ADAPTABLE CAT *The puma* (Puma concolor) *is found in large parts of North, Central, and South America and can live in many different habitats. It has a variety of common names, such as cougar and mountain lion.*

### ⚠ CONSERVATION

Poachers, livestock farmers, and roadkills all threaten the survival of wild cats. The destruction of their habitats makes their situation worse. Several species of cat have become extinct and many are now endangered. Conservationists are keeping a constant watch on their populations and are trying to discourage poaching.

### FACTFILE

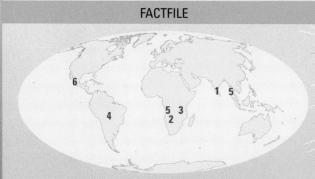

The numbers show where the featured cats are found.

■ **The animals** There are about 38 species of cat. Wild cats are found throughout Europe, Asia, Africa, and the Americas, in mountains, forests, grasslands, and deserts. Most of them are good climbers, and several are excellent swimmers.

**Size comparison**

## My thick **fur** keeps me well **insulated**.

The Siberian tiger grows a long coat to keep it warm in the cold winters. The coat also becomes paler to help it blend into the snow.

▶ ENDANGERED *The Siberian tiger* (Panthera tigris altaica) *is the largest living cat. The species is critically endangered and is rarely seen in the wild.*

# Tiger
*Panthera tigris*

- **Length** 2.8 m (9¼ ft)
- **Weight** 260 kg (573 lb)
- **Speed** 55 kph (34 mph)
- **Location** Southern and eastern Asia

Although the tiger is **large**, it can stalk its prey almost silently. It hunts mainly at night and pounces on its victims, such as deer or wild pigs, from close range. Tigers' stripes vary in width and number, and **no two cats are the same.**

# Caracal
*Caracal caracal*

- **Length** 91 cm (36 in)
- **Weight** 19 kg (42 lb)
- **Speed** 55 kph (34 mph)
- **Location** Africa, western and southwestern Asia

The caracal has long legs and is known for the way it can **spring up** into the air and catch low-flying birds in its front paws. It also eats other animals, such as rodents, hares and even small antelopes. This cat lives mostly on the ground, but **can climb well**.

# Cheetah
*Acinonyx jubatus*

- **Length** 1.5 m (5 ft)
- **Weight** 72 kg (160 lb)
- **Speed** 100 kph (62 mph)
- **Location** Africa, western Asia

The cheetah is **famous for its speed**. It is the fastest land animal, but can keep going for just 10 to 20 seconds. It is a **sociable** cat. Young cheetahs stay with their mother for up to two years. Brothers may stay together for several years.

# Ocelot
*Leopardus pardalis*

- **Length** 1 m (3 ft)
- **Weight** 16 kg (35 lb)
- **Location** Southern USA to central and South America

This **solitary cat** is very adaptable. It lives in a variety of habitats and eats lots of different food. Its favourite food is small rodents, but it will also eat lizards, fish, birds, snakes and even turtles. Its spotted coat has led to it being one of the **most hunted** species of cat and it is now endangered.

# Leopard
*Panthera pardus*

- **Length** 1.9 m (6¼ ft)
- **Weight** 90 kg (200 lb)
- **Location** Africa, southern Asia

The leopard relies on **stealth** rather than speed to catch its prey. It can kill larger and heavier animals, such as wildebeest and antelopes. All leopards are spotted, even the black panther, shown here, which is a leopard with **dark skin and fur**.

# Bobcat
*Lynx rufus*

- **Length** 1.1 m (3⅗ ft)
- **Weight** 15.5 kg (34 lb)
- **Location** Southern Canada, USA, Mexico

This is the most common wild cat in North America. It gets its name from its short, **"bobbed" tail**. The bobcat hunts mainly rabbits and hares, but will also eat rodents, bats, birds, deer, and carrion when its favourite food is scarce. It is a solitary, **secretive** animal and does most of its hunting at dawn and dusk.

# Lion *teamwork*

Lions are the only cats that live and hunt in groups. These groups are called prides and contain between 4 and 35 animals. By working together, they can take down animals larger than themselves. Female lions do most of the work.

## WORKING TOGETHER
*The female members of a pride team up to hunt large animals such as zebra, antelopes, and buffalo. After stalking to within 30 m (100 ft), they fan out to encircle their prey.*

## Lion
*Panthera leo*

- **Length** 1.7–2.5 m (5½–8¼ ft)
- **Weight** 150–250 kg (330–550 lb)
- **Location** Africa (sub Sahara), South Asia (Gir Forest, West India)

Lions are the most sociable of all big cats, which makes them **great teamworkers.** Most live in Africa, where their colouring blends in well with the dry grassy plains, making it **hard for prey to spot them** approaching. The smaller Asiatic lion (*Panthera leo persica*) lives in the Gir Forest in India.

▶ JOBS FOR THE GIRLS *On a hunt, lionesses have different jobs to do according to what they are best at. Some chase and direct prey; others ambush and kill.*

# Shush!
# Take it **slowly**.

Female lions are sleek and powerful. They do not have a mane like males, because it would impede them as they hunt. They creep up silently on their prey, before swiftly moving in for the kill.

## BOYS FIRST

*...er a successful kill* *...the females, the* *...le arrives to take* *...share. Although it* *...n't done any of the* *...rk, it is always* *...owed to feed first.* *...role in the pride is* *...defend territory,* *...ich it does by* *...ing around,* *...ring, and leaving* *...scent on trees.*

## Who is the scavenger?

A male lion that does not have any females to hunt for him may take food from other hunters, such as hyenas. He will wait for a pack of hyenas to do all the hard work of a kill, and then bully them away to enjoy the feast himself. Once he is full, vultures will usually dive in to strip any remaining meat from the carcass.

# A *world* of cats

Wild cats range in size from the black-footed cat, about the size of a small pet cat, to the tiger, whose body can be the length of a small car. But all cats are accomplished hunters, and all move and hunt in similar ways, stalking their prey with stealth and patience.

**Bobcat**
*Lynx rufus*

**Cheetah**
*Acinonyx jubatus*

**Lion**
*Panthera leo*

**Wild cat**
*Felis silvestris*

**Jungle cat**
*Felis chaus*

**Sand cat**
*Felis margarita*

**Black panther**
*These cats are either leopards (Panthera pardus) or jaguars (Panthera onca) that have black fur.*

MAMMALS

**Canadian lynx**
*Lynx canadensis*

**Caracal**
*Caracal caracal*

**Ocelot**
*Leopardus pardalis*

LARGEST CAT
**Tiger**
*Panthera tigris*

A tiger hunts largely at night, but its coat provides effective camouflage during the day.

SMALLEST CAT
**Black-footed cat**
*Felis nigripes*

**Serval**
*Leptailurus serval*

**Domestic cat**
*Felis catus*

**Fishing cat**
*Prionailurus viverrinus*

75

# Playing *to survive*

Playing is a good way to learn. When young mammals tumble around together and chase each other, they are picking up hunting and fighting skills, which will be vital for their survival in later life. They learn coordination and control and gain experience of situations which will help them when they have to fend for themselves.

TAKING OVER *Young males leave their family when they reach adulthood, and wait until they are strong enough to fight for leadership of their own pride. Once in charge, they tolerate their own cubs, but kill those of the previous leader.*

## GAINING EXPERIENCE

Lion cubs tumble, prowl, and pounce around. As well as enjoying themselves and learning useful skills, they are establishing their position in the "pecking order" within their family. They also discover – in a controlled, safe environment – what risks they can take and what could happen if they put themselves in unnecessary danger.

▶ GONE FISHING
*Bear cubs learn from their mother by following her and copying what she does. An important lesson for brown bear cubs is fishing. They watch their mother while she fishes for salmon, then imitate her until they know how to catch the fish for themselves.*

## Retract those claws, kids. They're **sharp**!

Like most cats, lions can retract their claws. When play-fighting, cubs keep in their claws and do not expose their teeth. In a real hunt, lions kill their prey by leaping on it and biting into the neck.

**Learning the ropes** Young tiger cubs love to wrestle with each other and with adults. In this way they learn how to test another animal's strength without the risk of being injured if they get it wrong. This playful form of fighting is also a good opportunity for the cubs to practise their suffocating grip on each other.

### FACTFILE

■ Young lions do not become independent until they are at least 16 months old. Females stay with their pride, while the males leave.

■ Tiger cubs start to take part in hunting expeditions when they are about five to six months old. They stay with their mother until they are 18 months to three years old.

■ Brown bear cubs remain with their mother for two to four years. Once they have left, the mother usually starts a new family.

# Weasels and *their relatives*

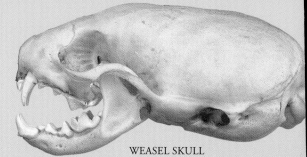

WEASEL SKULL

Weasels belong to a family of animals called mustelids. Their relatives include otters, badgers, and martens. Many mustelids are small but they are strong and can be fierce hunters. They live in a variety of habitats everywhere except Australia, New Zealand, and Antarctica.

▲ HUNTER'S HEAD *A weasel's head is little wider than its neck, which allows it to get through small holes. Like other meat-eaters, it has very sharp canine teeth. It kills its prey of voles and mice with a quick bite to the back of the neck.*

**Pine marten**
*Martes martes*

## COMMON FEATURES

Most mustelids have a long flexible body, short legs, and a long tail. They have five toes on each foot with non-retractable, curved claws. They have an acute sense of smell, which they use for hunting. Many of these animals, especially the sable, have been hunted by humans for their soft, thick fur.

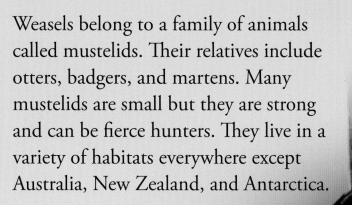

### FACTFILE

■ **Terrestrial, or land-based, mustelids** include the weasel, the striped skunk, and the stoat.

■ **Arborial, or tree-based, mustelids** include the European pine marten and the American marten.

■ **Semi-aquatic mustelids** include the European mink and the European polecat. They live near water.

■ **Fully aquatic mustelids** include the giant otter, sea otter, and river otters. They spend most of their time in water.

■ **Burrowing mustelids** include the Eurasian badger, honey badger, and the wolverine. They live in burrows.

▶ AGILE HUNTER
*The European pine marten is an excellent climber and often hunts for prey in trees. But it hunts mainly on the ground, feeding on small rodents, birds, insects, and fruit.*

# Weasel

*...stela nivalis*

- **Length** 24 cm (9½ in)
- **Weight** 250 g (9 oz)
- **Location** North America, Europe to northern, ...tral, and eastern Asia

...e weasel is one of the **smallest** mustelids. ...s small enough to chase mice into ...eir burrows. It must eat one-third ...its body weight every ...y, and so it ...nts **day and** ...ght. It is like ...stoat, but does ...t have a black ...p to its tail.

# Eurasian badger

*Meles meles*

- **Length** 90 cm (35 in)
- **Weight** 34 kg (75 lb)
- **Location** Europe to eastern Asia

Unlike most mustelids, the Eurasian badger lives in groups. It has a burrow called a **sett**, which is a system of tunnels and chambers. It hunts at night and **eats a varied diet,** from worms to small birds.

MAMMALS

# ...riped skunk

*...phitis mephitis*

- **Length** 75 cm (30 in)
- **Weight** 3 kg (6½ lb)
- **Location** Central Canada to northern Mexico

...edators should keep well away from skunks. ...ey are known for spraying a **nasty-smelling** ...quid over an enemy's head! The smell is so ...rong it can be smelt up to 1 km (½ mile) away. Striped skunks live alone, but they may join others in winter to shelter in burrows or even **under buildings**.

# European polecat

*Mustela putorius*

- **Length** 50 cm (20 in)
- **Weight** 1.5 kg (3 lb)
- **Location** Europe

This animal is probably the ancestor of the pet ferret. It **swims well** and can catch fish to eat, but it prefers to eat small mammals, reptiles, and birds. If it is threatened, the polecat **produces a strong smell** to persuade its enemy to keep back.

# Wolverine

*Gulo gulo*

- **Length** 105 cm (41 in)
- **Weight** 32 kg (70 lb)
- **Location** Canada, northwestern USA, northern Europe to northern and eastern Asia

This bear-like creature is a **fierce** predator and has strong jaws for crushing bones. It is also called **the glutton** – a word we use for a greedy person!

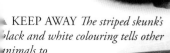

KEEP AWAY *The striped skunk's black and white colouring tells other ...nimals to ...eep away.*

# Giant otter

*Pteronura brasiliensis*

- **Length** 1.4 m (4.5 ft)
- **Weight** 32 kg (70 lb)
- **Location** Northern and central South America

The giant otter is the **largest** mustelid in terms of length. It feeds mainly on fish and crabs, which it catches with its mouth. Groups of up to ten otters live in **dens** or burrows beside a river.

# At home *with sea otters*

This is the only species of otter that spends its whole life at sea. Its food includes fish, crabs, molluscs, and sea urchins, and it has strong teeth for crushing the shells. A social animal, the sea otter lives in groups called rafts, separated into male and female rafts.

## I love to **float** on my back in the sea.

Sea otters spend a lot of time floating on their back with their paws out of the water. They eat and sleep on their back, and mother sea otters nurse their pups while floating on the surface.

SAFELY STOWED *Sea otters are found in beds of giant kelp, a type of seaweed. They often use the kelp to anchor themselves while they sleep. Mothers also wrap their pups in kelp to keep them safe while they go fishing.*

# Sea otter
*Enhydra lutris*

- **Length** 1.3 m (4¼ ft)
- **Weight** 28 kg (62 lb)
- **Location** North Pacific ocean

Unlike most sea mammals, the sea otter does not have blubber under its skin to keep it warm. **Thick fur** traps a layer of air so that the otter's skin never gets wet. In fact, a sea otter has more hairs on a fingernail-sized patch of its skin then a person has on their head!

▲ USING TOOLS *The sea otter has learned to use tools to open shellfish and sea urchins. While floating on its back, it cracks open the shell on a rock it carries on its tummy.*

## PROTECTED SPECIES

Once hunted for its fur, the sea otter nearly became extinct in some areas. It is now a protected species and its numbers are increasing in certain places. Efforts are being made to relocate it to other areas.

▲ UNDERWATER *This excellent swimmer has a strong, flat tail that it uses as a rudder and flipper-like hind feet. It dives to forage for food on the sea bed and its large lungs allow it to stay under the water for several minutes.*

MAMMALS

81

# Civets *and relatives*

These cat-like animals belong to two families (the Viverridae and Herpestidae). There are about 70 species, and they include civets, mongooses, and genets. Many are fierce predators, some are solitary, while others work together in social colonies.

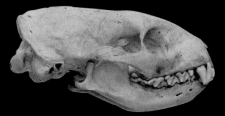

▲ SKULL AND JAW *This is an Egyptian mongoose skull (Herpestes ichneumon). The long face is typical of animals in these families, which, though related to cats and hyenas, have more snap to their bite with more teeth.*

## BODY PARTS

Civets and their relatives have a long body, short legs, and a long tail. They have thick coats, often marked with spots or stripes. They have scent glands under their tail, and if an enemy comes too close, some will spray a nasty-smelling liquid.

I'm a **tree climber.**

The spotted genet is an excellent climber. It hunts for birds at night when they are roosting and not so likely to escape. They also forage for eggs, rodents, insects, and small reptiles.

CAT-LIKE *The large spotted genet (Genetta tigrina) looks a bit like a cat. But its snout is more pointed and it can only partly retract its claws when they are not being used.*

## FACTFILE

■ The oriental linsang (*Prionodon pardicolor*) of southeast Asia uses its tail to balance and brake as it climbs.

■ The binturong (*Arctictis binturong*) of southeast Asia is one of only a few carnivores with a prehensile tail.

■ The fossa (*Cryptoprocta ferox*) is the largest carnivore to live on the island of Madagascar.

5

4 5

4 5

3 5 2
1

The numbers show where the featured animals are found.

# Yellow mongoose
*Cynictis penicillata*

**15**

**1**

- **Height** 33 cm (13 in)
- **Tail** 25 cm (10 in)
- **Weight** 800 g (29 oz)
- **Location** Southern Africa

The yellow mongoose is sometimes called the **red meerkat** and it often shares burrows with meerkats. It lives in colonies containing **one breeding pair** and up to 20 of their young and other relatives.

# Striped civet
*Fossa fossana*

**10**

**2**

- **Length** 45 cm (18 in)
- **Tail** 25 cm (10 in)
- **Weight** 2 kg (4½ lb)
- **Location** Madagascar

This **shy, nocturnal** civet hunts for small animals on the forest floor. It can store fat in its tail as **preparation** for winter when food may be scarce.

# Meerkat
*Suricata suricatta*

**12**

**3**

- **Length** 35 cm (14 in)
- **Tail** 25 cm (10 in)
- **Weight** 975 g (35 oz)
- **Location** Southern Africa

Meerkats live in burrows. They often take over old burrows of ground squirrels, which they enlarge by digging with their long front claws. Their claws are also useful for finding insects, spiders, roots, and bulbs to eat. **These sociable creatures form colonies** of up to 30 animals. While the colony is searching for food, some **act as lookouts** and warn if a predator is nearby. The colony then dives for cover.

LINE WATCH *Adult meerkats keep a watchful eye ready to alert the colony to danger.*

# Banded mongoose
*Mungos mungo*

**10**

**4**

- **Length** 45 cm (18 in)
- **Tail** 23 cm (9 in)
- **Weight** 2.5 kg (5½ lb)
- **Location** Africa

Mongooses eat lots of different foods, from termites to birds' eggs, but they are known for the way they **attack snakes.** Their thick fur helps to protect them from being bitten, and they are **partially immune to poisonous snake bites.**

# Dwarf mongoose
*Helogale parvula*

**10**

**5**

- **Length** 28 cm (11 in)
- **Tail** 19 cm (7½ in)
- **Weight** 350 g (13 oz)
- **Location** Eastern and southern Africa

As its name suggests, this is the **smallest mongoose.** It forms packs of from 2 to 20 animals that live and feed together – on insects, lizards, snakes, birds, eggs, and mice. Female dwarf mongooses have up to six young, and the **whole pack help** to look after them.

MAMMALS

# Seals and sea lions

These sea mammals belong to an order of animals called pinnipeds. They spend most of their time at sea and cannot move around so well on land. They haul themselves out on to rocky or sandy beaches to breed. All species have fur and long whiskers.

TRUE SEAL
SKELETON

SEA LION
SKELETON

## WATER MAMMALS

Seals and sea lions have a layer of blubber under the skin, which keeps them warm. They have flippers, instead of legs, and can close their ears and nostrils when they dive. Their large eyes help them to see well under the water.

▲ DIFFERENCES
*A true seal has back flippers that point backwards. A sea lion can rotate its back flippers forward for moving on land.*

▲ COLONY *During the breeding season, several thousand Cape fur seals come on shore and form colonies.*

**Northern elephant seal**
*Mirounga angustirostris*

## FACTFILE

■ **Number of species:** There are 34 species of pinniped in three families. There are 19 true seals, 14 eared seals (sealions and fur seals), and 1 walrus (*see pp 86–87*).
■ **Key features:** They are all carnivorous. Seals and sea lions feed mainly on fish and small crustaceans called krill.

True seals have no external ears. They include the bearded seal (*Erignathus barbatus*), top left, the grey seal, and the common seal. Eared seals have small external ears. They include the Californian sea lion (*Zalophus californianus*), bottom left, and the Cape fur seal.

SWIMMERS *Seals and sea lions are designed for swimming, with a streamlined body and powerful flippers. In water, they are agile and graceful.*

# Californian sea lion
*lophus californianus*

- **Length** 2.4 m (7¾ ft)
- **Weight** 390 kg (860 lb)
- **Location** Western USA

ke all sea lions, Californian sea lions an **support themselves** n their front flippers n land. They are fast wimmers, reaching speeds f 40 kph (25 mph). They are **layful** animals and can ometimes be seen surfing nd leaping out of he water.

# Steller's sea lion
*Eumetopias jubatus*

- **Length** 3.5 m (11 ft)
- **Weight** 1,100 kg (2,425 lb)
- **Location** North Pacific coast

This is the **largest** sea lion, and a male might weigh three times as much as a female. Males are aggressive and fight each other for mates. This species is **in danger** because it has been hunted and its food is decreasing due to overfishing.

# Grey seal
*Halichoerus grypus*

- **Length** 2.5 m (8¼ ft)
- **Weight** 310 kg (680 lbs)
- **Location** North Atlantic, Baltic Sea

Grey seal pups are born with soft, **white fur**. They shed this within three weeks and grow a grey coat. The Latin name for this seal means "hook-nosed sea pig" and the male particularly has a long, **hooked nose**.

# Common seal
*hoca vitulina*

- **Length** 1.9 m ¾ ft)
- **Weight** 170 kg 375 lb)
- **Location** North Atlantic and North Pacific coasts

Also known as the harbour seal, he common seal is the **most widespread** pinniped. Common seals do not gather in uch large groups as other seals although they do rest on rocky shores, mud flats, and sandy beaches. They do not travel more than about 20 km (12 miles) from the shore.

# Southern elephant seal
*Mirounga leonina*

- **Length** 6 m (20 ft)
- **Weight** 5,000 kg (11,000 lb)
- **Location** Antarctic and subantarctic waters

Male southern elephant seals are four or five times the weight of the females. The males have a **huge nose**, which looks a bit like an elephant's trunk. When they are fighting for females during the breeding season, they **inflate** their nose and roar at their rivals.

# Antarctic fur seal
*Arctocephalus gazella*

- **Length** 1.70 m (5½ ft)
- **Weight** 130 kg (286 lb)
- **Location** Antarctic and subantarctic waters

Fur seals have a layer of **soft underfur** as well as the short fur that most seals have. This keeps them dry and warm. Male seals arrive first at the breeding ground on a rocky island, and **fight for territory**. When the females arrive, about five females join each male.

OFTEN SEEN *The Antarctic fur seal is one of the most common fur seals.*

# Cape fur seal
*Arctocephalus pusillus*

- **Length** 2.3 m (7½ ft)
- **Weight** 360 kg (794 lb)
- **Location** Southern Africa, Southeastern Australia, Tasmania

Cape fur seals spend most of the time at sea, but they do not swim far from land. Mother fur seals spend several days at sea, feeding, and **return to their pups regularly** to feed them. The pups **play together** while their mothers are away.

# Walrus
*Odobenus rosmarus*

- **Length** 3.6 m (12 ft)
- **Weight** 2,000 kg (4,400 lb)
- **Location** Arctic waters

40

The walrus belongs to the same order of animals as seals and sea lions – the pinnipeds. It dives to between 10 and 50 m (33–164 ft) to find food on the seabed, using its whiskers and snout. It will **stay under water for up to 10 minutes.**

## USEFUL TUSKS

The walrus is the only member of the pinnipeds to have tusks, which can grow to nearly 1 m (3 ft) long on males. They are basically overgrown canines. The males use their tusks as weapons when they compete with each other for breeding sites during the breeding season.

**Sunbathing** When walruses lie in the sun their skin turns pink, as if they were sunburnt. This is because the arteries that take blood to the skin's surface expand. Blood flows to the skin cells and absorbs heat from the sun. This is one way in which walruses keep warm.

▲ SAFETY IN NUMBERS *Mother walruses are protective of their young. In fact, all the adults help to protect the pups from predators. They swim in a tight group, keeping the pups carefully guarded in the middle.*

# I am the *walrus*

The walrus lives in Arctic waters. It is hunted by killer whales so it prefers shallower waters and comes ashore to breed. Walruses are social animals and gather on land and on ice floes in large herds containing hundreds of animals. Space can get very tight!

ICE MAN *This walrus is resting on pack ice in northeast Canada. Its thick skin and blubber keep it warm. It can also contract the blood vessels close to its skin to reduce heat loss.*

# Look!
# I have my own
# **ice picks!**

Both male and female walruses have tusks. They are useful for helping to haul the walrus out of the water and onto the ice – they are purpose-built ice picks!

# Elephants

These giant animals are the largest living land mammal. With their long, mobile trunks; curved, white tusks; and large, flapping ears, elephants are instantly recognizable. But what many do not know is that there are three different elephant species – one living in Asia and two from Africa.

### FACTFILE

- **Family:** Elephantidae
- **Number of species:** Three
- **Key features:** Distinctive trunk used as a "fifth limb"; upper incisors elongated into large, curved tusks in bulls; large, fan-shaped ears; thick, wrinkly skin.

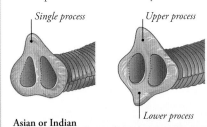

*Single process*  *Upper process*

*Lower process*

**Asian or Indian elephant**    **African elephant**

SAY HELLO *Elephants often greet each other by standing close and twining their long trunks. The sense of touch is extremely important in elephant society.*

# sian elephant
*phas maximus*

**Head–body length** 5.5–6.4 m (18–21 ft)
**Shoulder height** 2.5–3 m (8–10 ft)
**Weight** Males 5,400 kg (11,905 lb); females 2,700 kg (5,952½ lb)
**Location** Southern and Southeast Asia

he Asian elephant is much smaller than its African ousins. Only the males have visible tusks. The Asian ephant population is **rapidly declining**. There may be wer than 60,000 individuals in the orld, including captive animals.

*The Asian elephant has smaller ears than its African cousin.*

# African bush elephant
*Loxodonta africana*

- **Head–body length** 5.5–7.5 m (18–24½ ft)
- **Shoulder height** 2.4–4.0 m (7⅞–13⅛ ft)
- **Weight** Males 6,300 kg (13,889 lb); females 3,500 (7,716 lb)
- **Location** Sub-Saharan Africa

The African bush elephant is the **world's largest land mammal**. These giants roam the African savanna, foraging for bark, branches, leaves, and grasses. A single adult needs to eat around 160 kg (350 lb) of food a day.

# ygmy elephant
*oxodonta cyclotis pumilio*

**Head–body length**
4–2.8 m (8–9¼ ft)
**Weight** 1,800–3,200 kg (4,000–7,000 lb)
**Location** Congo Basin of Central Africa

ome zoologists think that these small elephants are a eparate species, but they are **forest elephants** whose ize may be due to environmental pressures such as estricted food.

# African forest elephant
*Loxodonta cyclotis*

- **Head–body length** 5.5–7.5 m (18–24½ ft)
- **Shoulder height** 1.6–2.8 m (5¼–9⅛ ft)
- **Weight** Males 6,000 kg (13,227⁷⁄₁₀ lb); females 2,700 kg (5,952½ lb)
- **Location** Central and West Africa

These elephants are smaller than their savanna relatives, and their **ears are more rounded**. The tusks are relatively straight and point downwards, which may be an adaptation to help them move through the dense lowland jungle. Sometimes, they wander along the edges of the forest, where they come into contact with bush elephants.

*The African forest elephant has yellow tusks.*

# Elephant family

Elephants have long held our fascination. These giant mammals have the biggest brains in the animal world. Since their intelligence is combined with great strength, it is no surprise that we have harnessed them as working animals. But people have also been the elephant's worst enemy thanks to competition for land and the ivory trade.

## I won't let you out of **my sight**.

Female elephants are called cows and their babies are calves. It is not only th mother that looks after her calf. Every cow in the family unit plays a part in helping to bring up the young elephants.

**FAMILY LIFE**
*Females live in family units made up of related cows and their young offspring. A cow and her calf are rarely more than a trunk's length apart.*

MAMMALS

▲ LONG REACH *Elephants can stand on their hind legs to reach high branches with especially tasty fresh green leaves.*

▲ PRECIOUS WATER *A water hole in the middle of the African savanna attracts animals from far and wide. Hot and thirsty elephants love to cool down in water holes.*

### ⚠ CONSERVATION

All elephant species are endangered. In parts of Asia and Africa, people compete with elephants for land. But the real damage was done before the 1989 worldwide ivory ban, when elephants were hunted for their tusks. The sale of ivory is now strictly controlled in most countries, and seized tusks have been publicly burned, but poachers still supply a black market.

# Dugongs and manatees

Manatees and dugongs are the only existing animals in the order of mammals called sirenians. They have a flat tail, paddle-like front limbs, but no hind limbs. They are the only marine mammals that feed purely on plants. An adult manatee will often eat up to nine per cent of its body weight per day.

## TOTALLY AQUATIC

Sirenians spend their whole life in water and never come on land. Manatees make long dives and can stay underwater for up to 15 minutes before they have to come to the surface to breathe. The dugong dives for only about one minute.

### I'm **not** in any hurry.

Manatees are large, slow-moving creatures. Their bodies contain a lot of gas, given off by all the plants they eat. This could make them rise to the surface, but they have heavy bones to help them stay underwater.

MANATEES *have tough skin, which can be up to 5 cm (2 in) thick. Underneath is a thinner layer of blubber. Because manatees live in warm water, they do not need lots of blubber.*

# West Indian manatee
*Trichechus manatus*

- **Length** 4.5 m (15 ft)
- **Weight** 600 kg (1,320 lb)
- **Location** Southeastern USA to northeastern South America, Caribbean

Manatees live in **shallow water** near the coast, and in nearby rivers and freshwater lagoons. Females have only **one calf** every two years. Mother and calf often "mouth" each other to help to keep the bond between them.

**▲ DUGONG**
*The end of a dugong's tail is crescent-shaped, or fluked, a bit like a whale's tail. It flaps it up and down to propel itself through the water and also steers with it.*

**▲ MANATEE**
*A manatee's tail is rounded and looks a bit like a beaver's tail. The manatee flaps it only about 30 times a minute to swim.*

**Grazers** Sirenians such as the dugong (*Dugong dugon*) graze on the seabed. They use their flexible upper lip to collect sea grasses and other plants, then crush the food between horny plates on their mouth. Finally, they grind it between their teeth before swallowing.

> ⚠️ **CONSERVATION**
>
> There are only about 130,000 sirenians left in the world. In the past they were hunted for their meat, skin, and oil. Now many manatees are injured or killed by boat propellers because they often sleep near the surface of the water and are difficult to see.

# Horses, asses, and zebras

There are four types of horse – Przewalski's wild horse, asses, zebras, and domestic horses (including ponies). They are called "odd-toed" animals because they have one toe on each foot. In the wild, they live out in the open where they can keep an eye out for predators.

## RUNNING WILD

There are many herds of horses and ponies living in the wild. They are descended from domestic horses. They include the mustangs of North America, the brumbies of Australia, and the white horses of the Camargue in France. Many breeds of pony live wild in Britain.

▼ ROUND UP *Many herds of wild mustangs in the USA are rounded up every year. The horses are gathered into corrals. Some are kept and domesticated for riding. The rest are returned to their life running wild.*

## FACTFILE

■ **Horses** All domestic and semi-wild horses and ponies are the same species. Przewalski's wild horse is a different species. It is the only truly wild horse.

■ **Zebras** The three species of zebra are Grevy's zebra, Burchell's zebra, and the mountain zebra. They have different patterns of stripes between species and between individuals.

■ **Asses** The Asian wild ass, or onager, the kiang, and the African wild ass are the three species of wild ass. The African wild ass is the ancestor of the domestic donkey.

▼ MIXTURES *A zebra/donkey cross is called a zedonk (right). A male donkey and female horse produce a mule (below right). A male horse and female donkey produce a hinny (below left).*

## African wild ass
*Equus africanus*

**25**

- **Height** 1.3 m (4¼ ft)
- **Weight** 230 kg (510 lb)
- **Speed** 70 kph (45 mph)
- **Location** E. Africa

The African wild ass lives in **hot, dry, rocky deserts**, where it eats almost any plant material it can find, from grass to thorny bushes. It can go without water for several days. The wild ass lives in herds of up to 50 individuals.

## Burchell's zebra
*Equus burchellii*

**9**

- **Height** 1.3 m (4¼ ft)
- **Weight** 385 kg (850 lb)
- **Speed** 55 kph (34 mph)
- **Location** E. and S. Africa

Also known as the common or plains zebra, Burchell's zebra is the only zebra with **stripes under its tummy**. It is widespread and herds containing several hundred animals are a common sight. The herds are made up of many family groups.

## Przewalski's wild horse
*Equus przewalski*

**34**

- **Height** 1.4 m (4½ ft)
- **Weight** 300 kg (660 lb)
- **Speed** 60 kph (37 mph)
- **Location** Mongolia

In the 1880s, these wild horses were found in Mongolia by **an explorer**. A few were taken to Europe to save the species. There are now small herds **living in zoos** around the world.

## Donkey
*Equus asinus*

**47**

- **Height** 1.2 m (4 ft)
- **Weight** 260 kg (573 lb)
- **Speed** 50 kph (30 mph)
- **Location** Kept domestically worldwide

Domestic donkeys are often kept as working animals or as pets. They are strong and can **carry heavy loads** over great distances with little food and water. Donkey **breeds vary in size** from miniature (less than 90 cm [36 in] high) to the French Poitou (up to 1.5 m [5 ft] high).

## Cape mountain zebra
*Equus zebra*

**20**

- **Height** 1.3 m (4¼ ft)
- **Weight** 390 kg (860 lb)
- **Speed** 55 kph (34 mph)
- **Location** South Africa

This zebra is a good climber and has **hard, pointed hoofs** to help it clamber up the steep, rocky slopes where it lives. Another difference between this and other zebras is that it has a fold of skin, called a **dewlap**, just under its throat.

## Grevy's zebra
*Equus grevyi*

**20**

- **Height** 1.5 m (5 ft)
- **Weight** 450 kg (990 lb)
- **Speed** 64 kph (40 mph)
- **Location** E. Africa

This is the **largest species** of zebra. It is not as social as the other zebras and does not form permanent herds. Female Grevy's zebras and their foals **roam freely**, looking for grass and other plants to eat. But they stay within the territory of their dominant male.

▲ DIFFERENCES
*Grevy's zebra can be identified by its large, round ears. It also has a V-shaped mark on its nose.*

## Mustang
*Equus caballus*

**25**

- **Height** 1.4–1.5 m (4½–5 ft)
- **Weight** 317–454 kg (700–1000 lb)
- **Speed** 64 kph (40 mph)
- **Location** Wild in North America

The mustang is descended from Spanish horses taken to the Americas in the 1500s. It is the same species as all **domestic horses** and ponies and comes in many different colours. This one is described as **bright bay**.

95

# Giraffe and okapi

Most people will have heard of a giraffe, but few know about the giraffe's smaller relative, the okapi. Both live in Africa, but they are found in different places. Giraffes roam the savanna and open woodlands in small herds. Okapis live alone and hide away in tropical rainforests.

# What do my **markings** say?

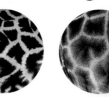

Giraffes have different skin patterns. Some have clear, chestnut patches (above left). Others have black patches (above centre) and some have small, blurry patches of yellow (above right).

## Giraffe
*Giraffa camelopardalis*

- **Height** 5.5 m (18 ft)
- **Weight** 1,900 kg (4,200 lb)
- **Speed** 56 kph (35 mph)
- **Location** Africa

Giraffes use their long, **dark tongues** and thin, mobile lips to pick off leaves and shoots from the treetops. The taller male giraffes eat the leaves from higher up the tree to **avoid competing** with the females.

## NECK LOCK

The giraffe is the tallest animal in the world thanks to its long neck. The bulls (males) use their necks to compete for the attention of the cows (females). In a display called "necking," the bulls lock necks and often clash heads. The winner earns the right to mate with the cows.

◀ TALL ORDER *The front legs of a giraffe are much longer than the back legs. So the giraffe spreads its front legs apart to drink at a water hole. The front legs are very strong. Giraffes use them to kick predators. One blow can kill a lion.*

▶ STRIPY SKIN
*With striking black-and-white stripes across its legs and rump, the okapi looks more like a zebra than a giraffe. Like giraffes, okapis have long necks and browse on soft twigs, leaves, and juicy shoots. Okapis are shy and the stripes help them to hide in the rainforests of central Africa. In fact, they are so shy people didn't even know they existed until 1901!*

HORNY HEAD *Giraffes have small horns, called ossicones, covered with skin. Baby giraffes are born with soft horns that turn hard as they grow older.*

MAMMALS

# Rhinoceroses

There are five species of rhinoceros living in the savannas of Africa or the swampy grasslands of Asia. They are large, heavy animals – only elephants and hippos are bigger. They have poor eyesight but make up for this with good senses of hearing and smell.

*All rhinoceroses like to wallow in mud. This cools them and protects their skin. Black rhinos look black because of mud dried on their skin.*

## RHINO HORNS

Rhinos have one or two horns, depending on the species. The horns are made of hair-like material called keratin, not bone – in fact, the same material that your hair and nails are made of. The horns are "perched" on top of the skull rather than being part of it.

▼ TWO HORNS *The white rhinoceros has two horns. The front horn is longer than the back horn and used for digging for water and plants.*

## I'm staying **close** to mum.

Young rhinoceroses are called calves. A female white rhinoceros usually has one calf every two to four years. The calf can run beside its mother after only three days.

# ndian rhinoceros
*hinoceros unicornis*

■ **Length** 3.8 m (12½ ft)
■ **Weight** 2,200 kg (4,850 lb)
■ **Location** Nepal and
 thern India

e **largest** of the Asian
inoceroses, the Indian
ino has only one horn.
eats trees and shrubs, but
ds out in the open, not
 forests. Its **hairless** skin
s lots of small lumps and
ngs down in heavy folds.
is makes the rhino look
 if it is wearing armour.

## CONSERVATION

All five species of rhinoceros are endangered. There are only about 60 Javan rhinos left in the world and the black rhinoceros is disappearing faster than any other mammal. Rhinos are in danger because they are killed for their horns. Rhino horn is used in China as a drug. In the Middle East horns are carved to make dagger handles. Some conservationists cut off rhinos' horns to make the animals worthless to poachers.

# White rhinoceros
*ratotherium simum*

■ **Length** 4 m (13 ft)
■ **Weight** 2,300 kg (5,070 lb)
■ **Location** East and southern Africa

he white rhinoceros is not really white, but
ey. Its name comes from the Afrikaans word
*eit* meaning "wide". This refers to its **wide,**
**raight mouth** which is ideal for eating grass.

# Javan rhinoceros
*Rhinoceros sondaicus*

■ **Length** 3.5 m (11½ ft)
■ **Weight** 1,400 kg (3,090 lb)
■ **Location** Southeast Asia

This rhino has only one horn, and some females have no horn at all. Like the Indian rhino, it has **no hair** except on its ears and the tip of its tail. This is one of the **rarest** large mammals in the world.

# Sumatran rhinoceros
*Dicerorhinus sumatrensis*

■ **Length** 3.2 m (10½ ft)
■ **Weight** 800 kg (1,764 lb)
■ **Location** South and Southeast Asia

This is the **smallest** rhinoceros. It is also the **hairiest** because it is covered with coarse, bristly hair. The Sumatran rhino lives in forests on hillsides, where it feeds on twigs, leaves, and fruits. It has two horns. The front one can grow to 90 cm (35 in) long.

# Black rhinoceros
*Diceros bicornis*

■ **Length** 3 m (10 ft)
■ **Weight** 1,300 kg (2,870 lb)
■ **Location** East and southern Africa

nlike the white rhino, the black rhino
eds on trees and shrubs. It has a **pointed**
**pper lip** which it can curl around twigs
nd shoots and pull them into its mouth to
e bitten off. The rhino is sometimes called
he hook-lipped rhinoceros. It is more
ggressive than the white rhino and may
harge without warning. Like other rhinos,
 can run surprisingly **fast for its size**
– 40 kph (25 mph) in short bursts,
which is the same as an Olympic sprinter!

# Battling hippos

The hippopotamus is one of Africa's largest mammals. It is also one of the continent's most dangerous animals. Males can weigh more than 3,048 kg (6,800 lb). They are also quick tempered and, when roused, can be lethal. Never get too close to a hippo.

BARING THEIR TEETH
*Hippos have enormous heads, with huge jaws. On the lower jaw are two dagger-like teeth. These razor-sharp fangs may be as long as 30 cm (12 in) and can be deadly in a fight.*

> I'm **boss** here. Challenge me and you'll be sorry!
>
> Male hippos often fight over territory. If roaring and splashing fails to drive off a rival, a bloody battle may break out. This could last for hours, ending only with the loser's death.

# Hippopotamus
*Hippopotamus amphibius*

40

- **Height** 1.5 m (5 ft)
- **Length** 5 m (16 ½ ft)
- **Weight** 3,000–4500 kg (6,600–9,900 lb)
- **Location** Africa

MAMMALS

Hippos **cannot sweat** to control their body temperature, so they spend their day **wallowing** in rivers and streams to keep cool. They are also protected from the baking African sun by an oily red liquid that oozes out from special glands in their skin. At night, they leave the water to graze on grass, wandering up to 5 km (3 miles) to find food.

▲ UNDERWATER *Hippos have webbed feet and can swim. The webbing allows them to spread their weight when they put their feet down: this helps them to walk along river beds. They can stay underwater for up to five minutes.*

▲ KEEPING WATCH *A hippo's eyes, nostrils, and ears are on top of its head. This means that it can breathe and look out for any trouble while almost totally submerged in water. Hippos can close off their nostrils and ears when underwater.*

## SURPRISE KILLERS

Hippos are thought to kill more people in Africa than any other wild animal. One minute, a hippo may appear harmless and docile, and the next, it is a rampaging killer. Hippos are known to swim under small boats, tip the occupants into the water and then attack with their huge, knife-like teeth.

## Dromedary
*Camelus dromedarius*

- **Height** 1.8–2.3 m (6–7½ ft)
- **Weight** 690 kg (1,500 lb)
- **Speed** 65 kph (40 mph)
- **Location** Northern and eastern Africa, western and southern Asia

This single-humped domestic camel is **extinct in the wild**. It eats a wide variety of plants, even salty and thorny ones, and scavenges on bones and dry carcasses.

▲ THIRSTY CREATURE
*Smaller than camels and dromedaries, vicuñas are not suited to dry conditions – they need water every day. Living high in the Andes in South America, they were once hunted so widely for their fur that they nearly became extinct.*

▲ ANCIENT SERVANT
*Native to the Andes, llamas were domesticated there thousands of years ago. Kept by the native people (and now bred all over the world) for their wool, their meat, and their skin, llamas also make excellent pack animals because they're sure-footed on rough, hilly ground.*

# Camels *and relatives*

If an animal has a split upper lip, one or two humps, long legs, and a funny rocking walk, then it's a camelid. Camelids walk this way because they move both their left legs together, then both their right legs together, in a special gait known as "pacing". Some species, such as llamas, are domesticated, while others, like vicuñas, are wild.

DESERT BEAST *The dromedary is perfectly adapted to desert life: its broad feet make it stable on shifting ground, its long lashes keep sand out of its eyes, and its nostrils close tight during dust storms. It has been used to carry loads for more than 4,000 years.*

### FACTFILE

- Bactrian camels have two humps. In winter, they grow a woolly brown coat, which they shed in spring. There are still a few wild bactrian camels in eastern Asia.

- Camels' feet have two large, evenly sized toes with a wide-cushioned pad underneath. This pad makes the animal particularly stable by spreading its weight evenly across the whole foot.

I can survive for **days and days** without any water.

Dromedaries can not only drink more than 50 litres (13 gallons) of water at a time, they can also store it; this allows them to survive for long periods without drinking. To conserve water, they produce very small amounts of sweat and urine.

◀ CAMEL HUMPS *are full of fat, which the animals store to provide them with an energy source when food is in short supply.*

MAMMALS

103

# Deer

With more than 40 species, deer can be found in most parts of the world. They are herbivorous and live in a range of habitats. Their most striking feature is their antlers, which grow on nearly all adult males.

▶ NEW PASTURES *In North America, reindeer are called caribou. In autumn, they form large herds of up to 500,000 animals and migrate slowly southwards to escape the extreme cold. In spring, they gather together again and migrate back northwards.*

## Reindeer
*Rangifer tarandus*

- **Height** 1.2 m (4 ft)
- **Weight** 300 kg (660 lb)
- **Speed** 60–80 kph (37–50 mph)
- **Location** N. North America, Greenland, N. Europe to E. Asia

Reindeer have an extremely **thick coat** to keep them warm in the cold of the far north. Their feet are furry, to give them grip on icy ground, and broad, to spread their weight and stop them sinking into the snow. Reindeer eat grass, leaves, and twigs, and also lichen, a moss-like plant. The female is the **only female deer to have antlers**.

## Indian spotted chevrotain
*Moschiola meminna*

- **Height** 35 cm (14 in)
- **Weight** 3 kg (6½ lb)
- **Location** S. Asia

Chevrotains are also known as **mouse deer**. They are not true deer and belong to a different animal family. They do not have antlers, but they do have two small tusks that point downwards. These tiny animals are **nocturnal** and prefer to live alone.

## FACTFILE

■ True deer belong to the family Cervidae. The two other families of deer are chevrotains (Tragulidae) and musk deer (Moschidae).

■ Many young deer are born with white spots to hide them from predators. They curl up and keep still in long vegetation.

■ Antlers are made of solid bone. They are shed after the rut in autumn and grow again in the spring, usually getting larger each year.

■ When antlers first grow they are covered with skin called velvet. This gradually rubs off in time for the rut.

■ Deer walk on two toes. A scent gland between the toes leaves a smell on the ground for other deer to follow.

■ Deer are native to Asia, Africa, the Americas, and Europe and have been introduced to Australia and New Zealand.

◄ ELK RUT *At the start of the breeding season, also known as the rut, male deer compete with each other for the right to breed with the females. They roar at each other and lock antlers to test each other's strength.*

# Chinese muntjac
*Muntiacus reevesi*

**10**

- ■ **Height** 55 cm (22 in)
- ■ **Weight** 18 kg (40 lb)
- ■ **Location** E. Asia

Male muntjacs have short, pointed antlers and **two short tusks**. They live mainly on their own. These deer are often called barking deer because they make loud, **bark-like calls** when they are alarmed and also during the breeding season.

# Elk
*Alces alces*

**27**

- ■ **Height** 2.3 m (7½ ft)
- ■ **Weight** 825 kg (1,820 lb)
- ■ **Speed** 55 kph (35 mph)
- ■ **Location** Alaska, Canada, N.Europe to N. and E. Asia

This is the **largest deer** and its antlers can grow up to 2 m (6½ ft) long. It is called the moose in North America. Elk eat twigs and bark and in summer often **wade into rivers** and lakes to eat water plants.

# White-tailed deer
*Odocoileus virginianus*

**10**

- ■ **Height** 1 m (3.3 ft)
- ■ **Weight** 215 kg (474 lb)
- ■ **Speed** 64 kph (40 mph)
- ■ **Location** S. Canada to N. South America

When the white-tailed deer is alarmed, it runs to safety with its long, bushy tail held up in the air. The **tail is white underneath**, and as the deer runs, the flashes of white warn other members of the herd of danger. This deer eats a variety of plant material, which is why it is able to survive in different **forest habitats**.

# Cattle and antelope

All these hoofed animals belong to the same family – the bovids. Some of them are huge and hairy; others are slim and delicate. The members of this group that have long, slender legs (such as springbok and impala) are known generally as "antelopes".

## FACTFILE

**Horny heads** All species in this family have pointed horns, which usually appear on both males and females. Horns do not branch like antlers, but they are often shaped in fantastic twists and spirals. A horn has a bony core covered by a sheath of tough material called keratin.

■ The desert-dwelling gemsbok has straight, ringed horns that can be 1.5 m (5 ft) in length.

■ The topi's horns form the shape of an "L". They are heavily ridged and point backwards.

■ The Asian water buffalo has the widest horn span of this group. It can reach 2 m (6½ ft) across.

■ Only male impalas have horns. These horns are ringed and lyre-shaped, and have heavy ridges.

## American bison
*Bison bison*

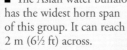

■ **Height** 1.5–2 m (5–6½ ft)
■ **Weight** 350–1,000 kg (770–2,200 lb)
■ **Location** North America

Bison are also sometimes called American buffalo. These huge animals roam in groups, spending the greater part of their day grazing and ruminating. The females, or cows, form herds with their calves under the leadership of a dominant female. The males, or bulls, live in separate herds and usually approach the cows only in the mating season. Rival bulls competing for cows **fight one another** in fierce head-to-head clashes.

▲ WRAPPED UP
*The bison's range extends to mountain areas, where the winters can be bitterly cold. With its massively thick coat and shaggy mane, the bison stays warm even when the temperature drops below zero.*

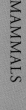

## Springbok

*Antidorcas marsupialis*

- **Height** 70–87 cm (2¼–3 ft)
- **Weight** 30–48 kg (66–106 lb)
- **Location** Southern Africa

When a springbok is frightened, or just excited, it bounces up and down on stiff legs. This leaping, called **"pronking"**, can lift the springbok as much as 3 m (nearly 10 ft) straight upwards. A frightened springbok may also open a skinfold on its back to reveal a **crest of white hairs**.

## Wild yak

*Bos grunniens*

- **Height** 2 m (6½ ft)
- **Weight** Up to 1,000 kg (2,200 lb)
- **Location** South and east Asia

Domesticated yaks are common in Asia, but wild yaks are **rare**. These hardy animals live in the icy, high-altitude steppes, and can survive on mosses and lichens. For protection against the cold they have a **double coat**. This has a dense underlayer and long top hairs.

## Impala

*Aepyceros melampus*

- **Height** 90 cm (3 ft)
- **Weight** 40–65 kg (88–143 lb)
- **Location** East and southern Africa

These small antelopes are very **agile**. They can leap high and run fast to escape predators such as leopards. A **scent released from glands** above their hind feet is thought to help a group of impala stay in touch with each other.

## Musk-ox

*Ovibos moschatus*

- **Height** 1.2–1.5 m (4–5 ft)
- **Weight** 200–410 kg (440–900 lb)
- **Location** North America, Greenland

Musk-oxen are found only in Arctic regions. They live in herds of one male with a group of females. If a herd is threatened by predators such as bears or wolves, the musk-oxen form **a defensive circle**, sheltering any young in the centre.

# Wildebeest *migration*

The wildebeest is a member of the cattle family. Huge herds roam the plains of eastern and southern Africa. In Tanzania's Serengeti National Park, more than a million wildebeest migrate with the seasons, moving from open grasslands to wooded savannah to find fresh grass.

DANGEROUS JOURNEY
*Migrating wildebeest will travel hundreds of kilometres to find fresh grass. At river crossings they are vulnerable to attacks from crocodiles, which lie in wait for them.*

# Common wildebeest
*Connochaetes taurinus*

- **Length** 1.5–2.4 m (5–8 ft)
- **Weight** 120–275 kg (260–610 lb)
- **Speed** 80 kph (50 mph)
- **Location** Eastern and southern Africa

The common wildebeest, or brindled gnu, can have **horns up to 80 cm** (31 in) long. Every spring, just before the calves are born, wildebeest seek out the richest pastures. This helps the females to produce milk for their calves that is full of health-giving nutrients.

MAMMALS

▲ *Migrating wildebeest can form herds more than a quarter of a million strong.*

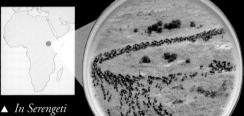

▲ *In Serengeti National Park, in Tanzania, the line of migrating wildebeest can be more than 40 km (25 miles) long.*

▲ *Wildebeest calves are born during the rainy season. They can stand and run within minutes of birth. Calves need to keep up with the herd, or they could end up as dinner for a hungry lion.*

# BIRDS

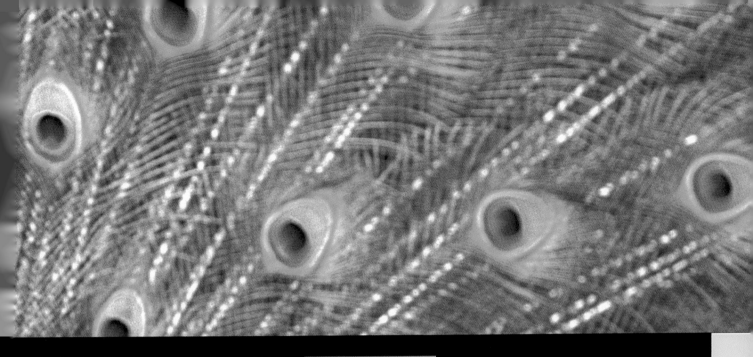

*Definition:* **Birds** are warm-blooded, egg-laying animals, most of which are able to fly. Their features include feathers, powerful wings, and hollow bones.

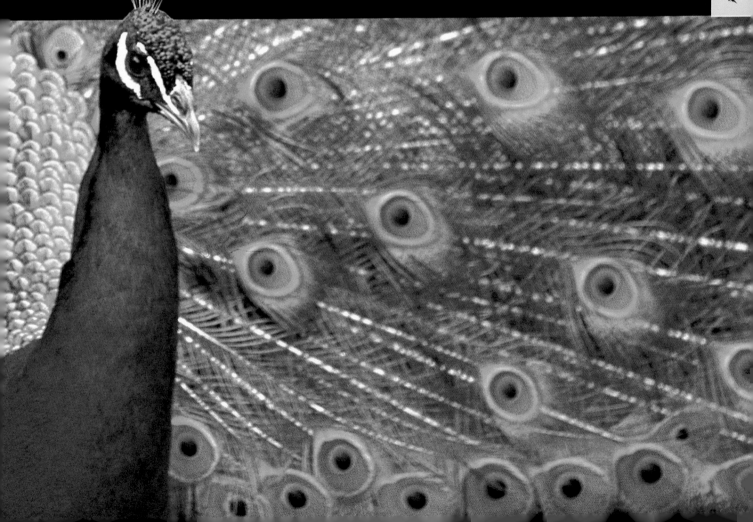

# What is a BIRD?

Birds are warm-blooded vertebrates, but they differ from other vertebrates in having feathered wings and bills instead of toothed jaws. Most can fly, and their bodies are specially adapted for this purpose.

*Wing feather*

*Down feathers*

*Contour feather*

## FACTFILE

There are almost 10,000 species of birds. They can loosely be split into groups of similar birds, including the following:

- **Flightless birds**, such as ostriches, rheas, emus, and penguins.

- **Waterbirds**, such as swans, ducks, and geese live on coasts, estuaries, or riverbanks.

- **Waders, gulls, and auks** live close to the coast and in wetlands.

- **Birds of prey**, such as falcons, vultures, and eagles, are expert predators.

- **Owls**, unlike birds of prey, are well adapted for hunting at night.

- **Fruit, nectar, and seed eaters**, such as toucans, parrots, and finches.

- **Passerines**, the largest group of birds.

*Tail feather*

**Blue and yellow macaw**
*Ara ararauna*

## FEATHERS

Feathers are formed from the same material as mammal hair – keratin – and they play an important role in protecting a bird from water and temperature changes. Flying birds have four different types of feathers: down, contour, tail, and wing.

▲ **DOWN FEATHERS** *are soft and form a warm underlayer.*

▲ **CONTOUR FEATHERS** *are small and provide a smooth covering over the body.*

▲ **TAIL FEATHERS** *are often symmetrical. They are used for flying and steering.*

▲ **WING FEATHERS** *are the flight feathers. They are long and rigid, providing the lift required for flight.*

# LIVING DINOSAURS

Many scientists now believe that birds are related to dinosaurs, because some dinosaurs appear to have been a mix of bird and reptile.

Fossilized Archaeopteryx

◀ *One of the earliest known birds was the pigeon-sized Archaeopteryx, which appeared about 150 million years ago.*

▶ *Archaeopteryx had toothed jaws, clawed fingers, and a long bony tail – all just like a dinosaur. But it also had feathers.*

# BONES FILLED WITH AIR

A bird's skeleton is lightweight, which helps to keep its body weight low for flying. In fact, many birds have feathers that weigh more than their skeleton!

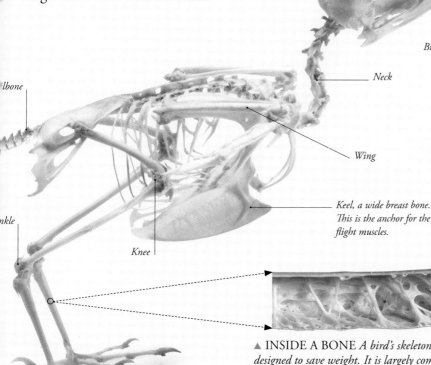

Skull

Eye socket

Bill

Neck

Wing

Tailbone

Ankle

Knee

Foot

Keel, a wide breast bone. This is the anchor for the flight muscles.

▲ INSIDE A BONE *A bird's skeleton is designed to save weight. It is largely composed of hollow bones with inner strengthening struts, as shown in this magnified picture.*

**Nests** Most birds build nests in which to lay their eggs. Nests are made from a huge variety of materials.

WOVEN GRASS NEST

**Eggs and young** Birds lay eggs, which hatch as chicks. These chicks are dependent on their parents for food and protection.

CHICK HATCHING

**Preening** Birds frequently clean and tidy their feathers to keep them in good condition. They waterproof the feathers with oil that they take from a gland at the base of the tail.

FEATHER CARE

# THE SHAPE OF A BILL

▲ FINCHES *are seed eaters and have a short, cone-shaped bill that is ideal for pecking up fallen seeds.*

▲ HUMMINGBIRDS *have long, narrow bills just perfect for extracting nectar from flowers.*

▲ PARROTS *have powerful bills, with a sharp hook to break into nuts and peel back fruit skins.*

▲ HERONS *have a long, strong, pointed bill to catch fish. They don't spear the fish, but catch it in the bill.*

▲ EAGLES *have sharp, hooked bills, which help them to tear up the prey they grasp in their talons.*

# A *world* of birds

There are about 9,000 species of birds with a huge variety of size, colour, and habitat. They all have wings and feathers, but not all of them can fly. Flightless birds include the ostrich, which runs fast on powerful legs. Penguins use their wings as flippers to speed through the water.

**Brown K**
*Apteryx mar*

**Blue-and-yellow macaw**
*Ara ararauna*

**Common crossbill**
*Loxia curvirostra*

**Toco toucan**
*Ramphastos toco*

**Yellow-fronted woodpecker**
*Melanerpes flavifrons*

**Red-billed hornbill**
*Tockus erythrorhynchus*

**Greater flamingo**
*Phoenicopterus roseus*

**Inca tern**
*Larosterna inca*

**Masked lapwing**
*Vanellus miles*

**Humboldt penguin**
*Spheniscus humboldti*

**Dalmatian pelican**
*Pelecanus crispus*

**Eurasian golden plover**
*Pluvialis apricaria*

**Wattled jacana**
*Jacana jacana*

**Chukar**
*Alectoris chukar*

**Dideric cuckoo**
*Chrysococcyx caprius*

**Common nightingale**
*Luscinia megarhynchos*

**Common pea**
*Pavo cristatus*

**dgerigar**
*lopsittacus undulatus*

**ed-tailed**
**awk**
*teo jamaicensis*

**Barn owl**
*Tyto alba*

**Laughing**
**kookaburra**
*Dacelo novaeguineae*

**Fire-tufted**
**barbet**
*Psilopogon*
*pyrolophus*

**Bearded**
**reedling**
*Panurus*
*biarmicus*

**Robin**
*Erithacus rubecula*

**Southern crested**
**caracara**
*Caracara plancus*

**Swallow-tailed**
**manakin**
*Chiroxiphia caudata*

**Scarlet ibis**
*Eudocimus ruber*

**Mallard**
*nas platyrhynchos*

**White helmet-**
**shrike**
*Prionops plumatus*

**LARGEST BIRD**
**Ostrich**
*Struthio camelus*

**SMALLEST BIRD**
**Bee hummingbird**
*Mellisuga helenae*

**Crowned crane**
*Balearica regulorum*

**King**
**penguin**
*Aptenodytes*
*patagonicus*

The ostrich
can be up to 280 cm
(108 in) tall. The **tiny**
**bee hummingbird**
is only 6 cm
(2¼ in) long.

**BIRDS**

115

# Birds of a *feather*

Not all birds can fly. These big birds are too heavy and they have small wings. Instead, they race across open countryside on their strong legs. But how can you tell an emu from an ostrich or a rhea from an emu? For a start, they come from different parts of the world.

BIRDS

## I am the **largest** bird.

Ostriches are the world's largest bird. They are also unlike other birds in having just two toes on each foot. The legs are powerful and will be used for defence to kick out at a predator if necessary.

OSTRICHES PREF
*to live in groups and a*
*rarely found on their o*
*In common with rheas*
*emus, the male bird us*
*cares for the eggs and cl*

116

# Ostrich
*Struthio camelus*

- **Height** 2–2.8 m (7–9 ft)
- **Weight** 160 kg (350 lb)
- **Speed** 70 kph (40 mph)
- **Location** W. to E. Africa (south of Sahara), southern Africa

This is the **world's largest and heaviest bird** – it is also the fastest runner. Powerful legs help to propel it forward by up to 5 metres (16 ft) at a time, and once it begins to run it can keep going for about 30 minutes. It feeds on plants (from which it gets water), insects, and lizards. Small stones are swallowed to help digestion.

# Common rhea
*Rhea americana*

- **Height** 1–1.5 m (3–5 ft)
- **Weight** 15–30 kg (33–66 lb)
- **Speed** 60 kph (37 mph)
- **Location** South America

The rhea is **also known as the American ostrich** as they look similar, but the rhea is actually about half the size. Rheas live in groups of about six individuals. They eat broad-leafed plants, seeds, fruit, insects, lizards, and small snakes. A male bird mates with up to 12 females then builds a nest where they lay eggs.

*The MALE looks after the eggs and then the newly hatched young. He will charge at anything that goes near, including the mothers.*

# Emu
*Dromaius novaehollandiae*

- **Height** 1.5–1.9 m (5–6 ft)
- **Weight** 60 kg (130 lb)
- **Speed** 50 kph (30 mph) with a 3 m- (10 ft-) stride
- **Location** Australia

**Australia's biggest bird**, the emu has drooping, fur-like feathers and **small wings**. It is named after the Portuguese word *ema*, meaning "large bird". Flocks may contain dozens of birds. They will eat berries, seeds, and insects, and will peck seeds from animal droppings.

# Birds of prey

Most of these meat-loving birds are skilled hunters, although vultures leave the killing to others, then feast on their left-overs. A bird's prey depends on its size. Some species target insects and worms; others can tackle a lamb or a young deer.

▶ FOOD PASS *Male kestrels hunt for food, but the female carries it home. She flies up to him, so he can drop his prey into her open beak. Then she flies off to feed their young.*

## Family groups

There are just over 300 different species of birds of prey (also called raptors). They are divided into five groups or families:

- **Eagles, hawks, kites, harriers, and Old World vultures**
- **Condors and New World vultures**
- **Ospreys**
- **Falcons**
- **Secretary bird** This family is unusual as it has just one member.

▶ STOOPING *Falcons spot their prey from high up in the sky, then dive down on it in a "stoop". Peregrine falcons reach speeds of up to 250 kph (155 mph) when stooping.*

## FACTFILE

- **Key features:** Most have a large head and large eyes with excellent vision. (It is thought that they can see four times as much detail as a human!) Many also have a keen sense of smell and very good hearing. Almost all have a powerful, hooked bill and strong feet, with sharp talons that they use to kill.
- **Size:** The smallest, the falconets of southeast Asia, are about the size of a sparrow, while condors can weigh up to 12.25 kg (27 lb) with a wingspan of just over 3 m (10 ft).

**Size comparison**

### Peregrine falcon
*Falco peregrinus*

15

- **Length** 34–50 cm (13–20 in)
- **Weight** 0.5–1.5 kg (1–3¼ lb)
- **Diet** Other birds
- **Location** Worldwide (except Antarctica)

The peregrine is **one of the fastest moving animals** on earth and one of the largest falcons. Females are almost twice the size of males, but both sexes are swift, efficient killers, chasing and swooping down on their prey. They are popular birds for falconry.

BIRDS

# Golden eagle
*Aquila chrysaetos*

- **Length** 75–90 cm (29½–35 in)
- **Weight** 3–6.5 kg (6½–14 lb)
- **Diet** Birds, reptiles and small mammals
- **Location** Europe, North America, Asia, North Africa

An impressive wingspan of 2.3 m (7½ ft) helps this bulky bird to soar elegantly across the sky, ready to swoop down on any prey it spots. It is often seen from a distance, but close encounters are rare. Its name comes from the **golden-brown feathers** around its neck.

*Large talons*

*Broad wings*

# White-backed vulture
*Gyps africanus*

- **Height** 94 cm (37 in)
- **Weight** 4–7 kg (8¾–15 lb)
- **Diet** Freshly dead animals (carrion)
- **Location** Central and southern Africa

Despite it size, this large bird **can be rather timid** compared with other scavengers. It will wait for others to open up a fresh carcass and is often pushed to one side when jostling for a share of the meat.

# Secretary bird
*Sagittarius serpentarius*

- **Length** 1.3–1.5 m (4–5 ft)
- **Weight** 2.5 kg–4.5 kg (5½–10 lb)
- **Diet** Snakes, insects and small rodents
- **Location** Central and southern Africa

Unlike any other bird of prey, this one has amazingly long legs. It **runs very fast** and chases its prey, which it stamps on when caught, digging in with its sharp talons.

# Northern goshawk
*Accipiter gentilis*

- **Height** 48–70 cm (19–28 in)
- **Weight** 1–1.5 kg (2¼ -3¼ lb)
- **Diet** Birds, reptiles and small mammals
- **Location** Europe, North America, Mexico, Asia

This bird is a **bold and cunning** hunter. Often it sits well hidden in a tree, ready to pounce on any unsuspecting prey that is passing by. It will happily tackle a large crow or a hare.

# Osprey
*Pandion haliaetus*

- **Height** 1.5–1.7 m (5–5½ ft)
- **Weight** 1.5–2 kg (3¼–4½ lb)
- **Diet** Fish
- **Location** Worldwide (except Antarctica)

This bird is perfectly **designed to catch fish**. It hovers patiently over lakes and rivers, waiting for a fish to swim close to the surface. Then it plunges in at lightning speed and grasps its prey firmly with its sharp claws. Talons that can move to grip both sides of the fish and small spines on the soles of the bird's feet help it to hold on to its catch.

# Andean condor
*Vultur gryphus*

- **Length** 1–1.3 m (3¼–4¼ ft)
- **Weight** 11–15 kg (24¼–33 lb)
- **Diet** Freshly dead animals (carrion)
- **Location** W. South America

This huge black vulture has the **largest wings** of any bird. It can hover around for hours, constantly on the look-out for freshly killed meat left by hunters and other animals. Deer and cattle are favourite foods. Males are bigger than females, unlike most birds of prey, and have a fleshy comb along the top of their head.

# Southern caracara
*Caracara plancus*

- **Height** 49–59 cm (19½–23 in)
- **Weight** 0.8–1.5 kg (1¾–3¼ lb)
- **Diet** Freshly dead animals (carrion), insects and small birds
- **Location** S. United States, Caribbean, South America

Caracaras feast mainly on the left-overs other animals leave behind. But they will also **steal food** from other birds, raid nests, and peck at passing insects.

**BIRDS**

119

## Bald eagle
*Haliaeetus leucocephalus*

- **Length** 71–96 cm (28–38 in)
- **Weight** 3–6.5 kg (6½–14 lb)
- **Diet** Fish, carrion, small animals and birds
- **Location** North America

The bald eagle is a large bird of prey, with a wingspan of up to 2.5 m (8 ft). It is known for its white head and neck, brown body, and white tail feathers, but this plumage does not develop until the bird is about five years old. **Females are larger than males.**

▲ NESTING *Bald eagles pair up for life, building a large nest in a tree or on the ground, which they will return to year after year, adding material each time. They will lay between one and three eggs a year, with both male and female tending them, but not all the chicks will survive.*

▲ FIGHTING FOR FOOD *Bald eagles will fight others for their food; it is sometimes easier to steal another bird's catch than hunt for their own. This happens more in winter, when food can be scarce.*

# Bald eagle

This eagle is named after its white head, though it is not bald: the head and neck are feathered. It is famou for being the national bird of the USA (since 1782), and it has been protected in North America since 1940. Its Latin name means "sea eagle".

## TIME FOR FISHING

The bald eagle is built to fish. Keen eyesight allows it to spot fish, helped on sunny days by the fact that its eyes have a bony ridge just above them to shade out the sun. Once grasped, a fish has no chance; a hind talon on each foot pierces the fish's body, while it is held securely by long front talons. It is a killer grip!

▲ A BALD EAGLE *can lift about half its weight. If a fish proves too heavy, the bird will swim to shore, using its immense wings as oars as it is unable to release the fish. However, occasionally a fish has proved so large it has pulled the eagle under and the bird has drowned.*

# Silent owls

This group of birds have mastered the skill of night hunting. Especially soft feathers mean they can swoop down almost silently on their unsuspecting prey, while hooked beaks and sharp talons help them to catch and kill very quickly.

### AN OWL'S SKULL

This diagram of an owl's skull shows how large the eyeball sockets are. Large eyes help the owl to see at night. However, an owl cannot move its eyes around. If it needs to look to the side, or even behind, it has to turn its whole head, an unusual ability in the animal world.

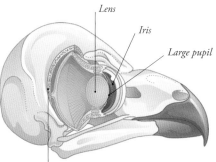

Lens

Iris

Large pupil

Eye is fixed in socket.

▲ VISION *Owls have vision that is specially adapted for night-time hunting.*

▲ CARE *Owls are attentive parents. Between one and five young are looked after in a cavity ○ tree hole, with the male bringing food and the female staying near by.*

◄ PELLETS *Owls usual swallow an animal whot and then regurgitate th indigestible fur, bones, an claws in the form of a pelle*

▼ FLIGHT *An owl flies fairly low – and silently.*

## FACTFILE

- **Number of species:** More than 200.
- **Key features:** Sharp talons, hooked bill, head that can swivel around, large eyes, soft plumage. Swallow prey whole and produce pellets containing the indigestible parts.
- **Size:** The largest is the Eagle owl (*Bubo bubo*) at up to 70 cm (28 in) in length. The smallest is the Least pygmy owl (*Glaucidium minutissimum*) at 12 cm (4¾ in) in length.

**Size comparison**

## owy owl

*tea scandiaca*

| | 10 | | | |

- **Height** 55–70 cm (22–27½ in)
- **Weight** 1–2.5 kg (2¼–5½ lb)
- **Diet** Lemmings, rabbits, hares, waterfowl
- **Location** Polar regions

is owl **lives further north** than
y other owl. Long, thick
athers extend over the
l and the toes,
eping the owl
credibly well
sulated.

## Spectacled owl

*Pulsatrix perspicillata*

| | 30 | | | |

- **Height** 43–52 cm (17–20½ in)
- **Weight** 600–1,000 g (21–35 oz)
- **Diet** Small mammals, insects, and crabs
- **Location** S. Mexico to C. South America

With the **ring of
white feathers**
around its eyes, it's
easy to see where this
owl gets its name from.
It usually makes its
home in dense
rainforest.

## Great horned owl

*Bubo virginianus*

- **Height** 50–60 cm (20–23½ in)
- **Weight** 675–2,500 g (1½–5½ lb)
- **Diet** Small mammals, insects, reptiles, amphibians, and birds
- **Location** North, Central, and South America

This owl has an **instantly recognisable hoot**.
It will choose a favourite perch, and when it
spots its prey will swoop silently down to
snatch it up. Females lay between one and five
eggs, and both the male and female will care
for the young for at least six weeks after
hatching. It is the largest American owl.

## el's fishing owl

*otopelia peli*

- **Height** 55–63 cm (22–25 in)
- **Weight** 2–2.5 kg (4½–5½ lb)
- **Diet** Fish and frogs
- **Location** Africa

s its name suggests, **this owl feeds on
sh**, in addition to frogs and any other
eshwater animals that it can catch. It
elps an animal to live near its food
ource, so the fishing owl's nest is always
ound in a tree hole at the edges of lakes,
vers, swamps, and marshes. Long,
urved talons help it to grasp and hold
nto its usually slippery prey.

## Barn owl

*Tyto alba*

| | | | | 2 | |

- **Height** 29–44 cm (11½–17 in)
- **Weight** 300–650 g (11–23 oz)
- **Diet** Small rodents
- **Location** North, Central, and South America, Europe, Asia, Africa, and Australia

This owl is the **most
widespread** of all
owls, and is found on
all continents apart
from Antarctica. It nests in
a hollow tree, or an
abandoned building. It has a
shriek rather than a hoot.

**BIRDS**

## Southern boobook
*Ninox novaeseelandiae*

- **Height** 30–35 cm (12–14 in)
- **Weight** 150–175 g (5–6 oz)
- **Diet** Insects, small mammals, and birds
- **Location** Australia (including Tasmania), S. New Guinea, S.E. Asia

This owl is **named for its
cry**, a distinctive two-
syllable "boo book".
It is Australia's
smallest owl, and
often hunts by
snatching flying
insects from
the air.

## Common scops owl
*Otus scops*

| | | 7 | | |

- **Height** 16–20 cm (6½–8 in)
- **Weight** 60–125 g (2⅛–4 oz)
- **Diet** Insects, spiders, worms, bats, and small birds
- **Location** Europe to C. Asia, Africa

This owl is hard to spot as its
plumage means it can almost
vanish when motionless
against a background of tree
bark. It will even sway, if
surprised, to imitate a branch
moving in the wind! **Its call is
a low whistle**, not a hoot.

# Gamebirds

The birds in this group usually live on the ground in a wide variety of habitats. Wild gamebirds, such as grouse and pheasants, have long been a food source for humans and hunted for sport, while their domestic relations, such as chickens, are a valuable source of meat and eggs.

## FACTFILE

■ **Number of species:** 280
■ **Key features:** Gamebirds are mainly ground dwellers. The cocks (males) of many species have spectacular plumage or brightly coloured patches of bare skin, while the hens (females) are usually very dull in colour. The cocks perform elaborate courtship displays to attract hens. Many gamebirds use camouflage to escape detection by predators.

The numbers show where the birds featured opposite are found.

◀ SHORT SPRINT *A pheasant launches into flight to escape from a predator. The strong flight muscles can support short bursts of speed but are useless for longer distances.*

BIRDS

FEATHER FAN *A peacock fans out his train of feathers to attract a peahen during courtship. He shakes the fan of erect feathers during the display to add to the effect.*

124

# ommon peafowl

*o cristatus*

**Length** 1.8–2.3 m (6–7½ ft)
**Weight** 4–6 kg (8¾–13 lb)
**Diet** Fruit, seeds, insects, snakes
**Location** India, Pakistan

w can mistake the spectacular sight of a
le peafowl (peacock) displaying his long
in of "tail" feathers. Each feather
ends from the bird's back, not
e tail, and ends with a
lourful "eye".

*Shimmering blue neck and breast.*

*Long train of "tail" feathers.*

▲ TRUE COLOURS *A bright feather train is a sign of a strong peacock, since it will attract predators as well as peahens.*

# Willow ptarmigan

*Lagopus lagopus*

- **Length** About 38 cm (15 in)
- **Weight** 550–700 g (20–25 oz)
- **Diet** Mosses, lichens, berries; chicks also eat insects
- **Location** N. Northern Hemisphere

These are hardy gamebirds, with **feathery legs** to insulate them from the cold winter. Most of these birds turn from reddish brown to white in winter as camouflage, but willow grouse from Scotland (known as red grouse) are an exception.

# emminck's tragopan

*agopan temminckii*

**Length** 64 cm (25 in)
**Weight** Not recorded
**Diet** Plants, insects
**Location** C. and S.E. Asia

During courtship, the cock **inflates his blue and red throat wattle,** which looks like a brightly coloured bib. If this show of strength impresses a hen, the pair will mate. The cock **mates with lots of hens** but plays no part in rearing his young.

# Helmeted guineafowl

*Numida meleagris*

- **Length** 55–58 cm (22–23 in)
- **Weight** 1.3 kg (3 lb)
- **Diet** Omnivorous
- **Location** Africa

As adults, the heads of these large, **compact** gamebirds lack any feathers, and they are topped with **yellow or red bony helmets** and decorated with patches of red and blue skin.

# Common pheasant

*Phasianus colchicus*

- **Length** Up to 90 cm (36 in)
- **Weight** 0.75–2 kg (1¾–4½ lb)
- **Diet** Plants, insects, small vertebrates
- **Location** Native to Asia

As one of the **most popular** gamebirds, the common pheasant has been introduced to many countries. The cock is much brighter than the hen, with **distinctive red wattles** (fleshy bulges) on the face to attract hens during courtship.

# Red jungle-fowl

*Gallus gallus*

- **Length** 80 cm (32 in)
- **Weight** 0.5–1.5 kg (1–3¼ lb)
- **Diet** Mainly seeds and small insects
- **Location** C. and S.E. Asia

The domestic **chicken is the descendant** of the red jungle-fowl, which lives around forests and the edges of villages and plantations.

# Mallee fowl

*Leipoa ocellata*

- **Length** 60 cm (24 in)
- **Weight** 2 kg (4½ lb)
- **Diet** Buds, fruits, seeds and the odd insect and spider
- **Location** S.W. Australia

Mallee fowl are unusual because they **do not lay on their eggs** to keep them warm. Like other megapodes, these birds build a **natural incubator,** laying their eggs in a pile of mud and rotting plant matter. The heat given off keeps the eggs warm.

▶ EGG COMPOST *If the eggs get too cold, the mallee fowl adds more mud and vegetation to its home-made incubator.*

125

# Seabirds and shorebirds

The birds of sea and shore live in or near the world's oceans. Seabirds spend most of their lives at sea but return to shore to breed. They are strong fliers and some can dive into the sea to catch fish. Shorebirds live along the coast. Many have long legs and probing bills to forage beneath the sand and mud for crustaceans, molluscs and marine worms.

## Ivory gull
*Pagophila eburnea*

- **Length** 40–43 cm (16–17 in)
- **Weight** 450–700 g (16–24 oz)
- **Diet** Fish, marine invertebrates, small mammals, and carrion
- **Location** High Arctic, from Canada and Greenland to northern Europe and Russia

Like all gulls, the ivory gull is a **scavenger**. It feeds on the remains left behind by predators such as polar bears. Little else is known about these birds since they live on the edge of the pack ice deep within the Arctic Circle.

### FACTFILE

- **Number of species:** Around 350
- **Key features:** Usually plain with bright body parts such as eyes or legs; bills come in many shapes and sizes, from long, slender bills used to probe in the mud, to short, compact bills for stabbing at prey; may have salt glands to expel the excess salt from seawater.

The numbers show where the featured animals are found.

FEEDING FRENZY *Every May, horseshoe crabs lay their eggs on the shores of Delaware Bay in the USA. The eggs are a feast for hungry shorebirds such as laughing gulls.*

## Herring gull
*...rus argentatus*

- **Length** 55–66 cm (22–26 in)
- **Weight** 0.8–1.5 kg (1¾–3¼ lb)
- **Diet** Fish, invertebrates, small birds, ...s, carrion, and human rubbish
- **Location** Northern Hemisphere

...ese large, noisy gulls
...e a common sight
...ong coastal regions,
...t they are also **found
...rther inland**, where
...ey scavenge
...a rubbish
...s and in
...y centres.

## Brown skua
*Catharacta antarctica*

- **Length** About 60 cm (24 in)
- **Weight** 1.6–1.9 kg (3½–4¼ lb)
- **Diet** Fish, marine invertebrates, small seabirds and their chicks, eggs, carrion
- **Location** Antarctic and sub-Antarctic zones around the Southern Ocean

In summer, brown skuas breed in sheltered rocky areas on the many islands of the Southern Ocean. A breeding pair **defend their nest fiercely**, flying at the heads of intruders with claws outstretched. The birds fly north in winter, spending a lot of time at sea.

## ...inged plover
*...haradrius hiaticula*

- **Length** 17–20 cm (7–8 in)
- **Weight** About 60 g (2¼ oz)
- **Diet** Mainly marine invertebrates
- **Location** Breeds in Arctic and northern temperate ...nes; many migrate to Africa and Asia for the winter

Ringed plovers are small, plump wading birds that **forage for food on beaches**, fields and tidal flats. As these birds tap their feet on the loose sand or mud, tiny marine worms and other invertebrates rise to the surface to be eaten.

## Avocet
*Recurvirostra avosetta*

- **Length** 40–45 cm (16–18 in)
- **Weight** About 400 g (14 oz)
- **Diet** Insects and crustaceans
- **Location** Europe, Africa, and Asia

When feeding, the distinctive avocet sweeps its **slender, upturned bill** from side to side through the water. Many avocets winter in southern Africa and Asia and then migrate north in the summer to breed.

## Common oystercatcher
*Haematopus ostralegus*

- **Length** About 42 cm (17 in)
- **Weight** About 540 g (19 oz)
- **Diet** Marine worms and shellfish
- **Location** Europe, Africa, and Asia

Shellfish such as limpets and mussels are favourite food for these striking birds, but they do **eat oysters** when they find them. They use their bright bills to prise the two halves of the shell apart and stab at the soft parts inside.

## ...Guillemot
*...ria aalge*

- **Length** 38–46 cm (15–18½ in)
- **Weight** 0.9–1 kg (2–2¼ lb)
- **Diet** Fish and marine invertebrates
- **Location** Across the Northern Hemisphere as far south as Mexico and North Africa

These **expert divers** can descend to depths of 40 metres (130 feet) or more when fishing. Common guillemots gather in **huge breeding colonies** on rocky cliffs and sea stacks. Three weeks after hatching, the chick leaves its nesting ledge and flies out to sea.

## Atlantic puffin
*Fratercula arctica*

- **Length** 25–30 cm (10–12 in)
- **Weight** 340–540 g (12–19 oz)
- **Diet** Mainly small fish
- **Location** High Arctic to the Mediterranean depending on the season

The **large, colourful bill** of the Atlantic puffin can hold a vast number of small fish such as capelin and sprat. When feeding, these striking seabirds gather in large groups, called rafts, a few miles offshore.

# Penguins

These flightless birds are found only in the seas and cold currents of the southern hemisphere. Penguins are fast, graceful swimmers, but on land they waddle awkwardly. To speed up a long journey over snow and ice, penguins sometimes toboggan on their bellies.

## LIVING IN COLONIES

Penguins spend a lot of their lives in water hunting for food. However, most species come on land in the warmer months to live in colonies and breed. Colonies can be made up of hundreds of thousands of birds. Penguins communicate by calls and visual displays when they are gathered in large groups.

**Anatomy** Penguins have plump bodies, short legs, and webbed feet. Their coat of dense feathers repels water and traps in body heat. Penguins have a thick layer of fat, called blubber, which insulates them from cold weather. Their wing bones are flattened to form flippers and solid to increase strength.

Skull

Neck

Eye socket

Bill

Tail bo...

Chest bone

Elbow

Wing

Foot

PENGUIN SKELETON

**King penguin**
*Aptenodytes patagonicus*

DIVING *Penguins can dive down to about 290 m (951 ft), flapping their wings to provide power. Some species can swim at speeds of 14 kph (9 mph).*

### FACTFILE

- **Number of species:** 17–20
- **Key features:** Live in colonies; fast swimmers.
- **Diet:** Fish, krill, and squid
- **Largest:** Emperor penguin, up to 115 cm (45 in) in height.
- **Smallest:** Little penguin, up to 45 cm (18 in) in height.

Little and Emperor penguins

2

3

4

5

1

7

6

The numbers show where the featured animals are found.

128

# Emperor penguin

*Aptenodytes forsteri*

- **Height** 110–115 cm (43–45 in)
- **Weight** 35–40 kg (77–88 lb)
- **Location** Southern Ocean, Antarctica

Emperor penguins are the only penguins to breed during the harsh Antarctic winter. After laying her single egg, the female goes back to the sea. Her **male partner looks after the egg for two months**, holding it on his feet beneath a flap of belly skin. All the males huddle together in a group to keep warm during winter storms. The females return to feed the chicks when they hatch.

FLUFFY *The grey down of emperor chicks is not waterproof, so they cannot go in the sea.*

# African penguin
*Spheniscus demersus*

- **Height** 60–70 cm (24–28 in)
- **Weight** 5 kg (11 lb)
- **Location** S.W. coast of Africa, Namibia

Also called the Cape or jackass penguin, this penguin **breeds in Africa**, coming ashore to nest in **burrows**. Over-fishing and oil spills have caused a shortage of food for the African penguin.

# Galápagos penguin
*Spheniscus mendiculus*

- **Height** 48–53 cm (19–20.8 in)
- **Weight** 2–2.5 kg (4½–5 lb)
- **Location** Galápagos Islands and Isabela Island

Galápagos penguins are **among the rarest** species of penguin. They live the farthest north and because of this they struggle to keep cool. To help heat escape from their bodies they **hold out their wings**.

# Royal penguin
*Eudyptes schlegeli*

- **Height** 70 cm (28 in)
- **Weight** 6 kg (13 lb)
- **Location** Antarctica

This is one of several species of penguins known as **crested penguins**, which have plumes on their head. A **female royal penguin lays two eggs**. The first egg, which is small, is kicked out of the nest. The reason for this is unknown.

# Humboldt penguin
*Spheniscus humboldti*

- **Height** 56–66 cm (22–26 in)
- **Weight** 4.5–5 kg (10–11 lb)
- **Location** Peru and N. Chile

Like all penguins, Humboldt penguins are very **sociable**. Their nesting burrows are always close together and the birds usually hunt in a group. Over-fishing in the area has reduced the Humboldt penguins' food supply and caused a **decline in their numbers**.

# Little penguin

*Eudyptula minor*

- **Height** 40–45 cm (16–18 in)
- **Weight** 1 kg (2¼ lb)
- **Location** S. and S.E. Australia, New Zealand, Tasman Sea, and Southern Ocean

This is the **smallest** penguin and the only one that stays offshore in the daytime. Most little penguins live in **sand or soil burrows**, but some make their homes among fallen rocks or under houses and sheds.

# Gentoo penguin

*Pygoscelis papua*

- **Height** 75–90 cm (30–35 in)
- **Weight** 8.5 kg (19 lb)
- **Location** Sub-Antarctic islands

No other penguin can swim as **fast underwater** as a gentoo penguin. These birds make their nests from stones and twigs piled up in a circular shape. They guard their property jealously. Arguments frequently break out in a gentoo colony because one bird has stolen a pebble from another's nest. The **chicks are cared for by both parents**.

# The *wandering* albatross

The wandering albatross is the world's largest seabird, with an incredible wing span that can reach 3.5 m (11 ft). Albatrosses spend much of their long lives soaring over the sea, on trips that cover thousands of kilometres. They come on land to breed.

GROWTH *Albatrosses take about nine years to mature into adults, before they seek a mate. They will pair up for life.*

# Ready to **fly**.

A wandering albatross has powerful flight muscles. Albatrosses have been observed following ships across oceans without stopping to rest. One bird travelled 6,000 km (3,700 miles) in 12 days.

## Wandering albatross
*Diomedea exulans*

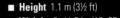

- **Height** 1.1 m (3½ ft)
- **Weight** 8–11.5 kg (18–25 lb)
- **Diet** Fish and squid
- **Location** Circumpolar around Antarctica

Although the wandering albatross has a large wingspan, each wing is actually just 23 cm (9 in) at its widest point. **Long narrow wings** allow the bird to glide on air currents with ease.

### CONSERVATION

Several species of albatross are under threat. Many have been accidentally killed when caught on baited hooks set out for fish, while others have lost eggs to foxes or rats. Efforts are now being made to protect them.

**BIRDS**

▲ NESTING *An albatross lays a single 10 cm- (4 in-) long egg in a nest made from mud, grass, and moss. Parents take it in turns to sit on the egg and will then feed the chick for the first nine months of its life. Albatrosses breed slowly, laying perhaps one egg every second year, so their success depends on the survival of these individual chicks.*

# Pelicans and relatives

These large birds include boobies, cormorants, gannets, and frigatebirds as well as the pelicans. Pelicans and their relatives are the only birds with webbing between all four toes, so most are strong swimmers. They all eat fish, but they catch their food in different ways.

## Brown pelican
*Pelecanus occidentalis*

■ **Length** 1–1.5 m (3¼–5 ft)
■ **Weight** Up to 5.5 kg (12 lb)
■ **Diet** Mainly fish
■ **Location** Caribbean and the Americas

This is the **smallest of the eight pelicans**, and it is the only one that dives in water to catch fish. It dives headfirst, mouth wide open, scooping up fish in its large throat pouch. The weight of the catch can often prevent the pelican from flying.

PELICAN PLUNGE *With wings folded back, these brown pelicans are ready to plunge into the sea to catch their next meal.*

## FACTFILE

■ **Number of species:** 67
■ **Key features:** Four webbed toes on each foot; diving species have small or closed nostrils (some breathe through their mouth); nest in large colonies.
■ **Distribution:** Found near coastal waters of most seas and oceans; also found around inland waters.
■ **Diet:** Mainly fish but some will eat crustaceans, molluscs and other marine invertebrates.

The numbers show where the featured birds are found.

# lue-footed booby
*a nebouxii*

20+

2

**Length** 80–85 cm (31–33 in)
**Weight** 1.5 kg (3¼ lb)
**Diet** Fish and squid
**Location** Mexico to northern South
erica and the Galápagos Islands

e **bright blue feet** that
ve this bird its name
ay a part in the male's
ating dance. He struts
front of his mate,
sing each foot
turn. She tucks
r head under her
ng as a sign of approval.

# Red-billed tropic bird
*Phaethon aethereus*

15+

3

- **Length** 78–80 cm (31–32 in)
- **Weight** 600–825 g (21–29 oz)
- **Diet** Squid and fish
- **Location** Tropical waters of the Atlantic, eastern
Pacific and northern Indian oceans

These small seabirds spend most of their lives
hundreds of kilometres from land, **flying high
above the ocean**. Red-billed tropic birds come
to land to breed, usually on remote tropical
islands. The female lays a single egg on a rocky
cliff ledge or directly on the ground. Although
they are poor swimmers, these birds plunge-
dive from great heights to catch their prey.
They are especially fond of flying fish.

### STREAM AND SCREAM
*These birds flick their tail
streamers and make screaming
calls in a spectacular, but
noisy, aerial courtship display.*

# rown booby
*la leucogaster*

25+

4

**Length** 64–85 cm (25–33½ in)
**Weight** 0.7–1.5 kg (1½–3¼ lb)
**Diet** Squid and fish
**Location** Tropical Pacific, Atlantic, and Indian oceans

The brown booby is **an expert
diver**, plunging into the ocean
from heights of 30 metres
(100 feet). The streamlined
shape of the bird helps it to cut
through the water to catch its
prey. Brown boobies also skim
the surface of the ocean,
picking off flying fish as
they leap from the water.

# Great cormorant
*Phalacrocorax carbo*

15

5

- **Length** 80–100 cm
(31–39 in)
- **Weight** Up to 3.5 kg (7¾ lb)
- **Diet** Mainly fish
- **Location** Eastern North America,
Greenland, Eurasia, central to
southern Africa

Great cormorants are sleek
and streamlined – the **ideal
shape for diving and
swimming**. These common
coastal seabirds can dive to
considerable depths, but they
often fish in shallow water.

# Galápagos cormorant
*Phalacrocorax harrisi*

?

6

- **Length** 100 cm
(39 in)
- **Weight** 2.5–
4 kg (5½–8¾ lb)
- **Diet** Mainly fish
- **Location** Galápagos Islands

The Galápagos cormorant lives
on the islands of Fernandina
and Isabela on the western
shores of the Galápagos. These
birds have **lost the ability to fly**. Instead, they
use their powerful legs and webbed feet to
swim after squid, octopus and eels, and other
small fish.

# Northern gannet
*Morus bassanus*

25+

7

- **Length** 80–110 cm (31–43 in)
- **Weight** 2.5–3 kg (5½–6½ lb)
- **Diet** Mainly fish
- **Location** North Atlantic
and Mediterranean

These gannets spend **most
of their lives at sea** but
nest in dense colonies
on steep rocky
cliffs and sea
stacks. A pair
breed for life,
using the same
nest year
after year.

# Great frigatebird
*Fregata minor*

40

8

- **Length** 85–105 cm (33–41 in)
- **Weight** 1–1.5 kg (2¼–3¼ lb)
- **Diet** Fish and squid
- **Location** Tropical Pacific, Atlantic, and Indian oceans

During courtship, groups of males shake
their wings and inflate their magnificent
**scarlet throat pouches** like balloons. The
female chooses a mate based on his display.

# Oriental darter
*Anhinga melanogaster*

?

9

- **Length** 85–97 cm (33–38 in)
- **Weight** 1–2 kg (2¼–4½ lb)
- **Diet** Fish
- **Location** Southern and
Southeast Asia

The Oriental darter is often
called the snakebird thanks
to its **long, snake-like
head**. This bird swims
with its body
submerged, but its
head and neck above
the water.

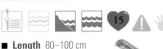

# Waterbirds

Some of these birds swim and dive, others wade in shallow lakes and swamps or even trot across the water surface on floating plants. Most waterbirds also fly well. Many swans and ducks migrate huge distances every year between their breeding grounds and the regions where they spend the winter.

## Mute swan
*Cygnus olor*

- **Height** 1.2–1.6 m (4–5¼ ft)
- **Weight** 9.5–12 kg (21–26 lb)
- **Diet** Aquatic plants, small fish, frogs, insects
- **Location** North America, Europe, Africa, Asia, Australia

Although they make less noise than other swans, mute swans are **not silent**. They call and sometimes hiss or snort. A mute swan can **fly at over 50 kph** (31 mph). Its wings make a loud creaking sound that can be heard as the swan passes overhead.

## FACTFILE

- **Key features:** Swimming birds such as ducks and swans have webbed feet and waterproof feathers. Some waterbirds feed while they are in the water, either by diving or dabbling for food. Others forage on land.

◀ HEAD FIRST
*Up-ending, known as dabbling, allows ducks and swans to extend their reach when they search for food in the water.*

LIFT OFF *To get its heavy body airborne, the mute swan needs a long runway. The bird launches itself with much inelegant pedalling of feet and flapping of wings.*

# lack swan

*gnus atratus*

- **Height** 1.1–1.4 m (3½–4½ ft)
- **Weight** 5–6 kg (11–13 lb)
- **Diet** Plants (mainly aquatic)
- **Location** Australia (including Tasmania), New Zealand

ese swans sometimes travel together in lonies numbering many thousands. They usually **nest together**, too, although some breeding pairs may stay apart from the rest. In Europe, black swans are kept as **ornamental** pets.

# Wattled jacana

*Jacana jacana*

- **Height** 17–25 cm (6½–10 in)
- **Weight** 90–125 g (3–4 oz)
- **Diet** Insects, aquatic invertebrates, rice seeds
- **Location** S. Central America, South America

Big, splayed feet spread this bird's weight and allow it to **walk on floating water plants** without sinking. The female wattled jacana usually takes **several mates**. She lays her eggs in floating nests.

# Great crested grebe

*Podiceps cristatus*

- **Height** 46–51 cm (18–20 in)
- **Weight** 0.6–1.5 kg (1¼–3¼ lb)
- **Diet** Fish, aquatic invertebrates
- **Location** Europe, Asia, Africa, Australia, New Zealand

The black head feathers and **spectacular frill** of the great crested grebe are displayed to full effect during the bird's courtship ceremony. A pair of grebes perform elaborate **dances in the water** and offer one another gifts of weeds.

# Goosander

*Mergus merganser*

- **Height** 58–66 cm (23–26 in)
- **Weight** 1.5–2 kg (3¼–4½ lb)
- **Diet** Fish
- **Location** North America, Europe, Asia

he goosander is an unusual duck because it as a long thin bill with **sharp "sawteeth"** long the edges. This means that the bird can et a firm grip on slippery fish. Goosanders unt by putting heir head below he surface of the water and **iving** for heir prey.

MALE GOOSANDER

# Mallard

*Anas platyrhynchos*

- **Height** 50–65 cm (19½–26 in)
- **Weight** 1–1.5 kg (2¼–3¼ lb)
- **Diet** Aquatic plants, grasses, small aquatic invertebrates
- **Location** North America, Greenland, Europe, and Asia

One of the **commonest** of all ducks, mallards are found across the northern hemisphere. Most domestic ducks are descended from the mallard. Both male and female mallards can be recognized by their noticeable **blue wing patch**.

*Dark green head*

MALE MALLARD

*Blue wing patch*

FEMALE MALLARD

# Muscovy duck

*Cairina moschata*

- **Height** 66–84 cm (26–33 in)
- **Weight** 2–4 kg (4½–8¾ lb)
- **Diet** Leaves, seeds, insects, small aquatic invertebrates
- **Location** Central America, N. South America

Domesticated muscovy ducks are kept all over the world and appear in many colour forms. Wild muscovy ducks have **black plumage** with some white feathers in their wings.

# Mandarin duck

*Aix galericulata*

- **Height** 41–49 cm (16–19 in)
- **Weight** 500–625 g (18–22 oz)
- **Diet** Plants, insects, snails
- **Location** N.W. Europe, E. Asia

These ducks are at home both in water and on land. They make their nests high in trees, safe from predators. The **fantastic plumage** of the male mandarin duck (seen here) has made this bird popular in captivity.

# Horned screamer

*Anhima cornuta*

- **Height** 80–95 cm (31–37 in)
- **Weight** 2–3 kg (4½–6½ lbs)
- **Diet** Leaves, grass, seeds
- **Location** N. South America

Screamers are **heavily built** birds that look rather like large domestic fowl. The horn that juts out from the head of the horned screamer is in fact a long **feather quill**. The bird's calls are hoots and honks rather than screams.

# Migration: *Snow geese*

Some birds fly thousands of kilometres each year, following "pathways" in the sky that are only visible to them. These snow geese, for example, follow well-established migration routes in search of richer feeding grounds or to return to their nesting grounds.

WE ARE FAMILY *Snow geese are sturdy birds. They have to be: it can take them more than 10 weeks to reach their nesting grounds, allowing for night-time rests. They fly in family groups within huge flocks.*

# Greater snow goose

*Anser caerulescens atlanticus*

- **Length** 69–83 cm (27–33 in)
- **Weight** Up to 2.7 kg (6 lb)
- **Speed** Up to 95 kph (60 mph)
- **Location** Canada, Greenland, E. North America

This goose is white, apart from the tips of its feathers, which are black. Some birds have a **blue-grey plumage**, and were once thought to be a different species, but they are now known to be the same. Pairs stay together for life.

▲ V-FORMATION *Why do migrating birds fly in a V-formation? It means that each bird is flying in the slipstream of the one in front, which is a lot less work and so saves energy. The lead bird changes frequently: it's a tiring place to be!*

▶ GRAZING *Snow geese graze on wetland rich with plant-life. They largely feed on aquatic plants, roots, grasses, and grains. They swallow small amounts of sand and grit to help them digest the plants.*

## ANNUAL MOVEMENT

Snow geese breed on the Arctic tundra, but fly some 5,000 km (3,000 miles) south away from the Arctic winter in September in enormous, noisy flocks, which may number more than 100,000 birds. They return to the Arctic in the following spring.

## Why are we "**snow**" geese?

Snow geese are named for their white colouring, which, when a large flock descends, looks a little like a blizzard of falling snow. Young birds have more grey feathers, flecked with white, which change to white in their first year.

## My feathers really **shine**.

A kingfisher's feathers shimmer because they are iridescent. The feathers have a fine layer on them that acts like a soap bubble and scatters light, so you see the vivid colours reflected back at you.

◄ FISH KING *The majestic kingfisher plunges headfirst into the water and grabs its prey in its long, straight bill.*

# Kingfishers and relatives

Kingfishers are famous for their fishing skills, but they have many relatives that live far from rivers and streams. These include bee-eaters, hoopoes, and hornbills. The birds in this group live in woodland habitats around the world.

### FACTFILE

- **Number of species:** 191
- **Key features:** Large heads and bills relative to the size of their compact bodies; legs usually short, with two toes fused near the base of the foot; many have bright plumage; all species nest in holes.
- **Body size:** The largest of these birds are the hornbills at lengths of up to 1.5 m (4¾ ft); the smallest are the todies at lengths of just 10 cm (4 in).

Size comparison

# Common kingfisher
*...do atthis*

- **Length** 16–19 cm (6½–7½ in)
- **Weight** 35 g (1¼ oz)
- **Diet** Mainly fish
- **Location** Eurasia, North Africa

Stand by any river or stream in Europe, and you might see a flash of brilliant colour as one of these **swift, active birds** flies past. The kingfisher returns to a favourite perch after a catch, striking the head of the unfortunate fish before swallowing it whole.

# Pied kingfisher
*Ceryle rudis*

- **Length** 25 cm (10 in)
- **Weight** 90 g (3¼ oz)
- **Diet** Fish
- **Location** Africa, southern Asia, and southeast Asia

The **breeding behaviour of these birds is rather unusual.** The breeding pair raises the young with the help of up to four other kingfishers. Often the helpers are young from a previous brood, but they may be completely unrelated. These birds are equally at home hunting in fresh water or salt water.

# European bee-eater
*Merops apiaster*

- **Length** 27–30 cm (11–12 in)
- **Weight** 70 g (2½ oz)
- **Diet** Stinging insects
- **Location** Europe, Central Asia and Africa

As its common name suggests, this **brightly coloured** bee-eater loves to eat stinging insects such as bees, hornets, and wasps. Before swallowing its meal, the bee-eater rubs the insect's tail against a perch and then squeezes the body in its bill to get rid of the sting. These birds **may eat 250 or more stinging insects** in this way **every day.**

# Great Indian hornbill
*...ceros bicornis*

- **Length** 1.5 m (5 ft)
- **Weight** 3 kg (6½ lb)
- **Diet** Fruits and small vertebrates
- **Location** Southern and southeast Asia

...he **large yellow helmet** on the head of ...is massive hornbill is **called a casque.** ...o one knows for sure what purpose the ...asque serves. It may have developed as ...way of attracting a mate, ...ut males have also ...een known ...o use it as ...battering ...am when fighting.

# Southern yellow-billed hornbill
*Tockus leucomelas*

- **Length** 50–60 cm (20–24 in)
- **Weight** 250 g (9 oz)
- **Diet** Fruits and insects
- **Location** Southern Africa

This hornbill is a **common sight on the savanna,** where it forages for insects, spiders, scorpions, and fruits such as figs. These birds **team up with dwarf mongooses and act as lookouts,** while the mongooses flush out locusts in return for the favour.

# Green wood hoopoe
*Phoeniculus purpureus*

- **Length** 44 cm (17¾ in)
- **Weight** 75 g (2½ oz)
- **Diet** Insects, earthworms, slugs, snails and spiders
- **Location** Sub-Saharan Africa

Yet another brightly coloured bird from this group, the green wood hoopoe is an **agile tree climber** that uses its slender, down-curved bill to probe the bark for insects and other invertebrates. These birds live in close-knit groups of up to 16, headed by a dominant breeding pair.

# Blue-crowned motmot
*Momotus momota*

- **Length** 46 cm (18½ in)
- **Weight** 150 g (5 oz)
- **Diet** Mainly insects
- **Location** Central America to central South America, Trinidad and Tobago

The colourful blue-crowned motmot **perches quietly for most of the day,** swinging its racquet-shaped tail feather like a pendulum.

# Laughing kookaburra
*Dacelo novaeguineae*

- **Length** 40–45 cm (16–18 in)
- **Weight** 350 g (13 oz)
- **Diet** Insects, snails, and small vertebrates
- **Location** Southern Australia (including Tasmania) and New Zealand

What this bird lacks in colour it makes up for with its raucous call. The kookaburra is the **largest of the kingfishers** and maintains its bulk by eating a range of small animals, such as frogs, birds, fish, and snakes.

## Lesser flamingo
*Phoeniconaias minor*

- **Height** Up to 1 m (3 ft)
- **Weight** Up to 2 kg (4½ lb)
- **Plumage** Sexes alike
- **Location** W., C., and southern Africa

This is the **smallest flamingo**, but it is also the most numerous. Like all flamingos, it likes company: some colonies contain more than one million birds! It feeds at dusk and after dark.

## AN UNUSUAL BILL

Flamingos wade in shallow water to feed, using their feet to stir up the muddy bottom. They feed with their heads almost upside-down, sweeping their specialized bill from side to side to filter out food particles. Large flamingos feed on crustaceans, molluscs, and worms. Small flamingos feed on microscopic algae.

BRINE SHRIMP

**Why so pink?** Flamingos get their pink colour from pigments in the food they eat. The pigment is made by algae, which are microscopic plant-like organisms. These are either swallowed by the flamingos, or they enter the bird's digestive system after the flamingo eats brine shrimp that have fed on the algae. It's a mini food chain!

# Flamingos

Flamingos nest in huge, noisy colonies consisting of many thousands of birds. These colourful birds are found in the tropics and subtropics. Their large nests are spaced so each roosting bird cannot quite reach its neighbour; a tactic that helps to prevent pecking!

I can sleep on **one** leg.

Flamingos will often stand on one leg. It is thought that this helps to lessen the amount of heat lost through the legs and feet.

FLAMINGOS *make their nests from flattened cones of mud, and a colony will lay eggs within the same few days. After a week or so, the chicks will join large creches.*

# Herons and relatives

Lanky legs, snake-like necks, and heavy, stabbing bills are features shared by many of these birds. The group includes storks, egrets, spoonbills, bitterns, and ibises. Most of them live near fresh water and eat fish. The herons are stealth-hunters that wait motionless for prey before making a lightning strike.

## FACTFILE

- **Number of species:** 115
- **Key features:** Most of these birds have splayed toes that enable them both to wade in shallow water and mud, and to stand in trees. They usually live alone, except in the breeding season. The majority are good flyers.

The numbers show where the featured animals are found

▼ ON THE RUN *The courtship displays of the grey heron include running and prancing with wings held open. The bird's big, rounded wings measure 1.5 metres (nearly 5 ft) from tip to tip.*

► GOOD CATCH
*The rare great white heron, a colour form of the great grey heron, lives only in the Florida Keys.*

## American bittern
*Botaurus lentiginosus*

- **Height** 58–86 cm (23–34 in)
- **Weight** 370–500 g (13–18 oz)
- **Location** North and Central America

In the reed beds where it lives, the bittern is disguised by its **striped plumage**. When it is startled, the bird **freezes**, with its head pointing straight upwards. This pose makes it even more unnoticeable. However, the bird's booming call means that it is easily heard.

## Scarlet ibis
*Eudocimus ruber*

- **Height** 55–70 cm (21½–28 in)
- **Weight** 600–750 g (21–27 oz)
- **Location** South America

The brilliant feathers of the scarlet ibis get some of their colour from pigments in the bird's food. Scarlet ibises like wet, muddy areas such as swamps, but for safety they build their nests in trees well above the water. If they can, they **nest on islands**, where their eggs and chicks are less likely to be in danger from predators.

# riated heron

*rides striatus*

- **eight** 43–50 cm (17–20 in)
- **Weight** 200–250 g (7–9 oz)
- **ocation** Africa, Asia, Australia, South America

o known as the green-backed heron, this
all, **secretive fish-eater** spends most of its
e hidden in dense cover. It sometimes
ks for its prey at night. The striated heron
a crafty hunter. It drops **bait**, such as an
ect, on the water
attract fish to
e surface.

# Marabou stork

*Leptoptilos crumeniferus*

- **Height** 1.1–1.5 m (3½–5 ft)
- **Weight** 4–9 kg (8¾–20 lb)
- **Location** Africa

A bald head and neck and **long
dangling throat sac** give the marabou
stork a most unusual appearance. When
it goes courting, the stork uses the
throat sac to make calls and grunts.
Marabou storks look magnificent in
the air, as they have a wingspan of
about 3 metres (10 ft). These birds eat
almost everything. Fish, insects, eggs,
other birds, and dead animals are all
on a marabou stork's menu.

# hoebill

*laeniceps rex*

- **Height** 1.2 m 4 ft)
- **Weight** 5.5–6.5 kg (12–14 lb)
- **Location** East central Africa

he colossal bill of this
traordinary-looking stork is
e shape of a wooden clog, hence
e bird's name. Sharp-tipped and
w-edged, the bill is a fearsome
ol for catching prey. A shoebill
n **crack the shell of a turtle** or
ap off the head of a small
rocodile. Shoebills live mostly
one. They pair up to share nest-
uilding and the care of chicks.

# Cattle egret

*Bubulcus ibis*

- **Height** 48–53 cm (19–21 in)
- **Weight** 300 g (11 oz)
- **Location** Southern Europe, Africa, South East Asia,
Australia, Central and South America

Once the cattle egret was
found only in Africa, but
it has spread into
many other regions.
In the breeding
season, cattle
egrets develop
**long plumes**
on their heads
and backs.

# Grey heron

*rdea cinerea*

- **Height** 90–98 cm (35–39 in)
- **Weight** 1.4 kg (3¼ lb)
- **Location** Europe, sub-Saharan Africa, Asia

*The long bill
has a sharp tip.*

While a grey heron waits
motionless, on the lookout
for fish, it stands with its long
neck kinked back. If it spots
prey, the heron takes **less than
a second to react**, shooting out
its neck and bill to grab the victim.

# Great blue heron

*Ardea herodias*

- **Height** 0.9–1.4 m (3–4½ ft)
- **Weight** 2.1–2.5 kg (4½–5½ lb)
- **Location** North America

With a wingspan of 1.8 metres
(6 ft) or more, this bird is **one of
the world's biggest herons**. The
great blue heron hunts for food
on land as well as in water.
Its diet includes rodents,
lizards, and even
snakes. The heron
may toss its prey
in the air before
gulping it down.

# African spoonbill

*Platalea alba*

- **Height** 90 cm (36 in)
- **Weight** 1.6 kg (3½ lb)
- **Location** Southern Africa

The African spoonbill goes
fishing by **sweeping its bill**
from side to side in the
water. Its food may
include water insects
and crustaceans,
as well as fish. The
bird traps its prey
between the
flattened tips
of its bill.

# Parrots

With their vivid colours and loud squawks and calls, parrots, and their relatives, are easily recognised. The group includes parakeets, macaws, lorikeets, cockatoos, cockatiels, and budgerigars. Many are popular as pets.

## FACTFILE

■ **Key features:** Hooked bill, large head, and short neck. Strong feet with sharp claws and two toes pointing forwards and two pointing backwards for a firm grip.

■ **Size:** Smallest are the pygmy parrots (genus: *Micropsitta*), which are about 8 cm (3 in) long. Largest is the Hyacinth macaw at 1 m (3¼ ft) long.

Size comparison

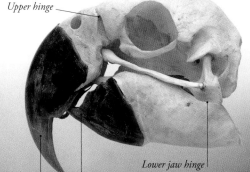

*Upper hinge*

*Lower jaw hinge*

*Upper bill*

*Lower bill (used for cracking nuts)*

**Versatile bill** A parrot's bill can move far more than you might think. This is because there is a highly flexible hinge joining the bird's upper bill to its skull. Parrots also use their strong, hooked upper bill like an extra foot, to help them grip the branches as they clamber through the trees.

SCARLET MACAW

FEEDING *Parrots have flexible feet that they use like hands. They often eat by grasping food with one foot and pulling bits off the food with their sharp, agile bill.*

## ...ed-fan parrot
*...optyus accipitrinus*

- **Length** 36 cm (14 in)
- **Weight** 200–300 g (7–11 oz)
- **Diet** Seeds, nuts, fruit, nectar, pollen, insects
- **Location** N. South America

Most of the time this parrot attracts little attention. But when it is frightened or excited, it raises its **bright red neck feathers** to form a fan that frames its face. This makes the bird look larger and possibly more scary to a potential predator.

## Rose-ringed parakeet
*Psittacula krameri*

- **Length** 40 cm (16 in)
- **Weight** 125 g (4 oz)
- **Diet** Seeds, nuts, fruit, flowers, nectar
- **Location** W. to E. Africa, S. and S.E. Asia

This bird can be found in more parts of the world than any other parrot. This is because many **released pet birds are breeding** in the wild in Europe and in North America.

## Rainbow lorikeet
*Trichoglossus haematodus*

- **Length** 30 cm (12 in)
- **Weight** 150 g (5 oz)
- **Diet** Pollen, nectar, fruit, seeds, insects
- **Location** New Guinea, S.E. Asia, S.W. Pacific, Australia (including Tasmania)

This is one of the most colourful of all parrots. Its feathers are usually a stunning mix of vivid colours, although some birds are duller than others. Lorikeets have **bristles on their tongues** to help them to gather pollen and nectar from flowers.

## ...udgerigar
*...lopsittacus undulatus*

- **Length** 18 cm (7 in)
- **Weight** 25 g (⅞ oz)
- **Diet** Seeds, grass, leaves
- **Location** Australia

...ost people know these ...endly birds as pets, but ...ge flocks of wild ...udgerigars are a familiar ...ght over the grasslands of ...ustralia. **Wild birds are always ...een**, with a yellow face and blue tail. ...ut since budgerigars were first introduced ...o Europe in 1840, careful breeding has ...oduced birds in many different colours.

**MANY COLOURS**
*In captivity, budgerigars are bred so that they come in a wide range of colours: blue, grey, green, yellow, violet, and even white.*

## Hyacinth macaw
*Anodorhynchus hyacinthinus*

- **Length** 1 m (3 ¼ ft)
- **Weight** 1.5 kg (3 ¼ lb)
- **Diet** Palm nuts, seeds, fruit, insects
- **Location** C. South America

These are the **largest of all parrots**, though half their length is made up of their tail! Often described as gentle giants, these highly intelligent birds love company and are usually seen in a group or with their mates. They stay with the same partner throughout their long lives.

## ...Galah
*...olophus roseicapillus*

- **Length** 35 cm (14 in)
- **Weight** 325 g (12 oz)
- **Diet** Seeds, grass, ...aves, fruit
- **Location** Australia ...ncluding Tasmania)

...he **noisy galah** is ...e most widespread ...nd the most ...ommon cockatoo of ...ll. It gathers in huge ...locks, and can be a ...est to farmers as it will ...aid fruits and seeds.

## Cockatiel
*Nymphicus hollandicus*

- **Length** 32 cm (12½ in)
- **Weight** 90 g (3¼ oz)
- **Diet** Seeds, nuts, fruit
- **Location** Australia

This is **the smallest cockatoo**, but its beautiful colouring and large, bright yellow crest make it a popular pet. The crest is lowered when it rests, and sometimes when it feeds. The underside of the tail is black for a male bird and yellow for a female.

## Kakapo
*Strigops habroptilus*

- **Length** 64 cm (25 in)
- **Weight** 2 kg (4½ lb)
- **Diet** Plant juices, grass, leaves, seeds, fruit, pollen
- **Location** New Zealand

**Kakapos cannot fly,** so are vulnerable to predators. They are extinct in the wild, but from 1987 to 1992 the few remaining birds were gathered up and taken to the safety of three predator-free islands off the New Zealand coast.

BIRDS

# Hummingbirds

These birds beat their wings in a figure-of-eight pattern, which gives them a lot of flight control. They are the only birds able to fly backwards and they can even fly upside down. They also hover, which is necessary when they use their long bills to probe flowers and drink the nectar within.

## My wings are **a blur!**

Small hummingbirds flap their wings about 4,200 times a minute. That's 70 times a second! A tiny bee hummingbird flaps its wings even faster, at about 200 times a second during courtship displays!

**Magenta-throated woodstar**
*Calliphlox bryantae*

DIET *Hummingbirds don't just feed on nectar. It would make a poor diet. They also catch insects and spiders, to add valuable protein, vitamins, and minerals.*

# Bee hummingbird

*Mellisuga helenae*

- **Height** 5–6 cm (2–2¼ in)
- **Weight** 2 g (¹⁄₁₆ oz)
- **Location** Cuba, Isle of Pines

Famed as **the smallest bird in the world**, the male bee hummingbird is smaller than the female. Unlike the female, it also has iridescent feathers around its head and neck. The females lay eggs no larger than peas, in tiny walnut-sized nests.

▲ IRIDESCENT FEATHERS *are a striking feature of most male hummingbirds. The feathers appear to have a metallic sheen. But why? It is to help the males to attract females. When he is looking for a female, the male searches for a perch in the sun, which causes the iridescent feathers to positively gleam.*

▶ NO HUMMINGBIRD *weighs more than 24 g (less than 1 oz). That is about the weight of a tablespoon of sugar. The largest hummingbird is the giant hummingbird.*

BIRDS

## FACTFILE

There are a number of different types of hummingbird, but all of them are found in the Americas. They all have a long, pointed bill that is designed to probe into flowers so the bird can drink nectar.

# Woodpeckers and toucans

These woodland birds all have striking bills – some huge and brightly coloured, others long, thin, and finely pointed like a dagger. They can also run up and down the sides of tree trunks with ease, thanks to their super-grip feet.

## FACTFILE

- **Number of species:** Just over 400 species, divided into six groups or families.
- **Key features:** Large bills and strong, parrot-like feet with two toes pointing forwards and two pointing backwards, for a firm grip.
- **Nest:** In holes, safely out of sight of predators.

Toes

Size comparison

◄ CACTUS NEST
*Gila woodpeckers (Melanerpes uropygialis) are unusual: they thrive in deserts, where there are unlikely to be any trees to nest in. Instead, they peck out nest holes in the large cacti that are common in the dry, hot areas of the southwest United States where this bird lives.*

**Strong skull** Woodpecker skulls are extra thick. This helps to cushion the brain, which is important for an animal that spends hours every day hammering away at trees with its bill. These birds also have an unusually long tongue, with a barbed or sticky tip for catching insects.

WOODPECKER
SKULL

FEEDING *Woodpeckers are born blind and helpless and rely on their parents for many months. This youngster takes a tasty morsel that its mother has carried back to the nest.*

## ufous-tailed jacamar
*bula ruficauda*

- **Length** 19–25 cm
  (2–10 in)
- **Weight** 18–30g
  (–1/16 oz)
- **Diet** Insects
- **Location** Central America
  d N. and C. South America

his beautiful bird, with
s shimmering green, red,
d gold feathers, likes to keep a
w profile. It spends most of the
y sitting quietly on a shaded
anch, only darting out
casionally to **spear a passing
sect** on its dagger-like bill.

## Green woodpecker
*Picus viridis*

- **Length** 30–33 cm (12–16 in)
- **Weight** 175–200 g (6–7 oz)
- **Diet** Insects, mainly ants
- **Location** Europe, W. Asia

The green woodpecker's tongue is nearly
twice the length of its bill, with a tip
covered in a sticky liquid to help trap
**ants, the bird's favourite food.** Although
green woodpeckers live in woods, where
they peck nest holes in the sides of trees,
they also spend a lot of time on the
ground, in gardens or parks, using their
pointed beaks to dig out any insects that
are crawling through the grass.

**NOISY BIRD** *The
loud "laughing"
cry of the green
woodpecker can be heard
far and wide over woods
and heaths during spring.*

## Greater honeyguide
*dicator indicator*

- **Length** 20 cm (8 in)
- **Weight** 50 kg (1¾ oz)
- **Diet** Bees and beeswax,
  es' eggs, ants
- **Location** Central and
  uthern Africa

oneyguides can **sniff out
ees' nests**, their main
urce of food, using their
en sense of smell. Some
frican tribes use the bird
o guide them to bees'
ests, so that they can
arvest the honey.

## Yellow-bellied sapsucker
*Sphyrapicus varius*

- **Length** 19–20 cm
  (7½–8½ in)
- **Weight** 50–80 g
  (1¾–2⅞ oz)
- **Diet** Tree sap, insects
- **Location** North and Central
  America, Caribbean

The sapsucker gets its
name because it **feeds on
the sugary sap** that it sucks
out of trees through holes it
drills in the trunk. In spring,
males drum on trees and other
objects to mark their territory.

## Great barbet
*Megalaima virens*

- **Length** 32 cm (12½ in)
- **Weight** 200–300 g (7–11 oz)
- **Diet** Fruit, nectar, insects
- **Location** Central and East Asia

Barbets use their large,
bristly, pointed bills to
dig out nest holes and to
peck into tree trunks in search
of a meal. This bird's plump
body, large head, and stubby,
rounded wings make it **a poor,
inelegant flyer**. It spends quite
a lot of its time bobbing along
the ground.

**BIRDS**

## Toco toucan
*Ramphastos toco*

- **Length** 53–60 cm (21–23½ in)
- **Weight** 550 g (20 oz)
- **Diet** Fruit, insects,
  irds' eggs
- **Location** N.E. to
  C. South America

This is one of the largest
and **most well known** of
all toucans. Its spectacular,
brightly coloured bill is
not solid, but has a
honeycomb-like structure,
making it much lighter
than it appears to be.

## Keel-billed toucan
*Ramphastos sulfuratus*

- **Length** 46–51 cm (18–20 in)
- **Weight** 275–550 g (10–20 oz)
- **Diet** Fruit, insects, reptile and birds' eggs
- **Location** Central and N. South America

Even for a toucan, this bird stands out for its
dazzling array of colours. Keel-billed toucans
do not fly very well, so spend most of their
time hopping along branches in search of
food. Having a long bill means they can
pick fruit that is often beyond the reach
of other birds. Once they have their
prize, they toss their heads back sharply,
open their surprisingly agile jaws wide
and **swallow the fruit whole**.

# Amazing *nests*

Birds' nests come in all shapes and sizes, from the tiny cup-shaped ones of songbirds to the massive platforms of eagles and the complex communal nests of weaver birds. All sorts of materials are used to build nests and some birds spend many weeks constructing them.

## WHY DO BIRDS BUILD NESTS?

Most birds build nests, but a nest is rarely a permanent home. Birds usually only start to build a nest when they are ready to breed. This is because they need a safe, warm place to lay their eggs, and for their newly hatched chicks to develop.

## NEST INGREDIENTS

Birds use many things for building their nests, including sticks, mud, feathers, stones, twigs, grass, and moss. Long-tailed tits even use sticky cobwebs to hold their moss nests together. They then camouflage the nest with lichen and use feathers to give it a soft lining.

WHITE TERN

**Out of reach** Many seagulls nest in colonies high up on the cliff face, away from possible predators. They build cup-shaped nests from twigs and plant materials along the rocky ledges.

**No nest** The white (or angel) tern does not build a nest. It just sticks its eggs in the fork of a tree branch, using only a glob of mucus to hold them in position.

**Family pile** Storks build huge nests by piling up sticks, often adding more sticks to the same nest year after year. They like to be up high, in tall trees or on the top of buildings or chimneys.

**Just move in** Most owls are not keen on nest building. They often lay their eggs in holes in tree trunks. These openings may have been hollowed out by another bird, or they may be natural.

BIRDS

## NEST SHAPES

Some nests are little more than a hole scraped in the ground and lined with pebbles. But many are complex structures, built to last.

▶ Orioles weave sack-like nests that they hang from the branches of trees. They use almost any materials, including bits of string.

◀ Weaver birds weave nests from shreds of leaves and grass. A long entrance tunnel is woven into the side or base.

◀ Many small birds make open, cup-shaped nests.

# Perching birds

More than half of all the bird species in the world belong to a group known as perching birds, or passerines. The feet of perching birds have three toes pointing forwards and one backwards. This allows them to get a firm grip on even the thinnest and bendiest branches.

My **feet** don't lose their grip even when I go to sleep.

When a bird lands, the weight of its body presses down on its toes. This makes the toes lock automatically round the branch in a tight grip.

### FACTFILE

Perching bird foot

Size comparison

■ **Number of species:** about 5,500.
■ **Key features:** specialized perching feet, with three toes pointing forwards and one back. Most perching birds have distinctive songs.
■ **Size:** The crows and ravens are the largest, with lengths of up to 65 cm (25½ in). The short-tailed pygmy tyrant is the smallest perching bird at just 7 cm (3 in) in length.

## GOOD SINGERS

Another special thing about perching birds is their ability to sing. They are often referred to as songbirds, and many of them have wonderful voices. Each species has a particular song, which may be made up of a wide range of notes. The best singers include the song thrush and the nightingale.

## Great tit
*Parus major*

| | | 15 | | | |

■ **Length**  14 cm (5½ in)
■ **Diet**  Insects, fruit, seeds
■ **Location**  Europe

This tit is seen everywhere from woodlands to town gardens. **Bold and bossy,** the great tit does not hesitate to drive smaller tits away from garden bird tables. Its distinctive two-note *"teacher, teacher"* call is easy to recognize.

# Woodpecker finch
*Camarhynchus pallidus*

- **Length** Not recorded
- **Diet** Insect larvae
- **Location** Galápagos Islands

This finch is a **rarity** among animals because **uses a tool to catch food**. The bird holds twig or cactus spine in its beak and probes in tree bark with the tool to lever out grubs.

# Robin
*Erithacus rubecula*

- **Length** 14 cm (5½ in)
- **Diet** Insects, worms, berries
- **Location** Europe, N. Africa, N.W. Asia

The "redbreast" is popular with gardeners in the UK for its **cheerful, bubbling song** and its appetite for harmful insect pests. Elsewhere in its range, the European robin is less inclined to associate with people. For all their charm, robins can be very **fierce** in defence of their territory.

# White-throated dipper
*Cinclus cinclus*

**Length** 18–21 cm (7–8¼ in)
**Diet** Small fish, crustaceans, molluscs, larvae
**Location** Europe, N. Africa, N. Asia

The dipper is found by fast-running streams and rivers. It swims well, and **can walk along riverbeds completely submerged** while it searches for food. When the dipper is not in the water, it perches on rocks by the riverbank, constantly bobbing its body up and down. This dipping action is how the bird got its name.

# Song thrush
*Turdus philomelos*

- **Length** 23 cm (9 in)
- **Diet** Berries, insects, worms, slugs, snails
- **Location** Europe, North Africa, N.W. Asia, Australia, New Zealand

Broken snail shells by a flat stone are a sign that a thrush has been eating there. **Numbers** of thrushes have **fallen dramatically** in Europe due to loss of their farmland habitat.

# Wren
*Troglodytes troglodytes*

- **Length** 9 cm (3½ in)
- **Diet** Insects and spiders
- **Location** Europe, N. America, N. Africa, Asia

This is a **very small bird** with a very loud voice. Wrens usually **live in dense hedges,** and can be heard before they are seen. In the breeding season, the male builds several nests for the female to choose from.

# Red-backed fairy-wren
*Malurus melanocephalus*

- **Length** 10–13 cm (4–5 in)
- **Diet** Insects, fruit, seeds
- **Location** N. and E. Australia

There are several different species of fairy-wren in Australia and Papua New Guinea. The red-backed wren, like all its fairy-wren relatives, has a **long tail** that it carries **cocked upright**. This wren builds its nests in dense undergrowth or among tall grasses. It is sometimes a garden visitor.

▲ SPLASH OF RED
*The vividly coloured red-backed wren is the smallest of all the fairy-wrens.*

# Red crossbill
*Loxia curvirostra*

- **Length** 17 cm (6½ in)
- **Diet** Seeds (from pine cones)
- **Location** North America, Europe, Asia

The crossbill's unusual **crossed-over beak** develops gradually, and is not seen in young birds. This beak is the perfect shape for breaking the seeds off pine cones.

# Japanese white-eye
*Zosterops japonicus*

- **Length** 10.5 cm (4 in)
- **Diet** Invertebrates, fruit, berries, nectar
- **Location** S. and S.E. Asia, Hawaii

White feathers ring this bird's eyes like a pair of spectacles. Japanese white-eyes are very common in Asia. They gather in flocks in gardens and woodlands. Their **varied diet** changes from season to season, according to what food is available.

◀ FLOWERS
*provide the Japanese white-eye with nectar and pollen.*

# Raggiana bird of paradise
*Paradisaea raggiana*

- **Length** 35 cm (14 in)
- **Diet** Fruit
- **Location** Papua New Guinea

There are many species of bird of paradise. The male birds usually have spectacular **flowing plumes**, which they show off in courtship rituals. Males of the type of bird of paradise shown here gather together to put on a mass display in front of the females.

# White wagtail
*Motacilla alba*

- **Length** 18 cm (7 in)
- **Diet** Insects, seeds
- **Location** Europe

The banks of rivers and streams, and the edges of ponds are good places to see a pied wagtail. This bird **loves to be near water**. A wagtail darts about in short, fast runs, flicking its tail, as it hunts for the insects that are the main part of its diet.

# Northern house martin
*Delichon urbicum*

- **Length** 12.5 cm (5 in)
- **Diet** Flying insects
- **Location** Europe, Africa (south of Sahara) and S.E. Asia

House martins like to be close to people. These birds nearly always use buildings as nesting sites. They stick their **mud nests** und the eaves of houses, in barns, and even under road bridges. About the only time a house martin comes down to the ground is when it is collecting mud for a nest. For most of its life, a martin stays in the air, wheeling and swooping in pursuit of flying insects.

# Short-tailed pygmy tyrant
*Myiornis ecaudatus*

- **Length** 6.5 cm (2½ in)
- **Diet** Insects
- **Location** N. and Central South America

This is one of the smallest birds in the world. Its tail is not much more than a tiny stub. The short-tailed pygmy tyrant belongs to a group of birds called tyrant flycatchers. These birds are **highly skilled at catching their insect prey** in mid-air. They are called "tyrants" because, despite their generally small size, they are very aggressive.

▶ PAIRED UP
*A breeding pair of ravens can be fierce when they are defending their territory. The couple may attack intruders or chase them over long distances.*

# ark-eyed junco
*co hyemalis*

- **ength** 14–16 cm (5½–6 in)
- **iet** Seeds, berries, invertebrates
- **ocation** North and Central America

...mmon in woodland, dark-eyed juncos ...ck together during autumn and winter, ...en the breeding season is over. The male ...nco sings at most times of the year.

# Zitting cisticola
*Cisticola juncidis*

- **Length** 10 cm (4 in)
- **Diet** Insects
- **Location** S. Europe, Africa, Asia, Australia

This warbler is **hard to see** because its colour blends in with the grasslands and scrublands where it lives. In flight, it makes a monotonous **two-note call**.

# Cliff swallow
*Petrochelidon pyrrhonota*

- **Length** 13–15 cm (5–6 in)
- **Diet** Flying insects
- **Location** Alaska, Mexico, South America

Buildings as well as cliffs are good nesting sites for cliff swallows. The birds plaster their **cone-shaped mud nests** on to vertical walls. These birds **migrate**, spending spring and summer in the north and going south for the winter.

▶ COLONIES
*Hundreds, or even thousands of cliff swallows may nest together at one site*

# ommon raven
*orvus corax*

- **Length** 65 cm (26½ in)
- **Diet** Fruit, nuts, eggs, carrion, small animals
- **Location** North and Central America, Europe, Asia, ...rth Africa

...he raven is one of the largest perching birds. ...is noted for its aerobatic flight, during ...hich it may twist and turn at high speed. ...ften, a raven rolls right over in mid-air and **flies upside down**. The bird makes various calls, including a hoarse croak.

# Red-whiskered bulbul
*Pycnonotus jocosus*

- **Length** 20 cm (8 in)
- **Diet** Berries, insects, nectar
- **Location** Asia; introduced into Australia and USA

Bright plumage and an **attractive song** have made the red-whiskered bulbul popular as a cage-bird. These birds are trapped in large numbers. They are still common but may soon need protection.

# Golden whistler
*Pachycephala pectoralis*

- **Length** 16–18 cm (6–7 in)
- **Diet** Insects, berries
- **Location** Indonesia, S. and E. Australia, Tasmania, Fiji

As its name suggests, the golden whistler is a fine songster. It has a loud, **tuneful voice** and a wide range of notes. Golden whistlers have particularly strong feet for gripping and a stout beak.

▼ COSY NEST
*Golden whistlers bind their nests with spiders' webs and line them with soft grass.*

1...

# Starlings

Starlings are a familiar sight in many countries throughout the world, roosting and flying in huge, noisy flocks. They nest in man-made or natural cavities, perhaps finding a space under roof tiles or a hole in a tree, and have proved immensely successful.

## FROM SMALL BEGINNINGS

Sixty starlings were deliberately released in New York City, in North America, in 1890 by a man who aimed to release into America all the birds named by Shakespeare. By the mid-1950s, starling numbers in North America had reached 50 million, and today there are thought to be some 200 million starlings.

## Common starling
*Sturnus vulgaris*

- **Length**  21 cm (8 ½ in)
- **Weight**  60–96 g (2–3¼ oz)
- **Diet**  Insects, earthworms, seeds, fruit
- **Location**  Worldwide except polar regions

Starlings are **stocky birds**, with speckled feathers that shimmer with iridescent purple and green. Their **beaks turn yellow** in the breeding season. They are noisy birds, and often mimic the calls of other birds, and even frogs or cats.

**Birds** fly in one of two ways: they either flap their wings continually, or they are able to glide on air currents, flapping their wings occasionally. Starlings are flappers, following straight flight lines and beating their wings rapidly to stay aloft.

▲ JUNIOR STARLING *Young birds have a brown plumage, and no iridescent feathers.*

*As the bird takes off, its feet are drawn up towards the body.*

*By flapping its wings up and down, the starling stays in the air.*

156

**Murmuration** Starlings gather in large flocks, and occasionally more than a million birds will gather. This is known as a murmuration and it will swoop and soar as one, each bird following its neighbour. Flocks as big as these make strange dark shapes in the sky.

# A *world* of eggs

No two bird eggs are exactly alike; they vary greatly in size, shape, colour, and texture, while the size of the egg doesn't always relate directly to the size of the bird. An egg laid by an ostrich is the world's largest bird's egg, but it is one of the smallest eggs in relation to the bird's body size.

**Common kingfisher**
*Alcedo atthis*

**Green broadl**
*Calyptomena viridis*

**Song thrush**
*Turdus philomlos*

**Eurasian nightjar**
*Caprimulgus europaeus*

**Black woodpecker**
*Dryocopus martius*

**Ringed plover**
*Charadrius hiaticula*

**Common oystercatcher**
*Haematopus ostralegus*

**Madagascar bulbul**
*Hypsipetes madagascariensis*

**Grey butcherbird**
*Cracticus torquatus*

**Tawny owl**
*Strix aluco*

**Emu**
*Dromaius novaehollandiae*

**Rose-ringed parakeet**
*Psittacula krameri*

**Rock wren**
*Salpinctes obsoletus*

**Southern cassowar**
*Casuarius casuarius*

**Herring gull**
*Larus argentatus*

**Black-winged cuckoo-shrike**
*Coracina melaschistos*

**Masked finfoot**
*Heliopais personatus*

**Egyptian vulture**
*Neophron percnopterus*

**ktail**
*aprolia*
*oriae*

**Dunnock**
*Prunella modularis*

**Great
snipe**
*Gallinago
media*

**Green wood-hoopoe**
*Phoeniculus purpureus*

**Grey catbird**
*Dumetella carolinensis*

**Richard's pipit**
*Anthus richardi*

**Cetti's warbler**
*Cettia cetti*

**American robin**
*Turdus migratorius*

**ommon quail**
*oturnix coturnix*

**Chimango caracara**
*Milvago chimango*

**Golden eagle**
*Aquila chrysaetos*

**Guillemot**
*Uria aalge*

**Eurasian curlew**
*Numenius arquata*

**Willow ptarmigan**
*Lagopus lagopus*

**eregrine falcon**
*alco peregrinus*

**Northern
lapwing**
*Vanellus
vanellus*

**Domestic chicken**
*Gallus domesticus*

**Greylag goose**
*Anser anser*

**Great crested grebe**
*Podiceps cristatus*

**Ostrich**
*Struthio camelus*

Ostrich eggs are cream in
colour with distinctive
pitted surfaces. The
eggshell is porcelain-
like in texture and
usually smooth
to touch.

15cm
(6 in)

**4,700** bee
hummingbird
eggs could fit
inside one
ostrich egg!

1cm
(½ in)

**Bee hummingbird**
*Mellisuga helenae*

159

# REPTILES

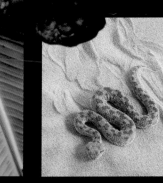

*Definition:* A **reptile** is a cold-blooded, usually egg-laying vertebrate. They are covered with scales or horny plates and they breathe through lungs.

# What is a REPTILE?

Reptiles once dominated the Earth. Fierce T-rexs and huge *Diplodocus* stalked the land, until their sudden extinction 65 million years ago. Although many dinosaurs were wiped out, other reptiles survived, and these creep around nearly every continent today.

## WHAT MAKES THEM DIFFERENT?

Like mammals and birds, reptiles are vertebrates (they have a backbone) and breathe air. However, unlike mammals, they are cold- blooded, they have scaly skin, and most species reproduce by laying eggs.

*Scaly skin*

It's not **furry**.
It's not **slimy**.
It's not **feathery**.
It must be a
**reptile**!

▲ TREE SNAKE *All reptiles have backbones, and some have extremely long and bendy ones, like this snake.*

### FACTFILE

There are five main groups of reptiles: lizards, snakes, tortoises and turtles, crocodilians, and the tuatara.

■ **Snakes:** Snake senses are sophisticated – they can find their prey with ease, and they make stealthy and cunning predators. They don't tend to chew their food, preferring to swallow it whole.

■ **Lizards:** This group is highly varied and very common, especially in warm countries. Many lizards can camouflage their skin to match their surroundings.

■ **Tuataras:** These animals can only be found on two small islands off the coast of New Zealand. They differ from lizards in lots of subtle ways.

■ **Crocodilians:** Crocodiles, caiman, and alligators make up this group. Most are freshwater inhabitants, but a few venture into the sea.

■ **Tortoises and turtles:** This group of reptiles had ancestors that swam alongside the dinosaurs. They are the only reptiles with a hard, protective shell.

◀ DINO COUSIN *"Dinosaur" means "terrible lizard" in Latin. Today's reptiles are close relatives of the dinosaurs.*

## SCALY SKIN

Reptiles have dry scaly or scale-like skin. The scales are made of keratin, the same material that makes hair, feathers, and fingernails. Some species of reptiles, like snakes, shed their skin as they grow.

▲ LIZARD SKIN

▲ SNAKE SKIN

▲ CROCODILE SKIN

## STURDY SKELETON

The different groups of reptiles have very different skeletons. This is the skeleton of a chameleon. Reptile skeletons are sturdy, making them suitable for life on land.

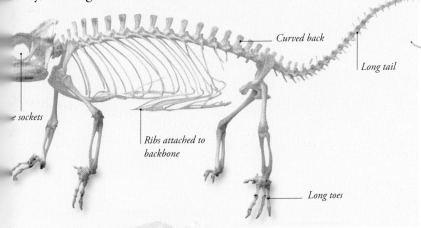

Curved back

Long tail

Eye sockets

Ribs attached to backbone

Long toes

## I'M FEELING COLD

Reptiles are often called "cold-blooded". This doesn't mean that their blood is cold. Their temperature depends on their surroundings. If the temperature doesn't suit them, some reptiles can hibernate until the temperatures are right again.

▼ SUNBATHING *If a reptile feels its blood is too cold, it will sunbathe to warm up.*

*Chameleon eggs*

## EGG BEGINNINGS

Most reptiles reproduce by laying eggs. Females lay their eggs in decayed wood, a nest of leaves and mud, or elsewhere on land. Reptiles do not sit on their eggs to incubate them like birds do.

◀ BIRTH DAY *A baby tortoise emerges from its egg.*

REPTILES

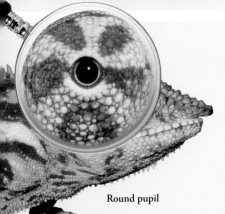

## LOOK INTO MY EYES...

Another unique characteristic of reptiles is their eyes. The shape of a reptile's pupil indicates whether the animal is active at night or during the day. Most reptiles active at night have slit-like pupils that can close tightly in bright light. Reptiles active in daytime have round pupils.

Round pupil

Slit-like pupil

# Reptile birthday

These turtles, like most reptiles, have to fend for themselves after they are born. There is safety in numbers so they all hatch at the same time, and usually during the night. Even so, it is estimated that just 1 in 1,000 baby turtles makes it to adulthood.

HEAD FOR WATER *The eggs hatch and hundreds of baby turtles emerge from nests in the sand. Instinctively, they head directly for the water, where they will have the best chance of survival. The babies can swim straight away.*

## BORN FROM EGGS

Most reptiles, including those that live mainly in water, reproduce by laying eggs on land. Reptile eggs often have a leathery shell that allows water and oxygen to pass through to the developing animal inside. Although many species of reptile lay their eggs, then leave, some reptiles, including the Nile crocodile, make attentive parents.

DAY 1
*Mum prepares a nest out of sand, mud, and weeds at the water's edge. She lays 20-60 eggs in the nest. They are protected by a tough, leathery shell.*

DAY 5
*Even though the mother crocodile stays close by and defends the nest, when she pops off for a cooling dip, the nest is often raided by predators.*

> I've got to get to the sea. I've got to get to the sea...

The mother turtle is long gone by the time these turtles hatch. They seem to know they have to make for the waves, and fast! Unfortunately, they have to run a gauntlet of predators as they grow, from seagulls to sharks.

**DAY 90**
*The eggs hatch. A baby croc uses its egg tooth to break the shell. Alerted by tiny grunts and chirps, the mother helps her babies out of the nest.*

**DAY 90**
*The mother carries the babies to the water where she will continue to watch and protect them for up to two years.*

### ⚠ TURTLE CONSERVATION

Sadly, the number of sea turtles has rapidly declined – for man-made reasons. These include disturbance of their nest sites due to beach tourism, collection of their eggs, pollution of the seas, and getting caught in fishing nets. To address the problem, beach reserves with assisted breeding programmes have been set up and turtle-friendly fishing nets have been introduced. Everyone is keeping their fingers crossed for these amazing creatures.

# Tortoises and turtles

Tortoises and turtles are among the longest-living animals on Earth. But they don't need to worry about losing their teeth as they get older, because they haven't got any. Instead they have a sharp, horny beak to cut and chew up their food with.

▲ DO NOT DISTURB *Tortoises and turtle[s] living in cooler parts of the world often hiberna[te] in winter, to avoid the cold and shortage of foo[d]*

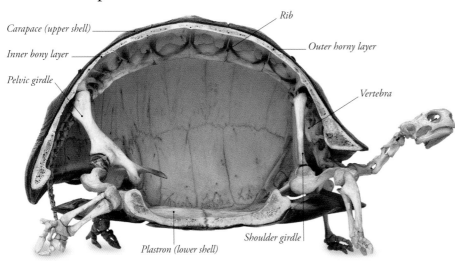

Carapace (upper shell)
Rib
Inner bony layer
Outer horny layer
Pelvic girdle
Vertebra
Plastron (lower shell)
Shoulder girdle

## SKELETON

Tortoises and turtles have an unusual skeleton. Their ribs and some of their vertebrae are fused to their upper shell. This means they cannot move their ribs to help pump air in and out of their lungs. Instead, they use muscles at the tops of their legs to do the pumping.

---

### FACTFILE

- **Number of species:** 293
- **Key features:** Tortoises live on dry land and have round, stumpy legs. Turtles spend most of their time in water and have flipper-like limbs. Freshwater turtles are often called terrapins. They all have a protective shell.

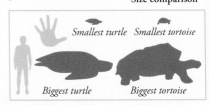

Size comparison

Smallest turtle   Smallest tortoise

Biggest turtle    Biggest tortoise

---

**I AM 150 YEARS OLD!**
*The Galápagos tortoise (Geochelone nigra) is the world's biggest at 1.2 m (4 ft) long. Some individuals have lived to be over 170 years old.*

## Desert tortoise
*...pherus agassizii*

**Height** 15–36 cm (6–14 in)
**Diet** Cacti, grass, some insects
**Location** S.W. USA, N.W. Mexico

...n exceptionally hot days, this tortoise will ...rrow into the sand, using its **shovel-shaped** ...et, to escape the baking desert heat, Males ...ay fight each other for a mate during the breeding season.

## Indian star tortoise
*Geochelone elegans*

**Height** Up to 28 cm (11 in)
**Diet** Grass, leaves, fruit
**Location** India, Pakistan, Sri Lanka

Its knobbly, high-domed shell, covered with **star-shaped markings**, make this tortoise one of the easiest to recognise. It is a **thirsty creature** and is usually only very active during the wet monsoon season. When it is dry, it tends to venture out just in the early morning or late afternoon.

## Hermann's tortoise
*Testudo hermanni*

**Height** 15–20 cm (6–8 in)
**Diet** Leaves, flowers, fruit
**Location** S.E. Europe, Mediterranean islands

This tortoise was once a **popular pet**, but its sale is now restricted by law. It usually **hibernates** for several months in winter, especially it if is very cold, and spends much of summer resting in the shade.

## Green turtle
*...helonia mydas*

**Length** 1–1,2 m (3¼–4 ft)
**Diet** Seaweed and algae; the young also eat jellyfish, ...olluscs, snails, worms, and sponges
**Location** Worldwide

...aving been **hunted** for centuries for their ...eat and eggs, green turtles are now **legally protected**. Special breeding beaches have been set up by conservationists to help save them from extinction.

## Leatherback turtle
*Dermochelys coriacea*

**Length** 1.3–1.8 m (4¼–6 ft)
**Diet** Jellyfish
**Location** Worldwide

Leatherbacks are the **biggest turtles**. Some weigh as much as 800 kg (1,770 lb). They also **swim great distances**. Individuals have been known to cross the Atlantic. Unlike other turtles, they have a leathery outer shell.

## Alligator snapping turtle
*Macrochelys temminckii*

**Length** 40–80 cm (16–32 in)
**Diet** Fish
**Location** S.E. USA

This is the world's **largest freshwater turtle**. Most of its day is spent with its scissor-sharp jaws wide open, as it lures fish towards them by wiggling a small, pink, wormlike tube on the floor of its mouth. Its hooked "beak" delivers a **deadly bite**.

## Common snake-necked turtle
*Chelodina longicollis*

**Length** 20–25 cm (8–10 in)
**Diet** Fish, crabs, lobsters, tadpoles
**Location** E. and S. Australia

This turtle uses its **exceptionally long neck** to "snorkel", while it hunts for food in rivers and streams. A long neck is also very handy for lunging at and **grasping prey**. The neck and head together are often longer than the shell.

## Loggerhead turtle
*Caretta caretta*

**Length** 70–100 cm (28–39 in)
**Diet** Shellfish, crabs, lobsters
**Location** Worldwide

Loggerheads get their name from their exceptionally **big head**. They also have large, powerful jaws, that can easily crunch their way through any passing shellfish, crab, or lobster. These turtles only breed every two years at the most and are **becoming rare**. Many of their breeding areas are now protected.

# Snakes

Snakes are highly evolved and deadly predators. They slither along on smooth bellies, hunting by stealth, eating all types of animals, from ants to alligators. The only way they can eat their prey is to swallow it whole, including the horns, hooves, and hair!

Forked tongue

Heat pits

◀ SENSES *Snakes have poor eyesight and hearing. They rely instead on their tongue, which they use to "taste" the air or touch the ground to follow a chemical scent left by their prey, and face pits that detect heat.*

New skin

Cast-off skin

▲ SKIN *Snakes shed their skin between four and eight times a year. Shedding starts around the mouth and nose. Once the skin is loose, the snake rubs against objects to help pull itself out.*

## FACTFILE

■ **Key features:** Snakes can move in three ways. Undulation is a side-to-side movement where the snake uses rough ground to push itself along. In tunnels a snake will concertina its coils against the walls to thrust itself forward. A snake also uses its belly scales to pull itself along.

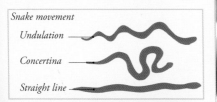

*Snake movement*

Undulation

Concertina

Straight line

## Anatomy

The skeleton of a snake is very simple. It consists of a skull, and hundreds of ribs set along a long, flexible backbone. The internal organs are mostly long and thin and are arranged to fit along the length of the snake. The jaws are loosely hinged to help swallow food.

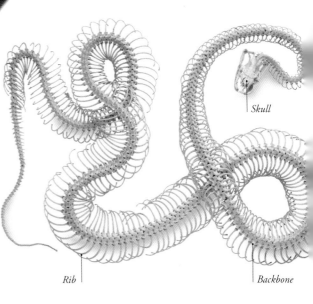

Skull

Rib

Backbone

## SEA SNAKES AND SEA KRAITS

**Sea snakes have flattened,** paddle-shaped tails and spend most of their lives at sea. Because they have lungs rather than gills they visit the surface regularly to breathe. Sea kraits are not sea snakes; they lay their eggs on land.

# Olive sea snake
*Aipysurus laevis*

- **Length** 1.8 m (6 ft)
- **Location** Australasia

The olive sea snake is found on coral reefs in Australia and New Guinea. Although **poisonous**, it only attacks if it is provoked. Its body is purplish brown with a light brown underside. These snakes are regarded as true sea snakes because they give birth to **live young in the water.**

# Banded sea krait
*Laticauda colubrina*

- **Height** 1–1.5m (3¼–5 ft)
- **Location** Southeast Asia

Sea kraits live in coastal waters where they hunt fish and eels. They are most **active at night.** Unlike sea snakes, kraits lay eggs on land and leave them to hatch. Sea kraits have **special scales** on their belly that help them to crawl on land.

▶ FANGS *Poisonous snakes have two hollow teeth that they use to inject their prey with venom. Venom kills or paralyses the animal, making it easier for the snake to swallow.*

# CONSTRICTORS

Constrictors are snakes that kill by wrapping their coils round their prey and squeezing hard so that the blood cannot flow around the victim's body. This stops the heart and prevents oxygen reaching the organs. When the animal stops struggling, the snake swallows it head first. Boas and pythons are typical constrictor snakes.

# Children's python
*Antaresia childreni*

- **Length** 75–100 cm (30–39 in)
- **Location** Northern Australia

This small python hides in caves and crevices where it **waits to ambush** lizards, birds, and small mammals. It will even eat bats. If threatened it will strike and bite an attacker, but it is not poisonous. Children's pythons are reddish brown in colour with **darker blotches**. They lay their eggs in hollow trees or caves.

# Anaconda
*Eunectes murinus*

- **Length** 6–10 m (20–33 ft)
- **Location** South America

The anaconda is the world's **heaviest snake,** and can weigh up to 250 kg (550 lb). Anacondas spend most of their time **submerged** in water, hiding in the plants along the edges of rivers and lakes. They are capable of killing capybaras and small deer and have even been known to attack fully grown caimans.

▼ BIG DINNER
*This anaconda has killed a caiman. It will not need to eat anything else for several months.*

REPTILES

169

# Emerald tree boa
*Corallus caninus*

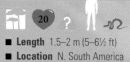

**20** ?

- **Length** 1.5–2 m (5–6½ ft)
- **Location** N. South America

The emerald tree boa is perfectly adapted for life in the treetops. Its **vivid colour** blends in with the rainforest foliage, while its muscular body firmly grips tree trunks and branches. These boas coil themselves around a branch with their heads hanging down, ready to strike a bird or mammal. The prey is speared by the snake's fangs before being **crushed** to death. Between three and 15 orange-red live young are born each season. They turn green after one year.

# arpet python
*elia spilota*

- **ength** 2–4 m (6½–13 ft)
- **ocation** Australia

rpet pythons are found across much of
stralia and in many different **habitats**. All
cies of carpet snakes have bold markings on
ghter-coloured background. They are **active**
**y and night**. Female carpet pythons lay up
50 eggs in hollow trees or rotting vegetation
d will **incubate** them until they hatch.

# Common boa constrictor
*Boa constrictor*

- **Length** 1–4 m (3½–13 ft)
- **Location** Central and South America

The common boa is a
large snake with
a narrow head and a
**pointed snout**. Boas are
good climbers and able
swimmers, but are also happy
to hunt on the ground. They
detect prey by scent rather
than by heat. Boa constrictors have distinctive
**dark markings** along their backs against a
pink, grey, or gold background. Female boas
produce live young.

▲ DISGUISE *The patterns
and colours of the boa
constrictor's skin help to break
up the snake's outline so that
it blends into the background.*

# ubber boa
*arina bottae*

- **Length** 35–80 cm (14–32 in)
- **Location** S.W. Canada, W. USA

his snake gets its common name
om the **rubbery** feel of its skin.
oth its head and tail are blunt,
aking them hard to tell apart.
hen threatened, the snake coils
self up and raises its tail to make
tackers think it is its head. Rubber
oas live underground, hunting for
nall animals in burrows and tree
oles. These snakes often **hibernate**
r long periods in winter.

# Reticulated python
*Python reticulatus*

- **Length** 6–10 m (20–33 ft)
- **Location** Southeast Asia

The reticulated python is one of the longest
snakes in the world and weighs up to 136 kg
(300 lb). These snakes have irregular
**diamond-shaped markings** in a variety of
colours. They are widely hunted for their skin,
which has led to them becoming increasingly
**rare in the wild**.

# Rosy boa
*harina trivirgata*

- **Length** 60–110 cm (23½–43 in)
- **Location** S.W. USA, N.W. Mexico

The rosy boa is a **burrowing snake** and lives
mostly beneath rocks and in crevices, where
t forages for food. Rosy boas are
ctually cream, grey, or buff in
olour with brown, orange, or
lack stripes running along the
engths of their bodies. They
are very **slow movers** and
have to ambush
their prey.

# African rock python
*Python sebae*

- **Length** 6–9 m (20–30 ft)
- **Location** Central and Southern Africa

African rock pythons are more
**aggressive** than other pythons and
will readily **bite** if harassed. They
live on grasslands and savannas,
often close to water. Farmers like
them because they eat cane rats
in the fields, but they are less
welcome on livestock farms
as they will also take larger
animals such as gazelles,
goats, and even crocodiles.

▼ NOTHING LEFT
*Every part of this gazelle
will be eaten by a rock
python, even though it
may take a whole year
for it to be digested.*

## FANG-TASTIC SNAKES!

The majority of snakes do not kill by constriction. Instead they use (often venomous) fangs to grab and kill prey. Most are harmless to humans but there is a small minority that add a LOT of "bite" to their bite! One strike from a taipan, for example, contains enough venom to kill 100 people. There are three different fang positions:

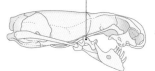

*Short, heavy jaw*

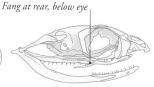

*Fang at rear, below eye*

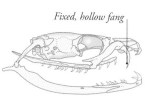

*Fixed, hollow fang*

### PRIMITIVE SNAKE
*Primitive snakes have a heavy skull and few teeth. Blind snakes, which feed only on small prey such as insects and their larvae, are primitive snakes.*

### REAR-FANGED SNAKE
*Rear-fanged snakes' fangs are grooved, not hollow, and their venom is usually weaker than front-fanged snakes. It is more to aid the digestive process than to kill.*

### FRONT-FANGED SNAKE
*The most familiar venomous snakes, such as rattlesnakes, are front-fanged. Their venom is potent and their fang position enables venom delivery during a strike or quick bite.*

**FATAL STRIKE** *This rattlesnake hunts by ambushing its victims, striking with venomous fangs before devouring its stunned, or dead, prey.*

REPTILES

## Milksnake
*Lampropeltis triangulum*

**30**

- **Length** 0.4–2 m (1¼–6½ ft)
- **Diet** Insects, frogs, small rodents, other snakes
- **Location** North America, Central America, N. South America

These colourful snakes are fairly common within their range, but rarely seen as they are **secretive**. They are usually found near forest edges, but can also be found in open woodlands, and grasslands near streams and rivers, on rocky hillsides, a in suburban areas and farmlands – in other words, just about anywhere.

## Grass snake
*Natrix natrix*

- **Length** 1.2–2 m (4–6½ ft)
- **Diet** Frogs, fish
- **Location** Europe to C. Asia, N.W. Africa

These non-venomous snakes often take to the water, and are **excellent swimmers**, feeding on frogs and fish. When they feel themselves to be in extreme danger, they **"play dead"** – a good surprise tactic.

## Western diamondback rattlesnake
*Crotalus atrox*

**25**

- **Length** 2 m (6½ ft)
- **Diet** Small mammals, birds, and lizards
- **Location** S. USA, N. Mexico

This is North America's most dangerous snake. Its "rattle" is a horny section at the end of its tail, which it vibrates when threatened. It is a **deadly predator** that stalks its prey, strikes, then swallows.

## uff adder
*s arietans*

- **ength** 1.8–2.4 m (6–8 ft)
- **iet** Small rodents (mice, rabbits) and birds
- **ocation** Africa

ne of the world's most dangerous snakes, puff adder is big, effectively camouflaged, **ghly venomous**, and aggressive. It strikes dily when annoyed or frightened, but ally **puffs up** or hisses loudly in warning. This snake has caused many human deaths.

## Mangrove snake
*Boiga dendrophila*

- **Length** 2.5 m (8 ft)
- **Diet** Small mammals, lizards, frogs, snakes, fish
- **Location** S.E. Asia

Dramatic colours warn predators that this is a venomous snake. The mangrove snake has a slightly flat body with a **ridge down its back**. Before striking, it draws back its head and flares its yellow lip scales.

## Corn snake
*Elaphe guttata*

- 20
- **Length** 1–1.8 m (3¼–6 ft)
- **Diet** Small rodents
- **Location** C. and S.E. USA

This eye-catching snake is not venomous, but it may strike to bite if threatened. It also **vibrates its tail** and excretes a foul-smelling musk to deter intruders. It is largely nocturnal, but may emerge in daytime in cooler weather.

## ndian cobra
*ja naja*

- 10
- **Length** 1.2–1.7 m (4–5½ ft)
- **Diet** Rodents
- **Location** S. Asia

ell known for emerging t of baskets, and eming to dance to a nake-charmer's music, is snake is **one of the ost dangerous in ndia** – with 10,000 talities each year. Cobras rise up and isplay their hoods hen they feel hreatened to appear s large as possible.

## Taipan
*Oxyuranus scutellatus*

- **Length** 2–3.6 m (6½–12 ft)
- **Diet** Mammals, birds, lizards
- **Location** S. New Guinea, N. Australia

The **most poisonous land snake in the world**, the taipan is the most feared snake in Australia. However, because an effective anti-venom has been developed, human fatalities are now relatively rare.

## Black mamba
*Dendv roaspis polylepis*

- 10
- **Length** 2.5–3.5 m (8¼–11 ft)
- **Diet** Small mammals and birds
- **Location** E. and Southern Africa

This is one of the most poisonous snakes, and probably **the fastest moving**. In short bursts it can overtake someone running, making it an extremely dangerous predator.

## Flying snake
*Chrysopelea ornata*

- **Length** 1–2 m (3–4 ft)
- **Diet** Small vertebrates
- **Location** South and S.E. Asia

Technically a glider rather than a flier, this snake **flattens its body** to twice the normal width to minimize air resistance. It reaches its take-off point by crawling up a tree, gripping the bark with its scales. The flying snake is **considered harmless** because its poison is not dangerous to humans.

# Lizards

Lizards are a large and varied group of reptiles that have successfully adapted to a wide range of habitats. Most lizards have four legs, a long tail, scaly skin, and reproduce by laying eggs.

*This lizard has lost the end of its tail*

*It can take up to two years to grow a new one*

▼ SUNBATHERS *Because lizards are cold blooded they need to spend time basking in the sun before they become fully active.*

*Dewlap*

*Five clawed toes*

*This pygmy chameleon is no bigger than a fingernail*

▲ CAMOUFLAGE *Many lizards ha patterned skin that helps them blend in their surroundings. This enables them to hide from predators or stalk their prey.*

## FACTFILE

■ **Key features:** Lizards typically have a tail longer than their body that some species can shed if attacked. Most have external ear openings, moveable eyelids, and a tongue that is notched or forked. Lizards also have sharp cusped or serrated teeth running along the edge of the jaw.

**Size comparison**

## Gila monster

*Heloderma suspectum*

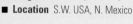

🍴 ❤ 60 ⚠ 👤 🦎

■ **Height** 45–60 cm (18–24 in)
■ **Location** S.W. USA, N. Mexico

Gila monsters live in desert and semi-arid regions, where they hide under rocks or in burrows. Their **beaded skin** is strongly marked with bands and blotches. Gilas are **venomous** and deliver their poison along grooves in the teeth of the lower jaw. They hunt mainly in the spring, usually for eggs and baby rabbits. After a large meal they store fat in the tail.

*Sharp teeth*

*Fat-storing tail*

*Bead-like scales*

▼ EGG THIEF *Lizards such as the Gila monster often raid nests for eggs and nestlings. They crush the egg with their jaws and let the contents trickle down their throat.*

## LEGLESS LIZARDS

**Amphisbaenians are a group of legless lizards** that are sometimes mistaken for worms or snakes. They have a cylindrical body and rings of scales that resemble the body segments of worms. Adapted to a life underground, the head is smooth and pointed for burrowing and the small rudimentary eyes are covered with a transparent scale. The nostrils point backwards to prevent them being filled with soil while tunnelling. Most amphisbaenians live in tropical regions, which provides them with the constantly warm soil temperatures they need to move underground.

Eye
Mouth

▲ EYES AND MOUTH
*Amphisbaenians have only limited vision. The lower jaw is set back to prevent soil entering while digging.*

▲ SCALES *Unlike snakes, the scales of amphisbaenians do not overlap and are arranged in rings, making them look like worm segments.*

▼ SKELETON *While they may look like worms from the outside, amphisbaenians have a skeleton similar to that of a snake. However, they also have bones that prove their ancestors had legs. Three Mexican species still have a pair of front legs.*

# Black and white amphisbaenian
*Amphisbaena fuliginosa*

- **Length** 30–45 cm (12–18 in)
- **Location** N. South America, Trinidad

Unlike most amphisbaenians, which are pinkish brown in colour, this species has a distinctive black and white skin. It spends most of its life underground but may come to the surface at night. Worm lizards move through the soil by pushing their body segments together like a concertina, which provides thrust for forward movement. This species feeds on any small vertebrates and insects it encounters, crushing them in its **powerful jaws**. It will shed its tail if necessary, but cannot grow a new one.

# Armadillo lizard
*Cordylus cataphractus*

| 20 | | | | |

**Length** 16–21 cm (6½–8½ in)
**Location** South Africa

These tiny lizards live in the deserts of South Africa. They have unusual **square-shaped scales** and a crest of spines along the neck and tail. If attacked they curl round and **bite their tail** to protect their soft belly, just like an armadillo. They also hide in crevices and puff themselves up so they cannot be dislodged. Armadillo lizards are live-bearers and sometimes live in colonies of up to 40 individuals.

# Frilled lizard
*Chlamydosaurus kingii*

| 20 | | | |

- **Length** 60–90 cm (24–36 in)
- **Location** N. Australia, New Guinea

Australia's frilled lizard is a spectacular sight when provoked. Rising up on its hind legs, it unfurls a wide **flap of skin around its neck** and hisses loudly. If this tactic doesn't work, it turns tail and runs for the safety of a tree. It comes down to forage for food, eating mainly insects, spiders, and other invertebrates.

▼ BIG FRILL *The neck frill of this lizard is stiffened with cartilage rods to make it stand away from the body.*

# Chameleons

With their bizarre swivelling eyes and amazing ability to change colour, it's no surprise that chameleons often have a special place in folklore. In Madagascar, they are protected by local superstitions and it is considered bad luck to kill one.

## I have a **twist in my tail**.

Chameleons have a long, grasping or "prehensile" tail that can be coiled tightly around branches to act as a secure anchor. When not in use the tail is usually held in a loose spiral.

## Panther chameleon
*Furcifer pardalis*

**5**

- **Length** 40–52 cm (16–20½ in)
- **Weight** 250 g (9 oz)
- **Location** Madagascar and Réunion Island, Indian Ocean

A large and **colourful** species, panther chameleons can change colour – females do this only when they are pregnant to signal they will not mate, but males flush any combination of red, green, or blue depending on their mood.

*The prehensile tail is used to grip branches*

## ALL CHANGE!
Special cells called chromatophores in the chameleon's skin contain a variety of pigments that can be displayed at the surface of the cell or hidden. Signals from the chameleon's brain tell each skin cell which colours to show and which to hide, in order to create an overall pattern to suit any occasion.

**VEILED CHAMELEON**
*The bony helmet or casque of some chameleons has several functions, including display and picking up low frequency sounds, like a dish.*

**COLOURFUL FEELINGS**
*Males use colour mainly to communicate. When rivals meet, they adopt aggressive postures and flush a range of colours to intimidate each other.*

*Each eye moves
independently*

## FANCY FOOTWORK
*The five toes on each of the
chameleon's feet are fused
together in groups of two and
three to form powerful
grippers that provide a secure
hold on narrow branches.*

*Long, sticky tongue*

### ▲ FOOD
*Chameleons eat mainly small
invertebrates such as insects and
spiders, which they catch using a
long, sticky tongue that can be
shot out at lightning speed and
with deadly accuracy.*

### ◀ NEST
*Female chameleons lay clutches of up to 50
rubbery eggs, usually in damp soil. The young
hatch into miniature versions of their parents
and must fend for themselves from day one.*

## CAMOUFLAGE
*A chameleon can display colours that match its
background. The disguise is perfected with gentle
swaying that mimics the movement of the tree.*

# Geckos, skinks, and others

Climbing aces of the lizard world, geckos can get a grip on anything with their sticky feet. They are common in the tropics. The slender skinks form the largest group of lizards. Their pointed heads and flattened bodies enable them to slip easily into cracks and crevices.

▼ TAKING TO THE AIR *is how Kuhl's flying gecko escapes enemies. It leaps from trees and glides with the help of webbed feet and skin flaps on its sides.*

▼ STICKY FEET *enable geckos to climb easily, even on smooth surfaces. Each toe pad is ridged and covered with tiny hair-like structures that cling firmly to everything they touch.*

Blue tongue

◄ TONGUE POKING *out, the blue-tongued skink defies an enemy. This defensive display, usually accompanied by loud hissing noises, often saves the skink from being attacked.*

Sticky toe pad

## Tokay
*Gekko gecko*

15

- ■ **Length** 18–36 cm (7–14 in)
- ■ **Diet** Insects, small vertebrates
- ■ **Location** Southeast Asia

Big and colourful, the tokay is one of the mo striking geckos. It is popular as a pet, despite being aggressive and having a **fierce bite**. When a tokay is annoyed it opens its mouth in a gape to show its **bright red tongue**. Ever other geckos have reason to be wary of the tokay. It is a **cannibal** and does not hesitate t eat geckos smaller than itself. The tokay gets its name because of its loud "tock-ay" call.

Pupil closes to a slit in daylight

### NIGHT VISION
*Because the tokay is active at night it has big goggle eyes to help it see in the dark. To shut out bright light, the pupils of the eyes close to a slit.*

Red tongue

## Leopard gecko
*Eublepharis macularius*

▮ | 25 | ⚠ | ✋ | 🦎

- **Length** 20–25 cm (8–10 in)
- **Diet** Spiders, crickets, worms, young mice
- **Location** South Asia

The tail of the leopard gecko is almost the same width as its body. The gecko uses this **plump tail** as a store for spare food, to be drawn on in times of shortage. Unlike most geckos, this species has **movable eyelids**, so it can blink. The leopard gecko is a popular pet and if kept in the right environment may live for more than 20 years.

## Ibiza wall lizard
*Podarcis pityusensis*

⛰ | 6 | ⚠ | ✋ | 🦎

- **Length** 15–21 cm (6–8½ in)
- **Diet** Insects
- **Location** Balearic Islands, introduced to Majorca

Slim, **agile**, and shy, Ibiza wall lizards usually run away or climb out of reach extremely quickly when startled. These lizards often gather together in **large groups**. They like sunning themselves on walls and rocks. Ibiza wall lizards are also sometimes seen in gardens, where they forage for food on scrap heaps.

▲ MANY COLOURS
*Ibiza wall lizards come in a wide variety of colours and markings. The males, one of which is shown here, are often blue with black patterning.*

*Red markings vary in individuals*

## Five-lined skink
*Eumeces fasciatus*

▮ | 🌱 | ❤ 6 | ⚠ | ✋ | 🦎

- **Length** 12.5–21.5 cm (5–8½ in)
- **Diet** Insects, spiders
- **Location** E. North America

The fine stripes that give this lizard its name are seen only in female and young skinks. **Males lose their stripes** when they become adult. Young skinks have bright blue tails (right). The lizards tend to live on the ground but can also be found in trees. They **like rotten logs** and tree stumps, which are a good source of insect food.

## Web-footed gecko
*Palmatogecko rangei*

🌵 | 5 | ⚠ | ✋ | 🦎

- **Length** 12–14 cm (4¾–5½in)
- **Diet** Crickets, spiders
- **Location** West southern Africa

The webbing between its toes stops this gecko from sinking into the sand of the deserts where it lives. During the day, the gecko **escapes the heat by staying in a tunnel** that it digs out. At night, it emerges to feed. The gecko's **huge eyes** help it to find prey.

## Madagascar giant day gecko
*Phelsuma madagascariensis*

▮ | ❤ 10 | ⚠ | ✋ | 🦎

- **Length** 22–30 cm (9–12 in)
- **Diet** Insects, spiders, fruit, pollen, nectar
- **Location** North Madagascar

There are several different types of day geckos and all of them are active during the daytime. The giant day gecko is one of the largest species.

Unlike its relatives, this gecko is **fiercely territorial**. The males drive away any other male that comes near their home ground.

## Broadley's flat lizard
*Platysaurus broadleyi*

≈ | ? | ❤ | ⚠ | ✋ | 🦎

- **Length** 15–20 cm (6–8 in)
- **Diet** Flies, berries
- **Location** Southern Africa

Broadley's flat lizard can squeeze itself into the narrowest of cracks, because its body and tail are so flattened. The male (below) is multi-coloured, but females and young are brown with pale stripes. They **live near waterfalls**, where they can find swarms of tiny flies to feed on.

## Black tegu
*Tupinambis teguixin*

▮ | ▮ | ≈ | 20 | ? | 🦎

- **Length** 90–135 cm (3–4½ ft)
- **Diet** Small vertebrates, snails, eggs, fruit, plants
- **Location** South America

This large, strong lizard can sometimes be aggressive. It is a **ground-dweller** and digs its own burrows. The black tegu is a good climber but prefers to stay on the ground most of the time. It often **lays its eggs in termite mounds** to protect them from predators.

# Iguanas, monitors, and relatives

Lizards come in all shapes and sizes. The largest lizard in the world is the Komodo dragon, which hunts animals such as deer and wild pigs. Others are tiny, and light enough to glide through the air.

◄ FEEDING
*Komodo dragons can eat 80 per cent of their body weight at one feeding. Dragons sometimes swallow smaller animals whole, regurgitating the horns, hooves, and hair later as pellets.*

## I am the **biggest lizard** of all.

Komodo dragons are not the sort of lizard most humans would want to bump into. They have thickly folded, scaly skin, a huge muscular tail, and powerful jaws that can tear off large chunks of flesh.

## Komodo dragon
*Varanus komodoensis*

- **Length** 2–3 m (6½–10 ft)
- **Location** Indonesia

Komodo dragons are the **top predator** on the islands where they live. Although they feed mainly on carrion, they will also ambush live prey. They can run quickly for short sprints and young dragons can climb trees. Dragons are usually **solitary** creatures.

# lumed basilisk

*iliscus plumifrons*

- **Length** 60–75 cm (23½–30 in)
- **Location** Central America

e plumed basilisk is a bright green lizard
at lives in trees overhanging streams and
nds. It has **three crests** along its head, neck,
d tail that it uses when swimming. This
ard has the unique ability to escape a
edator by running very quickly across the
rface of a pond on its hind feet.

# Thorny devil

*Moloch horridus*

- **Length** 15–18 cm (6–7 in)
- **Location** Australia

Thorny devils are small, spiky lizards
that live in the Australian
desert. Their **spines**
protect them against
predators and also act as
channels to **collect water**
for drinking. Devils eat only
one type of black ant. They
will sit by an ants' nest
for hours, eating up to
3,000 ants one by one.

**SCARY DEVIL**
*The spines of thorny
devils are not their
only defence. They
can also take in air
to inflate their size.*

*Spiny scale*

# Rainbow lizard

*agama agama*

- **Height** 30–40 cm (12–16 in)
- **Location** Africa

ainbow lizards are usually brownish grey, but
he males develop a blue body and tail and an
**orange-red head after basking** in the sun.
ainbow lizards live in open habitats and
re often found near buildings.
he rainbow's tail is twice
s long as its body.

# Flying lizard

*Draco spilonotus*

- **Height** 15–20 cm (6–8 in)
- **Location** Southeast Asia

Flying lizards have flaps of skin along their
ribs that they can stretch out to form a **"wing"**
on either side of their body. They use these
wings like a parachute to escape predators and
glide to safety. Another
flap under the
chin is used to
**attract mates**
and threaten
rivals.

# Green iguana

*Iguana iguana*

- **Height** 1.75–2 m (5½–6½ ft)
- **Location** Central and South America

Green iguanas are found across most of
northern South America, particularly the
Amazon rainforest. Iguanas have a **fleshy
dewlap** under the chin and a crest of spiky
scales running down their back. Although
they are agile climbers, iguanas can also
**swim, using their tail** to propel them
through the water.

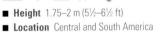

# Nile monitor

*Varanus niloticus*

- **Height** 1.5–18 m (4½–5½ ft)
- **Location** Central Africa

The Nile monitor lives near water, where it
feeds on crabs, molluscs, and fish as well as
small birds and eggs. In cooler climates Nile
monitors hibernate together in **communal
dens**. If threatened by crocodiles or pythons,
they will use their teeth, claws, and tail to
defend themselves. Females lay their eggs
in **termite mounds**.

# Marine iguana

*Amblyrhynchus cristatus*

- **Height** 50–100 cm (20–39 in)
- **Location** Galápagos Islands

Marine iguanas live on the rocky
shores of the Galápagos Islands off the
coast of Ecuador. They are the only
iguanas to **swim in salt water**, diving for
the algae on which they feed. They can only
spend a short time in the cold sea and have to
bask in the sun to warm up again. During this
time they are vulnerable to predators.

# Crocodiles and alligators

Large, scaly reptiles including crocodiles and alligators are collectively known as crocodilians. They live on land and in water and are excellent swimmers, using their tails to propel themselves along. Their jaws are strong enough to crush bones when they close, but so weak when they open, that they can be held together by hand.

Nostrils close when under water.

Skin is covered in armour-plates, called osteoderms.

## Dwarf crocodile
*Osteolaemus tetraspis*

- **Length** 1.7 m (5½ ft)
- **Weight** 31 kg (70 lb)
- **Diet** Fish, frogs, toads; young eat worms and insects
- **Location** West and Central Africa

Among the **smallest** of crocodiles, this is one of the most aggressive. During the day, it burrows among tree trunks at the water's edge and **at night it hunts.** The female usually lays about 10 eggs. When they hatch, she carries each baby to the water in her mouth.

▼ *Crocodilians are cold blooded, so they depend on the temperature of their environment to warm up or cool down.*

## Spectacled caiman
*Caiman crocodilus*

- **Length** 2–2.5 m (6½–8 ft)
- **Weight** 45 kg (99 lb)
- **Diet** Reptiles, fish, waterbirds
- **Location** Central America, northern South America

This crocodile has a **bony ridge** around its eyes that look like glasses. It spends almost all its time in fresh water, floating on the surface during the day and hunting at night. It is a good swimmer and hunts fish such as piranhas and catfish. It also **snatches mammals,** including wild pigs, that come to the water to drink.

▼ *Crocodilians have see-through eyelids that they close when they are under water.*

## Gharial
*Gavialis gangeticus*

- **Length** 4–7 m (13–23 ft)
- **Weight** 100 kg (220 lb)
- **Diet** Fish, frogs, insects
- **Location** Northern India

A crocodile with a long, **narrow snout,** the gharial rarely leaves the water. It is one of the largest crocodilians and cannot walk on land, so it **belly slides** across the ground.

# The first crocodilians.

Crocodiles appeared with the first dinosaurs, about 200 million years ago. They have remained virtually unchanged ever since.

▶ KILLING TIME
*As it waits for prey, a crocodilian floats almost completely submerged. Only its nostrils and eyes are above the water.*

## Slender snouted crocodile

*Crocodylus cataphractus*

- **Length** 3–4.2 m (10–14 ft)
- **Diet** Crabs, frogs, fish, birds, and small mammals
- **Location** Central and West Africa

**Grey-green** to almost black, this crocodile lives in rivers, lakes, and coastal waters. Although it prefers fresh water, it can tolerate salt water and may **swim over to islands** near the African mainland. Females lay between 13 and 27 eggs in riverbank nests.

▲ *A crocodilian can open its mouth wide under water – a flap of skin on its throat stops water going into its lungs.*

## American alligator

*Alligator mississippiensis*

- **Length** 2.8–5 m (9¼–16 ft)
- **Weight** 453 kg (1,000 lb)
- **Diet** Fish, small mammals, birds
- **Location** S.E. USA

A large, **heavy predator,** the American alligator lives mostly in the rivers, lakes, and **swamps** of Florida and Louisiana, USA. Females lay 25–60 eggs. The young have yellow and black stripes. They stay with their mother for up to three years.

## Nile crocodile

*Crocodylus niloticus*

- **Length** 3.5–6 m (11–20 ft)
- **Weight** 225 kg (500 lb)
- **Diet** Fish and large mammals including antelopes, zebras, and buffaloes
- **Location** Africa, western Madagascar

This crocodile feeds on fish, as well as larger animals including antelopes and zebras. It **pulls big prey into the water**, then spins round and round to tear off chunks that it can swallow.

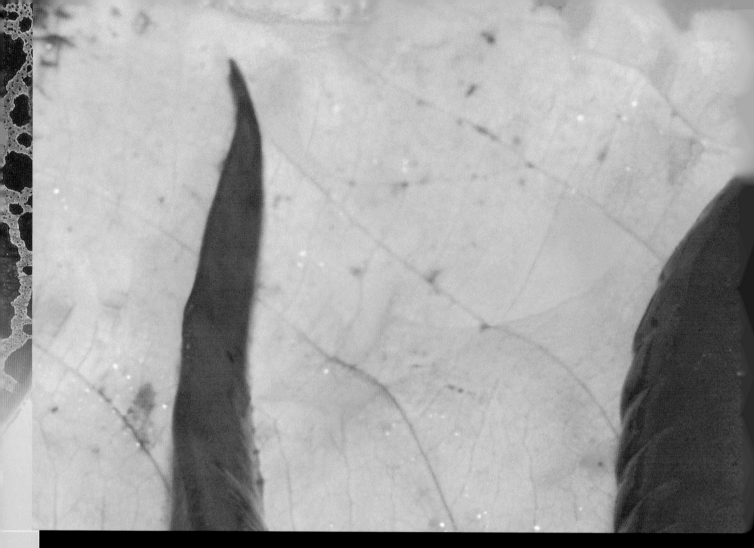

# AMPHIBIANS

*Definition:* **Amphibians** comprise three groups: newts and salamanders, frogs and toads, and caecilians. They are cold-blooded and live both in water and on land.

# What is an AMPHIBIAN?

Amphibians have three life stages: eggs, larvae, and adults. Many amphibians start life in water, and breathe through gills, then change into adults that can live on land, and breathe through lungs. This happens in a process called "metamorphosis".

## IT'S A FROG'S LIFE

... and a toad's, and a newt's, and a salamander's, and a caecilian's. All these creatures are amphibians. The least well-known of these is the caecilian. It is a worm-like animal, rarely seen by humans because it lives either in soil burrows or underwater. It has a good sense of smell to sniff out earthworms, which it catches with sharp, curved teeth.

◄ CAECILIAN LIFE CYCLE
*Caecilians have varied life cycles: some lay eggs, while some keep the eggs in their body until they are ready to hatch into larvae.*

I might go **ashore** now for a bit of a wander.

Amphibians are equally at home on land or in water.

### FACTFILE

There are three groups of amphibians: frogs and toads, newts and salamanders, and caecilians. Altogether there are 5,000 species.

■ **Frogs and toads**
Frog and toad larvae are called "tadpoles". They eat algae until they become adults when they become carnivorous.

■ **Newts and salamanders**
These animals have tails and short legs. They are carnivorous in both their larva and adult stages.

■ **Caecilians**
These form a small group. They have long, thin bodies and no legs. They only live in tropical, humid places.

## A LONG WALK HOME

Most amphibians live on land as adults but return to water to breed. Some species migrate long distances to get back to the same pond where they started out themselves. In some cases this can mean a mass of frogs moving across rough terrain during the breeding season to get "home".

► EGG-CELLENT
*When frogs find a pond, they mate and lay their eggs.*

186

## SPECIAL SKIN

The skin of an amphibian is hairless and smooth, and highly specialized. It is very thin and absorbent – thin enough to breathe through. Mucus glands keep it damp, which helps gases pass through.

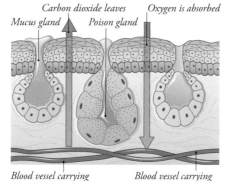

Carbon dioxide leaves
Oxygen is absorbed
Mucus gland
Poison gland
Blood vessel carrying oxygenated blood.
Blood vessel carrying deoxygenated blood.

▲ SPOT THE FROG *Many amphibians have amazing camouflage. It's as though their skin has been painted to make them disappear.*

## STURDY SKELETON

Amphibians have a fairly simple body structure, well adapted to life in water and on land. They have large eye sockets to make room for their big eyes, and wide mouths to fit in large prey.

Wide mouth

Long toes

◄ LEAP FROG
*The structure of a frog skeleton reveals clearly how it moves. It looks poised to leap. It has a short squat body, wide mouth, and large eye sockets (all the better to see its prey!).*

Four fingers

Ribs

Spine

Five toes

Long back legs

SALAMANDER STRUT
*This creature uses its legs to walk on land, and its long tail to propel it through the water. Its long backbone is unusually flexible.*

## MORPHING

Most amphibians start life in water, as one egg among a cluster of eggs (in the case of frogs, this is called "frogspawn"). After a few weeks the eggs hatch into larvae. These are like little fish with tails – they swim and breathe through gills. Gradually they start to change and develop lungs until metamorphosis is complete and they can leave the water.

Newt egg

Two weeks later – newt larva hatches

Three to four months later – adult newt

▲ NEWT LIFE CYCLE
*Like frogs, newts have an egg, larvae, and adult stage. They keep their tails.*

Adult frog (16 weeks)

Frogspawn

Froglet (12 weeks old)

Tadpole (recently hatched)

Front legs (nine weeks)

Long back limbs (six to nine weeks)

▲ FROG LIFE CYCLE
*Frogs start out as frogspawn, which hatches into tadpoles. Legs gradually grow, the tail shrinks, and finally they become frogs.*

# Salamanders and newts

## It's **hair raising** being a newt!

This great crested newt is still a baby. It spends all its time under water, breathing through its long feathery gills. At about four months old, its gills shrink and disappear. It begins to breathe air through lungs and is ready to leave the water.

There is no real difference between newts and salamanders. Newts are a subgroup of salamanders which means all newts are salamanders, but not all salamanders are newts! Newts generally spend more of their adult life in water than salmanders. Both groups are amphibians.

188

# Chinese giant salamander
*...rias davidianus*

**Length** 1.8 m (6 ft)
**Diet** Fish and crustaceans
**Location** China

...is is the **largest
...phibian** in the world.
...ives in mountain streams,
...ferring fast-running water,
...d hunts mainly at night for
...imps, fish, and insects. Certain males
...ke masterful fathers. In the mating
...son, one male controls the movements
...all breeding pairs in his territory and
...er **guards all the eggs** until they hatch.

# ...ire salamander
*...lamandra salamandra*

**Length** 18–28 cm (7–11 in)
**Diet** Worms, slugs, and insects
**Location** N.W. Africa, Europe, W. Asia

...he **yellow markings** on this sturdy creature
...arn predators that it is poisonous, and would
...ake a disgusting meal. It often
...ves on mountain slopes in
...oodland. During the cold
...inter months, it curls up
...nderground, in a cosy hole.
...emerges when it's
...armer, especially
...fter rain, to eat
...ugs and worms.

# Jordan's salamander
*Plethodon jordani*

**Length** 8.5–18.5 cm (3¼–7½ in)
**Diet** Millipedes, beetles, and insect larvae
**Location** E. USA

This salamander is also distasteful to predators,
thanks to a **slime that oozes from its tail**. Its
breeding habits show the varied behaviour of
salamanders: males breed every year, females
breed every two years.

# Pacific giant salamander
*Dicamptodon tenebrosus*

**Length** 17–34 cm (6½–13½ in)
**Diet** Invertebrates, other amphibians,
snakes, and mice
**Location** S.W. Canada, N.W. USA

This large salamander lives in or around
streams, and **comes out at night**. Some never
leave the water, and never lose their gills, and
some do leave the water and do lose their gills!
Their numbers have dipped because of logging
and the resulting silting up of streams.

# Great crested newt
*...riturus cristatus*

**Length** 10–14 cm (4–5½ in)
**Diet** Insects, worms, woodlice, slugs, and snails
**Location** Europe, Central Asia

...his is a male great crested newt; you can tell
...y the **crest on his back** that develops during
...he breeding season. He does a complex dance
...nder water to attract a female. After mating,
...he female **lays one egg at a time**, and wraps
...ach one in a leaf. It's a big job as she lays more
...han 200 eggs and they can take up to four
...months to wrap.

# Emperor crocodile salamander
*Tylotriton shanjing*

**Length** 14–18 cm (5½–7 in)
**Diet** Worms, fish
**Location** Southern and southeast Asia

During the winter or dry weather, this **warty
newt** stays underground. It comes out for the
monsoon, when it rains a lot. It then makes a
journey to a breeding pond and sticks its eggs
on to water plants.

# Olm
*Proteus anguinus*

**Length** 20–30 cm (8–12 in)
**Diet** Invertebrates
**Location** Southern Europe

This is one of the few amphibians that
**makes its home in a cave**, sometimes many
kilometres inside the Earth. It lives in total
darkness, and is **near-blind**. It eats bugs and
larvae in underground streams, and never
leaves the water.

# Frogs and toads

These cold-blooded creatures form the largest and best-known group of amphibians. They come in a variety of shapes, sizes, and colours. The goliath frog is as big as a cat, but some are so small they can fit on your fingernail.

▲ WELCOME TO MY PAD *The male of each species has a different call. The grey treefrog (Hyla chrysoscelis) has a vocal sac that fills with air to produce a really loud call. On hearing it, females know where they can find a mate.*

LEAP FROG *Frogs can crawl, climb, and hop along, and are able to leap 10 times their body length. They launch themselves out of danger, like this tiger-striped leaf frog.*

## FACTFILE

- **Number of species:** Almost 4,500.
- **Key features:** Short body, long hind legs, moist skin, no tail.
- There is no clear way to tell the difference between frogs and toads.
- Frogs usually have smooth, moist skin, are slimy, and jump. They spend most of their lives in or near water.
- Toads tend to be dry, warty-looking, and walk rather than jump. They spend more time living on land.
- A group of frogs is called an "army". A group of toads is called a "knot".

# reen treefrog

*ia caerulea*

**ength** 5–10 cm (2–4 in)
**abit** Terrestrial
**ocation** S. New Guinea, N. and E. Australia

s frog is well known for its **tame** behaviour,
d its habit of living in or near buildings.
ight hunter, it eats mosquitoes, bugs, and
n mice, so is a **much appreciated guest.**
e skin has also been helpful to humans –
a substance in it
can be used to
treat high
blood pressure.

# Mexican burrowing toad

*Rhinophrynus dorsalis*

- **Length** 6–8 cm (2¼–3¼ in)
- **Habit** Terrestrial/burrowing
- **Location** Southern USA to Central America

This **bloated** toad spends most of its life
underground, burrowing into soft soil, slurping
up ants and termites. It only comes out after
heavy rain to breed. As rain falls any time, it
**doesn't have a breeding season** and its low
"whoo-oa" call
can be heard
all year.

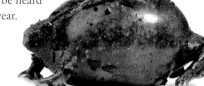

# Asian treefrog

*Megophrys montana*

- **Length** 7–14 cm (2¾–5½ in)
- **Habit** Mostly terrestrial
- **Location** Southeast Asia

This forest floor frog does an amazing
impression of a dead leaf. Its pointy snout,
**hooded eyes**, and sharp folds in
its skin add to the effect.
The frog **stays still**
and waits for its
prey – scorpions
or small crabs –
to pass by.

# ed-eyed treefrog

*alychnis callidryas*

**Length** 4–7 cm (1½–2¾ in)
**Habit** Terrestrial
**Location** Central America

any scientists believe the red-eyed treefrog
veloped its **vivid scarlet peepers** to shock
edators into questioning their meal choice.
ny small hesitation gives the frog the split
second it needs to leap
to safety. Red-eyed tree
frogs are **nocturnal**,
and feed on moths and
crickets which they
catch with their long,
sticky tongues.

# Grey treefrog

*Hyla chrysoscelis*

- **Length** 3–6 cm (1¼–2¼ in)
- **Habit** Mostly terrestrial
- **Location** S. Canada, C. and E. USA

These small frogs are well camouflaged to hide
amongst the lichen-covered tree branches they
live on. They are never far from water. Their
tadpoles have round bodies and high tails,
which **turn red** when there are predators
nearby. They change
from tadpoles to
young adults
in as little
as two
months.

# Golden mantella

*Mantella aurantiaca*

- **Length** 2–3 cm (¾–1¼ in)
- **Habit** Wholly terrestrial
- **Location** Western and central Madagascar

Although this
frog is **not toxic**,
it looks like it is to
predators! Its bright
orange colour mimics that
of the golden poison dart frog
and is a very effective deterrent. Golden
mantellas are small land frogs and hunt by
day, eating any insects they can fit in their
mouths. They often **live in colonies**, with
twice as many males in them as females.

# North American bullfrog

*ana catesbeiana*

**Length** 9–20 cm (3½–8 in)
**Habit** Mostly aquatic
**Location** S.E. Canada, W., C., and E. USA

hese big frogs have a **big appetite**! They will
at almost anything that moves and that they
an swallow, including invertebrates and small
ammals, birds, reptiles, fish, and even turtles
nd other frogs. They usually live
mong vegetation along
he edge of large,
low-moving
ivers and
treams.

# Goliath bullfrog

*Conraua goliath*

- **Length** 10–40 cm (4–16 in)
- **Habit** Mostly aquatic
- **Location** Cameroon, Equatorial Guinea

The Goliath is the **biggest
frog in the world**, and can
leap the length of a car. It is
shy, sharp-eyed, and quick to
**dive out of sight**. The eggs and
tadpoles of its early stages give
no hint of its future giant size as
they are not much larger than
those of any other of the world's
frogs. Only after metamorphosis
does it begin to grow and grow.

**AMPHIBIANS**

## I think I'm in **love**!

Frogs and toads gather in breeding ponds. Here they mate, the female lays eggs, and then they take off again. The survival rate is low. Out of 2,000 eggs fewer than five frogs or toads will make it back to the same pond to breed there.

EUROPEAN COMMON TOADS *pair up in breeding ponds in spring. The female is much bigger than the male, especially at this time of year, when she is laden with eggs.*

## oulenger's Asian tree toad

*stibes hosii*

- **ength** 5–10 cm (2–4 in)
- **here** Mostly on land
- **ocation** S.E. Asia

usually for a
d, this one is a
d climber. It
es to "hang out"
the branches of
es over rivers. The
ale lays long strings
oadspawn in rivers
the **tadpoles**
e **sucker-like**
uths** to cling
to rocks.

## Oriental fire-bellied toad

*Bombina orientalis*

- **Length** 3–5 cm (1¼–2 in)
- **Where** Mostly in water
- **Location** E. and S.E Asia

This toad has a **bright
orange belly** for a reason
– when threatened it arches its
back, flattens its body, and lifts its
legs over its head to display the
vivid colours – and hopefully
scare off any predator. It **lives
in mountain streams** near
the coast, and hides
under rocks and logs
during winter.

## urinam toad

*a pipa*

- **Length** 5–20 cm (2–8 in)
- **Where** Always in water
- **Location** N. South America

pa pipa* has powerful
d legs to swim fast,
d **feelers on its fingers**
help it find prey in
uddy water. When the
male lays her eggs, they
e absorbed into the skin
her back, where they
evelop in capsules** and
erge as mini-toads.

## Midwife toad

*Ayltes obstetricans*

- **Length** 3–5 cm (1¼–2 in)
- **Where** Mostly in water
- **Location** W. and C. Europe

This toad has a very
**unusual way of
breeding**. The female lays
large, yolk-filled eggs in
strings, which are
transferred to the male during mating.
The male then wraps these strings around
his legs, and carries them around until
they are ready to hatch. At which point,
he pops them into a pool.

## uropean common toad

*ufo bufo*

- **Length** 8–20 cm (3¼–8 in)
- **Where** Mostly on land
- **Location** N.W. Africa, Europe to Central Asia

*Bufo bufo* is Europe's most
widespread amphibian. Apart
from during the breeding
season, the toad spends its
time on land, **hunting slugs
and insects**. If threatened it
stands on tiptoe, with rigid
legs, and **takes gulps of air**
to puff up its body. It is
mainly nocturnal.

## African clawed toad

*Xenopus laevis*

- **Length** 6–13 cm (2¼–5 in)
- **Where** Mostly in water
- **Location** Southern Africa

With **eyes on the top of
its head** to spy food above,
and long fingers to shovel
small fish and insect larvae
into its mouth, this toad is
a **voracious underwater
feeder**. Its skin colours
make effective camouflage –
good protection from
hungry herons.

# Marine toad

The world's largest toad has a hidden weapon. Its skin is highly toxic, and results in death to any animal that attacks it. If it is squeezed – or even threatened – a creamy white venom will ooze from glands on its shoulders and body. An animal that eats this venom may die rather quickly.

STAY BACK! *As well as using venom, the marine toad will raise itself up if threatened, to look far larger then it is. Most predators have learnt to take extreme care with a marine toad.*

## Be careful... I **eat** small snakes!

Marine toads do eat snakes, but some snakes, like the toad-eater snake shown here, can eat marine toads without being affected by the toad's toxins. However, this toad may be too big a mouthful for this particular snake. Marine toads are stocky, and find it easier to walk on flat rather than bumpy ground.

# Marine toad
*Bufo marinus*

- **Length** 5–23 cm (2–9 in)
- **Weight** Up to 2 kg (4 lb)
- **Habit** Mostly terrestrial
- **Location** Central America. South America. Introduced to Australia and elsewhere.

You can see white toxins seeping out of large **glands on the shoulder** of this marine toad. These toads tend to be active at night, choosing to hide during the day under leaves or stones, or burrowing down into loose soil.

### ⚠ CONSERVATION

The marine, or cane toad was first introduced to Australia in 1935, but its numbers have grown rapidly and it is now a serious pest. It has successfully competed against Australia's frogs and toads for space and food, and caused native animal deaths.

## NEW GENERATIONS

Marine toads lay a lot of eggs – it's estimated about 30,000 at a time. Though perhaps just a few of these make it to adulthood, it's partly why marine toads are so successful. The eggs hatch in three days, and the young grow rapidly.

AMPHIBIANS

▲ DIET *Marine toads will eat anything they can catch. Their diet consists largely of insects, but may include a variety of rodents, smaller frogs and toads, and snakes. If hungry, they will even eat their own young. They are common near houses, where they will eat dog food if it is left out.*

# Poison dart frogs

These jewel-like frogs of the jungle are colourful for a reason – bright colours warn predators that they are highly toxic. In fact, the family name comes from the use by local tribes of the frogs' powerful venom to tip their blowgun darts when hunting.

### FACTFILE

- There are about 120 species of dart frogs.
- Nearly all species are brightly coloured.
- Most are small.
- They live in the tropical rainforests of Central and South America.
- Males buzz and chirp to attract females.
- They have tiny suction cups on their toes that cling to slippery leaves and branches.
- They eat termites, ants, flies, crickets, and other insects, which they catch with quick flicks of their sticky tongues.

*Glands in a poison dart frog's skin ooze poison.*

▲ BREEDING AMONG THE TREES
*The male looks after the eggs in most poison dart frog families. He guards them and keeps them moist by collecting water. When the tadpoles are ready to hatch, he lets them wriggle onto his back and carries them to a suitable pool of water.*

◄ THE MOST POISONOUS FROG *on Earth is the golden poison dart frog – with enough poison in its skin to kill ten men. These frogs can be very dangerous and are thought to be the only animal that can kill a man by touch alone. It is one of the biggest poison dart frogs, reaching lengths of 5 cm (2 in).*

BEAUTY WITH BITE
*The spots, stripes, and brilliant colours may look pretty, but to predators, they mean only one thing:*
DON'T EAT THEM.

# Blue poison dart frog
*Dendrobates azureus*

| | **10** | ⚠ | 🖐 | 🐸 |

- **Length** 5 cm (2 in)
- **Where** Forest floor
- **Location** Suriname

...ly discovered in 1968, ...e poison dart frogs ...active during the day ...d can be found hiding ...mong boulders and ...ris near streams. ...ey **lack toe** ...ebbing** and are ...or swimmers, so ...ey are **never found** ...the water.

# Green poison dart frog
*Dendrobates auratus*

| | **8** | ⚠ | 🖐 | 🐸 |

- **Length** 3–6 cm (1–2¼ in)
- **Where** Forest floor
- **Location** Central and South America, Hawaii

These little frogs have one habit that is unusual among amphibians – the **females take the lead** in mating. She entices the male to mate by beating him on the back with her hind feet. People have introduced them to Hawaii where they have flourished. In highly populated areas, they sometimes **leave their eggs in broken bottles** or discarded cans.

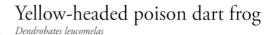

▲ FLOOR HOPPER
*Green poison dart frogs, like all adult dart frogs, are found on the floor of rainforests. They prefer living near small streams or pools.*

# Lehmann's poison dart frog
*Dendrobates lehmanni*

| | **?** | ⚠ | 🖐 | 🐸 |

- **Length** 3 cm (1¼ in)
- **Where** Forest floor, low bushes
- **Location** Colombia

...his frog is also known as the red-...anded poison dart frog. It is listed as **...ritically endangered** because it lives in ...st one area of rainforest that is less than ...0 km² (4 sq miles). Groups of frogs are ...pread about within this area with no ...ontact between each group. This puts ...his little frog at even greater risk. ...nfortunately, the quality and extent ...f their habitat is still in decline.

# Yellow-headed poison dart frog
*Dendrobates leucomelas*

| | **7** | ⚠ | 🖐 | 🐸 |

- **Length** 3–5 cm (1¼–2 in)
- **Where** Forest floor, sometimes in trees
- **Location** Northern South America

The male of this species is **very territorial**. If another male of its kind happens into its territory, it will grasp it belly to belly, and make **a loud buzzing noise** in its ear. Another name for this frog is the bumble bee frog.

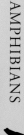

AMPHIBIANS

# Harlequin poison dart frog
*Dendrobates histrionicus*

| | **10** | ⚠ | 🖐 | 🐸 |

- **Length** 3–4 cm (1–1½ in)
- **Where** Forest floor
- **Location** W. Equador, Columbia

This is one of the **most poisonous** of these frogs, as well as one of the smallest. The poison that oozes from every bit of its body is collected from the **toxic bugs** it eats and then deposited in its skin.

# Strawberry poison dart frog
*Dendrobates pumilio*

| | **10** | ⚠ | 🖐 | 🐸 |

- **Length** 2–2.5 cm (¾–1 in)
- **Where** Forest floor
- **Location** S. Central America

This little frog is also small, but less poisonous than the harlequin dart frog. It would still give a predator a **nasty stomachache**, though. Its **colour can vary** from bright red, to brown, blue, or green, depending on where it lives. It is most commonly found in the humid rainforests of Costa Rica.

# Frogs *and* toads

Frogs and toads form the largest group of amphibians. There's actually no clear difference between them. They range in size from the tiny Brazilian gold frog to the enormous goliath bullfrog, both shown here at their maximum life sizes.

**Green treefrog**
*Litoria caerulea*

**Tomato frog**
*Dyscophus antongilii*

**North American bullfrog**
*Rana catesbeiana*

The goliath bullfrog can reach just over 40 cm (15¾ in) in length. The Brazilian gold frog is just under 1 cm (⅜ in).

**BIGGEST FROG**
**Goliath bullfrog**
*Conraua goliath*

**Solomon Islands horned frog**
*Ceratobatrachus guentheri*

**Green mantella frog**
*Mantella viridis*

**SMALLEST FROG**
**Brazilian gold frog**
*Psyllophryne didactyla*

**Monte Iberia Eleuth frog**
*Eleutherodactylus iberia*

**Yellow-headed poison frog**
*Dendrobates leucomelas*

**Emerald glass frog**
*Centrolene prosoblepon*

**European treefrog**
*Hyla arborea*

**Golden poison frog**
*Phyllobates terribilis*

**Malabar flying frog**
*Rhacophorus malabarcius*

**Red-eyed treefrog**
*Agalychnis callidryas*

**Natterjack toad**
*Bufo calamita*

**Mexican burrowing toad**
*Rhinophrynus dorsalis*

**Turtle frog**
*Myobatrachus gouldii*

**Asian treefrog**
*Megophrys montana*

**Surinam horned frog**
*Ceratophrys cornuta*

rsley frog
*dytes punctatus*

**Green toad**
*Bufo viridis*

**Surinam toad**
*Pipa pipa*

**Woodhouse's toad**
*Bufo woodhousii*

**Red spotted toad**
*Bufo punctatus*

Couch's spadefoot toad
*Scaphiopus couchii*

**Marine toad**
*Bufo marinus*

199

FISH

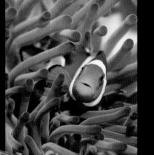
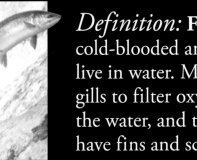

*Definition:* **Fish** are cold-blooded animals that live in water. Most have gills to filter oxygen from the water, and the majority have fins and scales.

# What is a FISH?

More than half of all vertebrates are fish. They first appeared on Earth some 500 million years ago. Most fish breathe using gills, have a body covered with scales, are cold-blooded, and move using fins. They live in fresh water or in the sea – and a few can survive in both.

## FACTFILE

There are just under 25,000 species of fish. They are broadly divided into three groups: jawless, cartilaginous, and bony.

■ **Jawless fish** (hagfish and lampreys) are eel-like and lack scales and jaws.

■ **Cartilaginous fish** include sharks, rays, and skates. They are covered with hard scales, have skeletons made of cartilage, not bone, and have sharp teeth.

■ **Bony fish** are the largest group. These fish have hard, bony skeletons.

■ **Sizes** range from a tiny minnow that reaches just 7 mm (¼ in) in length to a whale shark, that can be 14 m (46 ft).

## FINS

Fish use their fins, combined with body movements, to propel themselves through the water and steer in the right direction. Some fins come in pairs. These are the pectoral (behind the head) and pelvic (on the underside). Other fins are unpaired: the dorsal (top), caudal (tail), and anal (nearest the tail).

CAUDAL (OR TAIL) FIN *In most bony fish this provides the power that propels the fish forwards.*

ANAL FIN *This fin acts as a stabilizer.*

PELVIC FINS *Paired pelvic fins add stability and may be used to slow the fish down.*

## NEW LIFE

Many fish begin life as eggs. They hatch out as larvae and change by stages into their adult form. Some fish hatch from eggs as tiny adults, while others are born as live young.

A baby trout hatches from an egg

Fish eggs

EGG SAC *The eggs of the dogfish develop inside a leathery sac, or "purse". Long threads anchor the egg sac to rocks or seaweed.*

## the inside

e skeleton of a bony fish is made up
hree main parts: the skull, the fin
leton, and the backbone.

Tail fin

Backbone

Dorsal fin

### SKULL AND TEETH
*The skull supports the jaws and gill arches. A fish may have teeth in its throat, the roof of its mouth, on its tongue, or in its jaws.*

Skull

Lower jaw

Pectoral fin

### ORSAL FIN
*is may be a single fin or it may be
arated into several fins. In most bony
hes, the dorsal fin is used for sudden
rection changes and it acts as a "keel"
keep the fish stable in the water.*

Liver

Stomach

*Some fish have "false teeth" in the throat*

## HOW FISH BREATHE

To live, fish need oxygen, which they obtain from the water. A fish takes in water through its mouth and sends it out through its gills (feathery structures found along the sides of the head). As the water flows out of the fish's body, the surfaces of the gills extract the oxygen, which then passes into the bloodstream.

OPERCULUM *This bony flap covers the gills.*

PECTORAL FINS *A fish uses these fins on either side of its head to change direction. The pectoral fins can also be used for tasting, touching, support, and to give the swimming fish a power boost.*

### Odd fish
Among the more unusual fish, there are those that appear to fly, others that have no jaws, and some that can "walk" out of water on their fins.

▼ LAMPREYS *have sucker pads instead of mouths. They latch on to prey with their teeth and either rasp off the flesh or suck blood.*

*Lampreys are jawless fish.*

▼ MUDSKIPPERS *can live out of water for long periods. They move over mudflats by using their pectoral fins to pull themselves along.*

▼ FLYING FISH *cannot really fly, but their large, winglike pectoral fins allow them to glide briefly above the water's surface.*

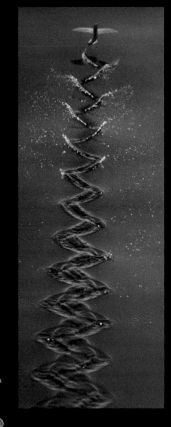

### Parental care
Some fish take an active part in caring for their young. Both parents may look after the eggs and tend the new hatchlings when they emerge. Parental duties can include feeding the young, fanning water over them to supply oxygen, and chasing away predators.

▲ YELLOWHEAD JAWFISH *The males carry eggs in their mouths until they are ready to hatch.*

▶ FATHERS *Male seahorses are unusual in that they carry their young. Female seahorses put their eggs in a pouch on the male's abdomen where they are fertilized and begin to develop.*

# A *world* of sharks

There are more than 350 species of shark.
They range from small pygmy sharks that are
just a little bit longer than the width of this
page to the whale shark, which can grow to
the length of a truck! Most have a pointed
nose and a triangular dorsal fin.

**Shortfin mako shark**
*Isurus oxyrinchus*

**Common smoothhound**
*Mustelus mustelus*

**Blacktip reef shark**
*Carcharhinus melanopterus*

**Porbeagle**
*Lamna nasus*

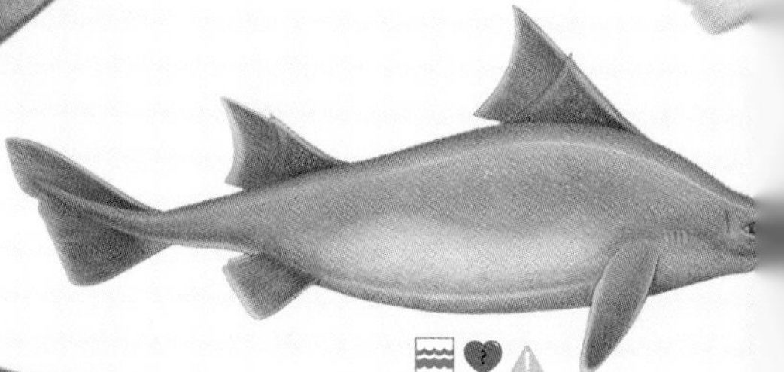

**Angular rough shark**
*Oxynotus centrina*

*The Port Jackson
shark is unusual
because it can breathe
when it is motionless.*

**Spined pygmy shark**
*Squaliosus laticaudus*

**Velvet belly lantern shark**
*Etmopterus spinax*

**Port Jackson shark**
*Heterodontus portusjacksoni*

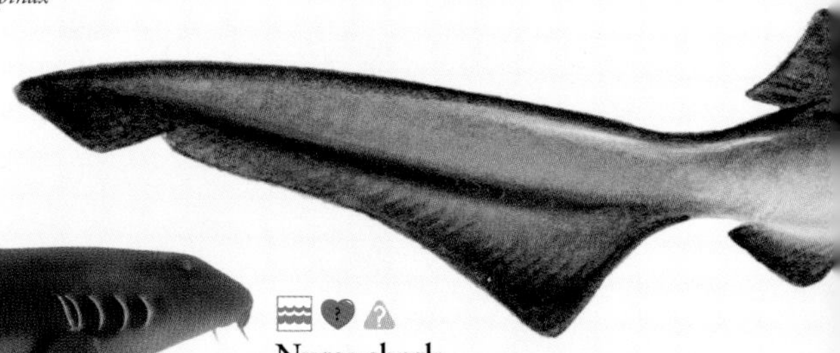

**Nurse shark**
*Ginglymostoma cirratum*

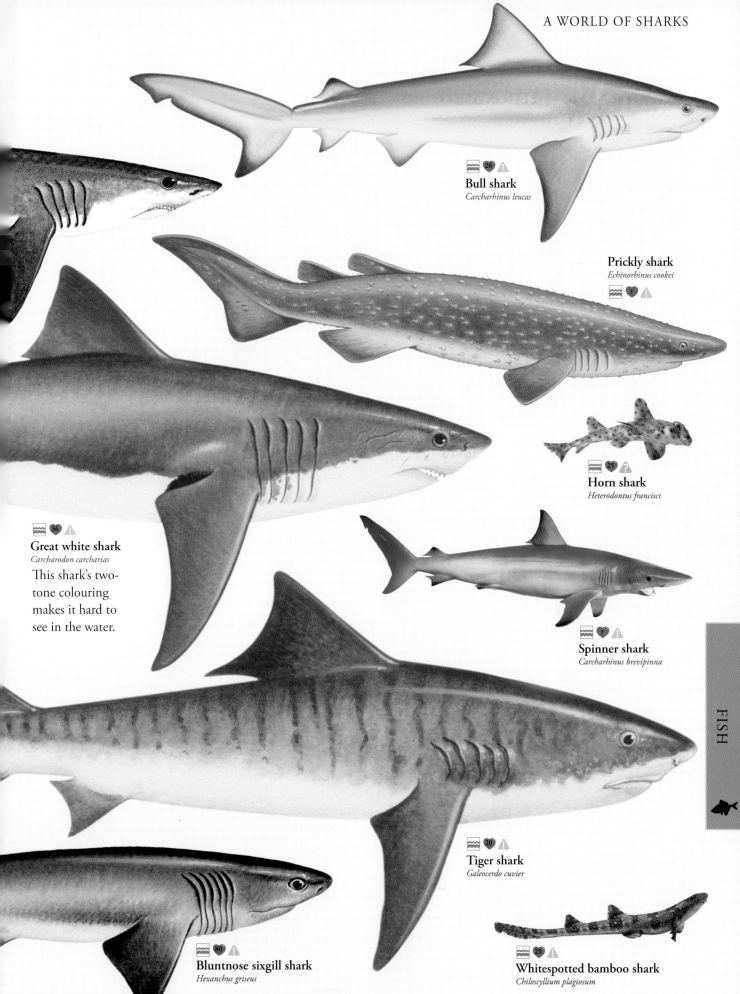

**Bull shark**
*Carcharhinus leucas*

**Prickly shark**
*Echinorhinus cookei*

**Horn shark**
*Heterodontus francisci*

**Great white shark**
*Carcharodon carcharias*
This shark's two-tone colouring makes it hard to see in the water.

**Spinner shark**
*Carcharhinus brevipinna*

**Tiger shark**
*Galeocerdo cuvier*

**Bluntnose sixgill shark**
*Hexanchus griseus*

**Whitespotted bamboo shark**
*Chiloscyllium plagiosum*

FISH

# Great hammerhead shark
*Sphyrna mokarran*

- **Length** 350–600 cm (11½–19½ ft)
- **Weight** 230–450 kg (500–1,000 lb)
- **Diet** Small sharks, rays, bony fishes, and squid
- **Location** Worldwide (warm temperate and tropical waters)

This is the **largest of nine species** of hammerhead. They live in warm coastal waters. Females produce 20–40 pups that are 70 cm (28 in) in length.

*Long upper tail lobe*

*Head flap*

*Pectoral fin*

## KEY FEATURES

Great hammerhead sharks have a wide head with an eye at both ends. The head moves in a constant sweeping motion so that the shark can see in every direction. Other characteristics are a first dorsal fin that is large and pointed, and teeth that are triangular with serrated edges.

▼ PREY *Hammerhead sharks are sometimes cannibalistic, but generally they live on a diet of fish, including rays. They eat other sharks, octopuses, squid, and crustaceans. Their favourite meal is stingray, which they pin down using their hammer-shaped head. They look fierce, but there have been few attacks on people.*

*Hammerhead sharks use their sensory organs to detect the electrical fields of their prey*

*Electrical field*

*Stingray hiding under the sand*

# The *big-headed* hammerhead

Hammerhead sharks stick together, and there can be up to 100 in a school. They are formidable hunters and are able to find hidden prey more effectively than typical sharks by using sensory organs in their head, which can pick up electrical signals in the water from potential prey.

FISH

# *Killer* sharks?

Most people think of sharks as sleek, fast-moving killers equipped with banks of viciously pointed teeth. Some sharks do live up to this description. But there are many other types, from sluggish, toothless giants to glow-in-the-dark fish not much bigger than a person's hand.

## Leopard shark
*Triakis semifasciata*

- **Length** 2 m (7 ft)
- **Weight** 32 kg (70 lb)
- **Diet** Crustaceans, worms, fish
- **Location** E. North Pacific coast

Sensory organs in the leopard shark's nose allow it to find and pull out prey buried in deep mud. The shark's **striking body patte** make it popular with fishermen.

## Spined pygmy shark
*Squaliolus laticaudus*

- **Length** 25 cm (10 in)
- **Weight** Not recorded
- **Diet** Squid, shrimp, small fish
- **Location** Atlantic, W. Indian Ocean, W. Pacific

This deep water species is **one of the smallest sharks** in the world. Unusually for a shark, it has a dorsal spine. Light-emitting organs in its belly glow in the dark. This may act as a disguise, confusing any predators swimming below.

## Whitetip reef shark
*Triaenodon obesus*

- **Length** 1.6–2 m (5–7 ft)
- **Weight** 18 kg (40 lb) and over
- **Diet** Fish, octopuses, crustaceans
- **Location** Tropical Pacific and Indian Oceans

Whitetip reef sharks **feed around coral heads**, where divers often meet them. These sharks are not usually aggressive towards people, although they have been known to grab fish from a diver's spear.

◀ **SEA FLOOR**
*These sharks rest on the sea floor or in underwater caves.*

## Whale shark
*Rhincodon typus*

- **Length** 12–14 m (39–46 ft)
- **Weight** 12,000 kg (26,500 lb) and over
- **Diet** Plankton, fish eggs
- **Location** Warm seas worldwide

This is the **biggest fish in the world**. Despite its name, the whale shark is not related to whales. With a mouth that may be up to 1.4 metres (4½ ft) wide, this shark looks dangerous but, in fact, it is quite harmless.

Slow moving and mostly solitary, whale sharks are usually seen cruising near the surface of the ocean. They feed largely by sucking water into their mouths to trap plankton – floating mats of tiny crustaceans and plants. Whale sharks give birth to live young and pregnant females have been found carrying hundreds of developing young.

**DEEP DIVER** *Whale sharks are capable of diving more than 1,000 metres (3,300 ft). They plunge to such depths in search of eggs released by spawning fish.*

FISH

# reat white shark

*harodon carcharias*

❤ 36 ⚠

**ength** 6–8 m (20–26 ft)
**eight** 2,000 kg (4,400 lb) and over
**iet** Seals, dolphins, and large fish
**ocation** Warm seas worldwide

e great white shark is one of the most feared
atures of the sea. There are many stories of
attacks on humans, although the shark's
utation as a man killer has been
ggerated. However, the great
ite's muscular, streamlined

body make it a swift and deadly predator.
With rows of sharp, pointed teeth designed
for **ripping and tearing**, the shark can take
the head off prey such as a seal with one bite.
Great white sharks live and hunt alone, but
they sometimes gather together to share a kill.
When feeding in groups, the sharks usually
show no aggression towards each other.

# Atlantic angel shark

*Squatina dumeril*

〰 ❤ ❓

■ **Length** 1.5 m (5 ft)
■ **Weight** 27 kg (60 lb) and over
■ **Diet** Small fish, molluscs
■ **Location** North Atlantic

Also known as the sand devil or monkfish,
this fish is one of several species of angel
sharks. It lives mostly **on the sea floor**,
keeping its flat body partly concealed in
the sand. When the shark spots its prey, it
bursts out of its hiding place to make a
sudden grab that takes the victim by
surprise. A potential meal
rarely escapes!

▲ TASTY SHARK
*The Atlantic angel shark is
fished for its succulent flesh.*

# hresher shark

*opias vulpinus*

〰 ❤ 28 ⚠

**Length** 5.5 m (18 ft)
**Weight** 450 kg (990 lb) and over
**Diet** Shoaling fish, such as herring and mackerel, squid
**Location** Warm seas worldwide

Jsing its immensely long tail like a whip, the
hresher shark rounds up its fish prey into tight
chools. The shark then often **stuns or kills its
ictims** with blows from its tail. Thresher
harks are strong swimmers and are occasionally
seen leaping right out
of the water.

# Basking shark

*Cetorhinus maximus*

〰 ❤ 40 ⚠

■ **Length** 10–15 m (33–49 ft)
■ **Weight** 6,000 kg (13,200 lb)
■ **Diet** Plankton
■ **Location** Cool to warm seas
worldwide

This giant shark is second in
size to the whale shark. It feeds
simply by swimming along with
its **vast mouth gaping wide**. As the
water rushes in, and then out again
through the fish's gills, sieve-like
projections filter out minute food
particles. The basking shark takes its
name from its habit of lolling in the
sun at the surface of the water.

◀ WHIPLASH
*The thresher's tail
may be more than
half the shark's
total length. Some
humans have received a swipe
from this formidable weapon.*

FISH

# Skates and rays

These fish appear to fly through the water, the larger ones using their fins almost as wings. They have a flattened shape and some live on the seabed, while others swim in open water. Some are able to stun unsuspecting fish with an electrical charge!

## Marbled electric ray
*Torpedo marmorata*

- **Length** 1 m (39 in)
- **Weight** 18 kg (40 lb)
- **Depth** 10–100 m (33-328 ft)
- **Location** Eastern Atlantic, Mediterranean

This ray creates **electric shocks** powerful enough to stun or kill other fish and contact with it can be dangerous for humans, but there are no reports of people actually dying after suffering a shock from it. There are stories that suggest the ancient Greeks may have used them to stun patients before surgery. It is nocturnal, and buries itself in the seabed during daylight hours.

## Long-nosed skate
*Dipturus oxyrinchus*

- **Length** 1.5 m (5 ft)
- **Weight** 17 kg (37 lb)
- **Depth** 15–900 m (50–3,000 ft)
- **Location** Eastern Atlantic, Mediterranean, Canary and Madeira Islands

The long-nosed skate is distinguished by its narrow, sharp nose, while its tail is armed with **three rows of spines**. It tends to rest on the seabed, almost buried but with its eyes just visible. Long-nosed skates are under threat, partly because they develop slowly: they take eleven years to mature to an age at which they can breed.

◄ FLYING THROUGH THE WATER *The long-nosed skate uses its pectoral fins in a sweeping motion to move through the water.*

## Common stingray
*Dasyatis pastinaca*

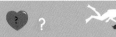

- **Length** 1.4 m (4½ ft)
- **Weight** 30 kg (66 lb)
- **Depth** 5–200 m (16–660 ft)
- **Location** Northeast Atlantic and Mediterranean Sea

▼ *Common stingrays are not aggressive – they prefer to flee rather than stay and confront their attacker.*

Common stingrays have **barbed spines full of venom** that can be up to 35 cm (14 in) long. The spines may break off when the common stingray attacks; however, these can grow back. These fish are caught and eaten, while oil is sometimes extracted from their wings.

FISH

210

# The *flying* **filter** feeders.

Manta rays use the **large lobes** on either side of the heads to *funnel* prey into their mouths. Water and prey goes into the mouth, but the water is *filtered* out through the gills while the prey is digested. Mantas prey on small fish as well as sifting plankton from sea water.

## Manta ray
*Manta birostris*

- **Width** 9 m (29½ ft)
- **Weight** 2,300 kg (5,000 lb)
- **Depth** 0–120 m (0–394 ft)
- **Location** Surface tropical waters worldwide, sometimes warm temperate areas.

This ray is **the biggest in the world**. It is also known as the devil ray, but because of its appearance not because it is aggressive: it ignores divers. Despite its size, this ray can leap out of the water, occasionally giving birth to its young while doing so.

## Undulate ray
*Raja undulata*

- **Length** 1.2 m (4 ft)
- **Weight** 7 kg (15 lb)
- **Depth** 45–200 m (150–660 ft)
- **Location** Eastern Atlantic and Mediterranean

▶ LAYING EGGS *Females are known to lay up to 15 eggs in muddy or sandy flats.*

The undulate ray is also known as **the painted ray** because of its detailed markings. In fact, it is a popular fish for large aquariums because of its markings. The undulate ray feeds on crabs, flatfish, and other seabed invertebrates.

◀ *Seen from below, an undulate ray looks completely different.*

## Blonde ray
*Raja brackyura*

- **Length** 1.25 m (40 in)
- **Weight** 14.3 kg (31½ lbs)
- **Depth** 10–380 m (33–1,247 ft)
- **Location** Eastern Atlantic

If you felt the back of this fish and it was smooth, you'd know that it was a young blonde ray, because the **adults develop prickles**. The young hatch from rectangular, horned egg cases in the summer months. Blonde rays have large eyes and a short snout. The outer angles of their wings are almost right-angles.

◀ WHERE ARE YOU? *The underside of a blonde ray is white, but the top is covered in small brown spots and larger, creamy spots. It camouflages itself well against stones on the sea floor.*

## Thornback ray
*Raja clavata*

- **Length** 105–120 cm (41–47 in)
- **Weight** 18 kg (39½ lb)
- **Depth** 20–577 m (66–1,900 ft)
- **Location** N.E. Atlantic, North Sea, Mediterranean, and the Black Sea

The thornback ray feeds on crustaceans such as shrimp and crab. They also eat small fish such as herring, sand eels, and flatfish. The thornback (as its name suggests) has **thorns on its fin and tail.** Females are longer than males.

▼ EGGS IN WAITING *Females lay their eggs in the summer, which then hatch during the winter.*

FISH

# Bony fish

Bony fish are the largest and most varied group of fish; 9 out of 10 types of fish are bony fish. Some live in salty oceans and seas, some live in fresh water, while a few can survive in both. However, they all share one thing in common: they have a light but strong internal skeleton.

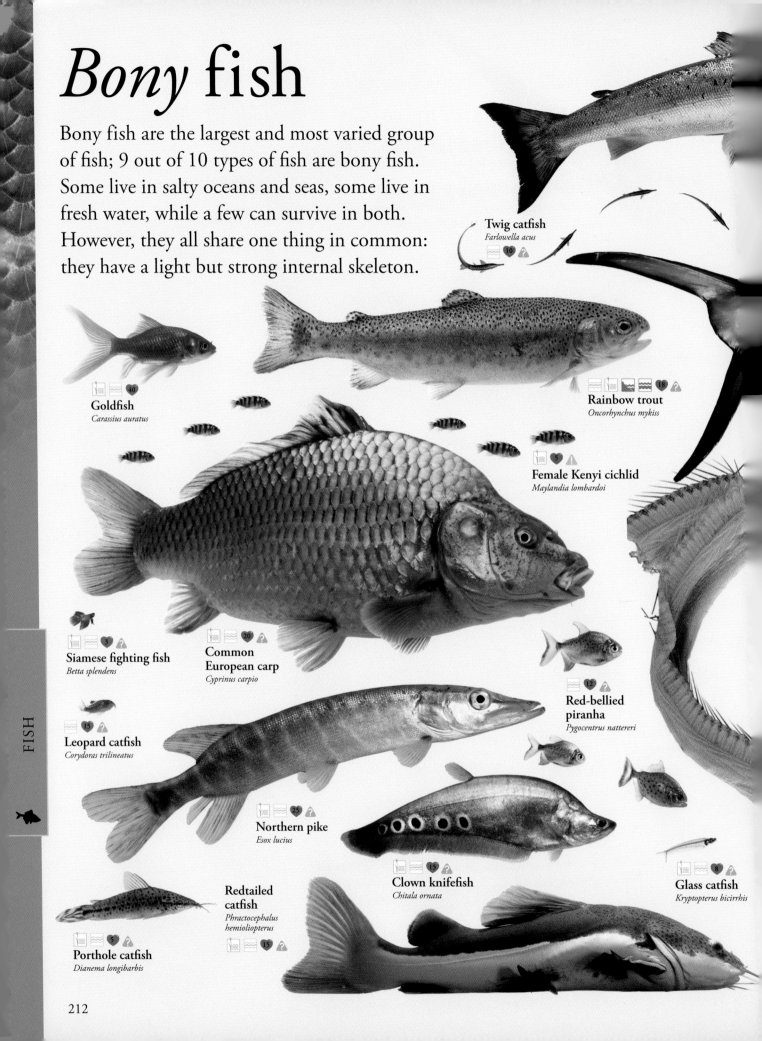

**Twig catfish**
*Farlowella acus*
10

**Goldfish**
*Carassius auratus*
40

**Rainbow trout**
*Oncorhynchus mykiss*
18

**Female Kenyi cichlid**
*Maylandia lombardoi*
5

**Siamese fighting fish**
*Betta splendens*
3

**Common European carp**
*Cyprinus carpio*
20

**Red-bellied piranha**
*Pygocentrus nattereri*
12

**Leopard catfish**
*Corydoras trilineatus*
15

**Northern pike**
*Esox lucius*
25

**Clown knifefish**
*Chitala ornata*
15

**Glass catfish**
*Kryptopterus bicirrhis*
8

**Redtailed catfish**
*Phractocephalus hemioliopterus*
15

**Porthole catfish**
*Dianema longibarbis*
5

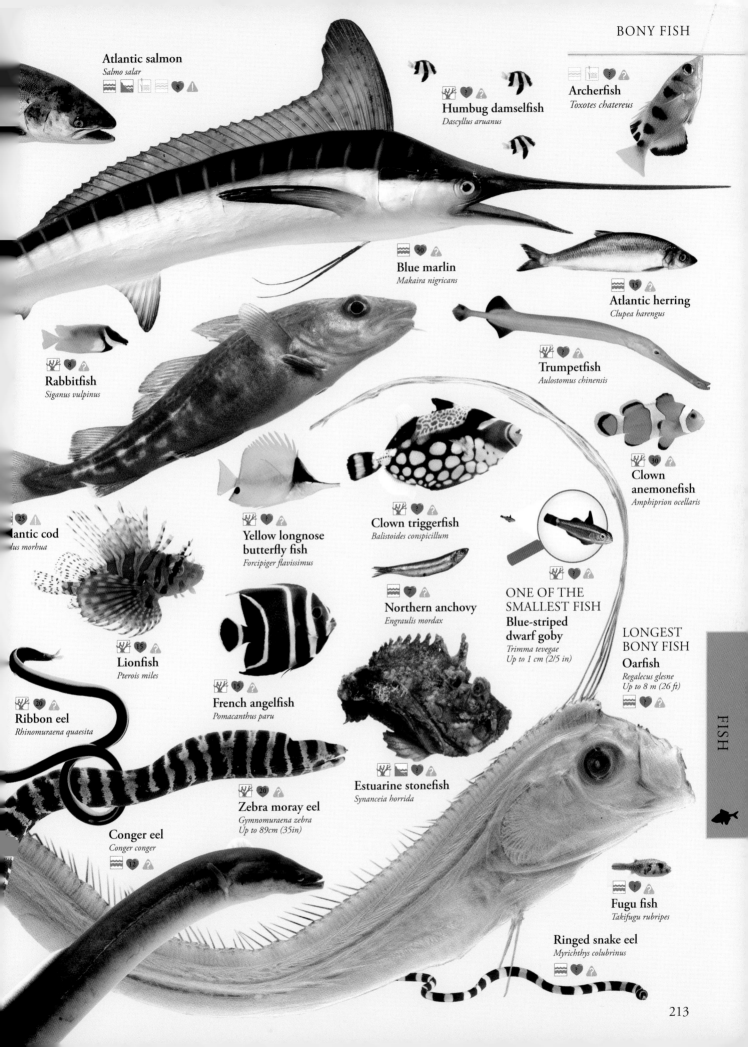

**Atlantic salmon**
*Salmo salar*

**Humbug damselfish**
*Dascyllus aruanus*

**Archerfish**
*Toxotes chatereus*

**Blue marlin**
*Makaira nigricans*

**Atlantic herring**
*Clupea harengus*

**Rabbitfish**
*Siganus vulpinus*

**Trumpetfish**
*Aulostomus chinensis*

**Clown anemonefish**
*Amphiprion ocellaris*

**Atlantic cod**
*...dus morhua*

**Yellow longnose butterfly fish**
*Forcipiger flavissimus*

**Clown triggerfish**
*Balistoides conspicillum*

**Lionfish**
*Pterois miles*

**Northern anchovy**
*Engraulis mordax*

ONE OF THE SMALLEST FISH
**Blue-striped dwarf goby**
*Trimma tevegae*
Up to 1 cm (2/5 in)

LONGEST BONY FISH
**Oarfish**
*Regalecus glesne*
Up to 8 m (26 ft)

**French angelfish**
*Pomacanthus paru*

**Ribbon eel**
*Rhinomuraena quaesita*

**Zebra moray eel**
*Gymnomuraena zebra*
Up to 89cm (35in)

**Estuarine stonefish**
*Synanceia horrida*

**Conger eel**
*Conger conger*

**Fugu fish**
*Takifugu rubripes*

**Ringed snake eel**
*Myrichthys colubrinus*

FISH

# SCHOOLS

There is safety in numbers for fish who swim in schools. They are able to confuse attackers as the size of the school can be bigger than the attacker itself. It is harder for a predator to isolate and catch a single fish among a fast-moving group. Fish in a school have an advantage over the fish who are after them because they have more pairs of eyes on the lookout!

## BAIT BALL

Copper sharks, or bronze whalers, swallow mouthfuls of sardines as they push their way through a bait ball, showering blood and fish scales around them. Bait balls are collections of fish that have been forced to swim tightly together.

## SCHOOL OR SHOAL?

Schooling fish swim close together in a syncronized fashion whereas a shoal is a looser collection of fish that swim in a group. Shoals can be made up of mixed groups of fish. Fish benefit from living in a shoal as they can search for food together, defend themselves from attacks, and have more chance of finding a mate.

▶ DIVING FOR DINNER
*Cape gannets dive into a baitball of sardines. They are plunge divers and will slam into shoals of fish from heights of up to 30 m (99 ft).*

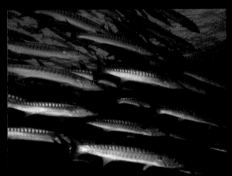

▲ PROTECTION FOR PREDATORS
*Fish who are predators also need to have protection from their attackers. Young barracudas live in shoals during the day to help each other keep safe and to look for food. However, most adult barracudas hunt alone.*

### HOW DO THEY WORK?

- Fish use vision and sensory systems to help them respond to slight movements around them. This ability allows them to swim in schools and shoals.
- If fish stand out in a shoal they are more likely to be noticed by predators. So fish join shoals of fish that are similar to themselves.
- Shoaling fish use different tactics when being attacked. They disperse into all directions, they flee away and then come back and swim past both sides of the attacker, or they split into smaller groups.

FISH

# *Fishing* for prey

Some fish are accomplished at fishing for prey. Heavy disguise helps them to hide from predators, but also to hide from potential victims. Equipped with a whip-like rod on their head that often has a lure at the end that looks like a small marine organism, they sit lazily and wait for their prey to fall for the bait.

## Angler
*Lophius piscatorius*

- **Length** 2 m (7 ft)
- **Weight** 57.7 kg (127 lb)
- **Location** E. North Atlantic, Mediterranean, Black Sea

The angler is called by a few other names; sea-devil, fishing-frog, or frog-fish. It is also known as the monkfish when it is sold as a fish to eat (like a few other fish). The angler is able to camouflage itself on the sea bed, helped by its broad, flattened body. It sits and waits for small fish to swim by and then opens its mouth and **sucks in its prey.** It has a large head and a wide jaw containing sharp teeth that slant inwards so it can stop prey from trying to escape from its mouth.

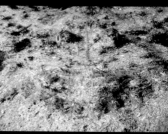

**Hidden away** It is difficult to see the angler on the sea bed as its marbled skin and flaps blend in so well with the sediment.

◄ SUPERB SHUFFLER *The angler has strong pectoral and pelvic fins that it uses to shuffle itself over the sea bed. It looks as if it is walking!*

## Smooth anglerfish
*Phyllophryne scortea*

- **Length** 10 cm (4 in)
- **Weight** Not recorded
- **Location** South Australia, Southern Ocean

Like the angler, the smooth anglerfish also goes by the name of the frog-fish. It is part of the large anglerfish family. The smooth anglerfish is a small fish with a large head. I differs from other anglerfishes as it has **thre extended dorsal fin spines** on its head. It uses the first dorsal spine like a fishing rod to attract other, smaller, fish, which are then sucked into its mouth.

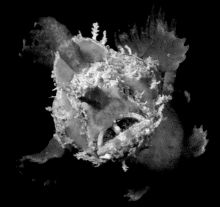

▲ WHERE AM I? *The smooth anglerfish mainly dwells on the bottom of the ocean. Its markings help to camouflage it against the ocean floor.*

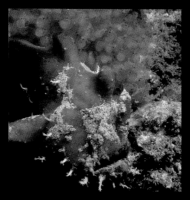

▲ PROTECTIVE PARENT
*A male smooth anglerfish guards eggs from predators. These have partially developed young inside them.*

# Warty frogfish
*Antennarius maculatus*

**Length** 15 cm (6 in)
**Weight** Not recorded
**Location** W. Pacific, Indian Ocean

The warty frogfish is another member of the anglerfish family. Many anglerfish live in the deep sea, but the warty frogfish lives in shallow waters – mainly in coral reefs. This fish is adorned with various patches and spots on its body. It eats other small fish and **occasionally it eats other warty frogfish.** A flap of coloured skin at the end of the long spine on its dorsal fin acts like bait on a fishing rod – it moves it to attract prey.

# Sargassum fish
*Histrio histrio*

- **Length** 20 cm (8 in)
- **Weight** 400 g (14 oz)
- **Location** Tropical and subtropical seas worldwide

This fish's Latin name means "the actor" because it blends in so well with the sargassum weeds in which it lives. The sargassum fish feeds by lying in wait for its prey, and these are hungry fish. It has been known to **swallow a fish as large as itself,** while adults are cannibalistic, which means they will eat each other. Sargassum fish are unusual in their courtship behaviour. Males pursue females by chasing them and nipping at them.

*The dorsal fin spine is used as a fishing rod and lure.*

▲ DINNER
*Sargassum fish live on a diet of small fish and crustaceans.*

# Estuarine stonefish
*Synanceia horrida*

- **Height** 60 cm (24 in)
- **Weight** Not recorded
- **Location** Indo Pacific

As its name suggests, the estuarine stonefish is able to hide on the gravelly sea bed without being seen by its prey. It is the **most venomous fish** in the world.

## HIDE AND WAIT

The estuarine stonefish does not have any scales on its body. Its colour and shape provide brilliant camouflage. It uses its pectoral fins to make a shallow hole on the sea floor. It then piles up sand and mud around itself to add to the illusion. Its head and eyes remain outside of the sand so that it can see its prey. The estuarine stonefish is a slow swimmer so it relies on catching fish that swim near to its hideout.

◄ VENOMOUS SPINES *The estuarine stonefish has 13 dorsal spines that have sharp tips and glands full of venom. If a human steps on one of the sharp spines it can be fatal.*

SHARP SPINES

Can you see me?

# *Giant* grouper

One of the largest of all the grouper fish, the giant grouper swims close to the bottom of the ocean in warm, shallow waters. It usually swims by itself and likes to stay in the same area, around coral reefs. It also swims in caves and near shipwrecks.

## DON'T
### come too close!

As its name suggests, the giant grouper is known for its size. It is the largest bony fish to live in coral reefs. The young are preyed upon by other fish, but adults are only at risk from humans.

# Giant grouper
*Epinephelus lanceolatus*

- **Length** 2.7 m (9 ft)
- **Weight** 400 kg (880 lb)
- **Location** Indian Ocean, W. and C. Pacific

The giant grouper is a fish of many names. It is known as the brown spotted cod, brindle bass, bumblebee grouper, and, in Australia, as the Queensland grouper. Its **colour changes** as it gets older. Young fish have irregular black and yellow markings. Adults are darker.

Tail fin | Heavy body

## FISHY FOOD

The giant grouper eats a range of food, including small sharks, fish, rays, and small sea turtles. Its main diet consists of crustaceans, such as spiny lobsters, and it occasionally eats crabs. As giant groupers are so big, they require plenty of food in order to survive.

▲ DIVERS *can usually approach the giant grouper without harm, but there are reports of fatalities.*

### ⚠ CONSERVATION

Giant groupers are being wiped out because of cyanide and the use of explosives for fishing on reefs. Their size and sluggish behaviour also makes them easy to hunt by spearfishing. Moves have been made to protect them in some areas, but some giant grouper species are struggling to survive.

FISH

219

# Deep-sea fish

Down in the depths of the oceans it is extremely cold and food and oxygen are scarce. It is also dark. Yet fish manage to survive here, having evolved to live in the harsh conditions. There is still a lot to learn about these deep-sea fish, as equipment to reach the deep sea is expensive. There's another problem too: deep-sea fish often die when taken out of their natural environment to be studied.

## Grrr...
## What are you looking at!

Some deep-sea fish have large eyes in order to make the most of what little light there is. Other fish have small eyes, but they have antennae sensitive to vibrations and an excellent sense of smell.

▲ POPULAR FOOD
*Lanternfish are an important source of food for many animals including tuna, sharks, whales, dolphins, grenadiers, sea birds, penguins, and large squid.*

# Metallic lanternfish
*...tophum affine*

- **Length** 8 cm (3 in)
- **Weight** Not recorded
- **Depth** 0–600 m (1,970 ft)
- **Location** E. and W. Atlantic

...etallic lanternfish have **thin, silvery scales.** ...ey have good vision because of their large ...es; these help them detect changes in light. ...etallic lanternfish have photophores that ...ok like small, bright studs on their flanks, ...dersides, and heads. These bright studs let ...t light in shades of green, yellow, or blue. ...otophores help groups of fish to see each ...her in darkly lit waters, enabling them to ...cognize each other and stay together.

# Sloane's viperfish
*Chauliodus sloani*

- **Length** 20–35 cm (8–14 in)
- **Weight** 30 g (1 oz)
- **Depth** 473–2,800 m (1,550–9,190 ft)
- **Location** Tropical, subtropical, and temperate waters worldwide

Sloane's viperfish is one of nine species of viperfish living in Earth's oceans. They swim up to depths of less than 600 m (1,970 ft) during the night as their prey is more plentiful in shallower waters. This fish has fearsome **fangs that are transparent!** The largest fangs won't fit in the mouth, so they protrude when the jaws close.

◀ LURING LIGHTS
*Sloane's viperfish have photophores along their sides and underside to lure prey.*

# Atlantic football fish
*...imantolophus groenlandicus*

- **Length of a female** 60 cm (2 ft)
- **Length of a male** 4 cm (1½ in)
- **Depth** 1,000 m (3,280 ft)
- **Location** Atlantic, Indian, and Pacific Ocean

...ootball fish are **poor swimmers,** especially ...e females, so they lie and wait for their prey ...o come by. Female ...ootball fish are ...uch bigger than ...ales and have larger ...ouths.

▶ LUMINOUS TAIL
*The tail of a pelican eel is ...uminous to attract prey. It moves its tail like a whip to propel itself forward in the water.*

# Lowcrest hatchetfish
*Argyropelecus sladeni*

- **Length** 7 cm (3 in)
- **Weight** Not recorded
- **Depth** 0–2,926 m (9,600 ft)
- **Location** Atlantic, Indian, and Pacific Oceans.

The lowcrest hatchetfish gets its name because its body is shaped like the blade of an axe. It can be found at great depths during the day, but at night it swims to shallower waters to feed. Hatchetfish use light as a form of **protective camouflage** – the photophores on their belly shine downwards to mimic light coming from above.

# Pelican eel
*Eurypharynx pelecanoides*

- **Length** 61–100 cm (24–39 in)
- **Weight** 1 kg (2 lb)
- **Depth** 500–7,625 m (1,640–25,000 ft)
- **Location** Tropical and subtropical waters worldwide

The pelican eel is also called the umbrella mouth gulper eel and is rarely seen by humans. Its **enormous mouth** is much wider than its body. Its stomach can expand so it can feed on fish much larger than itself.

# Frilled shark
*Chlamydoselachus anguineus*

- **Length** 2 m (7 ft)
- **Weight** Not recorded
- **Depth** 50–1,500 m (165–4,920 ft)
- **Location** Worldwide

The frilled shark has an **eel-like body** and looks quite different from typical sharks. This species reproduces infrequently. It can take up to two years after fertilization for the female frilled shark to give birth.

# Yellow goosefish
*Lophius litulon*

- **Length** 150 cm (59 in)
- **Weight** 40 kg (88 lb)
- **Depth** 25–560 m (82–1,840 ft)
- **Location** Northwest Pacific: Japan, Korea, and the Yellow and East China Seas

The yellow goosefish is fished for food; its liver is considered a delicacy in Japan while elsewhere it is sold as "monkfish". It is also used in Chinese medicine. **Females are larger than males.**

FISH

221

# *Spawning* salmon

The life cycle of the sockeye salmon shown here is anadromous. This means that they are born in fresh water, then migrate to the ocean, before returning to fresh water in order to breed (which is also called spawning). On spawning, the sockeye salmon turns a dramatic bright red.

## ON A MISSION

From birth to the point at which they return to spawn, some four years later, these sockeye salmon may have travelled up to 1,500 km (930 miles). At the end of its amazing journey, each female will lay more than 4,000 eggs.

# Atlantic salmon
*Salmo salar*

- **Length** 1.5 m (5 ft)
- **Weight** 46.8 kg (100 lb)
- **Status** Locally common
- **Location** N.E. North America, W. and N. Europe, and North Atlantic

Atlantic salmon are farmed as a source of food. They are **strong swimmers with powerful tails** that give them the ability to leap up waterfalls and weirs on their way back up the fresh water streams where they spawn. Most salmon die after spawning, but the Atlantic salmon sometimes survive and head back to the ocean.

## AN OBSTACLE COURSE

Salmon have well-developed swimming muscles that are useful on their long journey from river to ocean and back. However, even their swimming skills can't save them from fishing nets. Salmon is a popular choice of food for people.

BEAR ATTACK
*Humans are not alone in enjoying a meal of salmon. Bears catch salmon when they return to fresh water rivers in the spawning season.*

FISH

# INVERTEBRATES

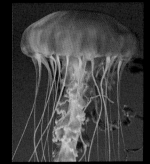

*Definition:* **Invertebrates** are animals without a backbone. They include insects, molluscs (such as snails and shellfish), sponges, jellyfish, and worms.

# What is an INVERTEBRATE?

Invertebrates are animals that have neither a backbone nor a bony internal skeleton. This group makes up more than 95 per cent of the animal kingdom. It is incredibly varied. Some invertebrates are little known, like the microscopic rotifers (animals that may be smaller than bacteria). Others are more familiar. Snails and spiders, fleas and flatworms, centipedes and corals: these are all invertebrates. There are simple invertebrates, such as sponges, that have no brain or internal organs. And there are complex ones, like the highly intelligent octopus.

◄ ARTHROPODA – INSECTS, ARACHNIDS, CRUSTACEANS (1,000,000 SPECIES) *Arthropods, as these animals are known as a group, have a hard outer covering. This covering, called an exoskeleton, is divided into sections. Examples of an exoskeleton are the shell of a crab and the casing of a beetle. Arthropods also have jointed limbs, which are arranged in pairs.*

◄ MOLLUSCA – SQUID, SNAILS, BIVALVES (60,000 SPECIES). *Most molluscs live inside a hardened shell of some sort. This may be a single shell, like that of a snail, or in two halves joined by a hinge, like that of a clam or a mussel. However, mollucs also include animals, such as the octopus and the cuttlefish, which have either no shell or an internal one.*

◄ CNIDARIA – JELLYFISH, CORALS, HYDRAS (11,000 SPECIES). *This group contains various aquatic animals, including jellyfish, sea anemones, and corals. Cnidarians, as they are called, all possess tentacles that bear stinging cells (cnidae). Some cnidarians can swim, others are attached to the sea bed.*

◄ ANNELIDA – EARTHWORMS, LEECHES, POLYCHAETES (12,000 SPECIES). *These are called annelid worms and they all have bodies that are divided into segments. The common earthworm belongs to this group. Polychaetes are also known as bristleworms. There are marine, freshwater, and land-dwelling annelids.*

◄ ECHINODERMATA – STARFISH, SEA URCHINS, SEA CUCUMBERS (7,000 SPECIES). *The common name of this group of marine animals is echinoderms. A key feature of many of them is an extremely prickly body. Nearly all echinoderms live on the sea floor and most of them can move about to feed.*

◄ PORIFERA – SPONGES (9,000 SPECIES). *Sponges may seem like plants but they are not. They are the simplest of all living animals. Their bodies are basically a tube of fibres. Sponges live attached to rocks on the sea floor. Water currents carry food into their bodies.*

## FACTFILE

An estimated five million species of invertebrates exist today. This could double as we learn more about the habitats of invertebrates.

- **Nematodes**, or roundworms, are possibly the most numerous creatures on Earth. Some are so tiny that as many as 90,000 can be counted on one rotting apple.

- **Invertebrates** sometimes gather together in huge numbers. One of the biggest locust swarms on record contained 72,000,000,000 insects and covered 1,200 km² (463 sq miles).

- **Octopuses** have shown that they are brainy. A female octopus in a German zoo watched keepers unscrewing the lids of jars of shrimps – and learned how to do it herself.

### Invertebrates from the past

One of the first invertebrate groups to appear on Earth were the sponges, some 600 million years ago. Fossils of soft-bodied invertebrates, like jellyfish, are rare. However, fossils of trilobites, crustacean-like arthropods, are abundant. Trilobites (above) survived for 300 million years, becoming extinct about 250 million years ago. Other fossil finds include giant griffonflies with 75 cm (30 in) wingspans, water-scorpions 2m (6½ ft) long, and giant marine molluscs with shells 9 m (30 ft) long.

### Living on others

Among the invertebrates are most of the world's parasites. These are animals that live on the outside or the inside of other animals, including humans. Many, though not all, are harmful. Common parasites include worms of various kinds that live in their host's intestines. Pests such as warble flies (above) lay eggs in the hair of mammals like horses and cattle. When the grubs hatch, they burrow into the skin, causing sores. Some insects lay their eggs on other insects, and the emerging grubs eat their host.

▲ IT TAKES TWO *butterflies to produce eggs. All insects start off as eggs, then pass through various stages, such as caterpillar and pupa, before becoming adult.*

## CREATING NEW LIFE

Invertebrates reproduce in various ways. Not all of them need to find a mate. Sponges and starfish can create new individuals from bits of their own bodies. In fact, if two sponges are put through a sieve and mixed up, they clump together to form a single animal. Many insects lay unfertilized eggs that hatch and develop into replicas of their parent. Stick insects, water fleas, and aphids all reproduce like this.

▼ SINGLE PARENTS *such as aphids can produce young from unfertilized eggs. This is a quick way of building up numbers.*

227

# Sponges

Sponges live at the bottom of virtually all seas. Although they grow rooted to the spot like plants, sponges are in fact simple animals. They were once among the most abundant forms of life in the oceans, and their skeletons formed vast reefs. These days they must jostle for space on the sea bed with corals and other marine organisms.

## SHAPES AND SIZES

The 5,000 different types of spong come in a range of shapes and size The smallest are simple tube-shap animals a few millimetres long. Th largest can reach a metre or more across and have bulbous, branchin shapes. Most species have a skelet made of a soft, springy material.

▼ TOXIC SPONGES *Many sponges, including this elephant ear sponge, grow on re Some contain toxic substances, which act as a defence against predators. These toxins are use in the manufacture of drugs and medicines.*

## Elephant ear sponge
*Ianthella basta*

■ **Location** Indian and Pacific Oceans and adjoining seas

These large, fan-shaped sponges intercept and feed off the water currents passing over the reefs. Their **springy skeleton** enables them to flex slightly so they are not damaged by stormy seas. There are several species of Ianthella, and they come in a variety of shapes, sizes, and colours.

**Elephant ear sponge**
*Ianthella basta*

### FACTFILE

■ **Anatomy** The sponge's body cells work together, but do not form organs, tissues, or obvious body parts. Sponges reproduce in two ways – by budding off tiny clones and by releasing sperm to fertilise egg cells.

■ **Feeding** Sponges obtain energy by taking in food. They collect this from sea water, which is taken in through tiny pores and passes through a system of channels in the body. The channels are lined with cells bearing tiny hairs that trap the food. The filtered water passes out again through an opening called the osculum.

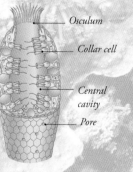

Osculum

Collar cell

Central cavity

Pore

FILTER SYSTEM *Sponges are known as "filter feeders".*

# Red sponge
*Latrunculia magnifica*

■ **Location** Red Sea and Arabian Sea

A dramatic-looking shallow water sponge that can grow into the branching structure seen below, or as a spreading crust on rocks. It **produces a toxic protein** called "latrunculin" to deter predators. This doesn't scare everyone and the sponge is still eaten by a species of sea slug. The sea slug stores the toxin in its own body and benefits from the toxin's protection without being poisoned itself.

# Breadcrumb sponge
*Halichondria panicea*

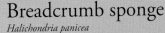

■ **Location** Atlantic Ocean, Baltic, and Mediterranean Sea

This sponge often grows on rocky overhangs in strong currents. It can reach up to 60 cm (24 in) across. The name refers to the **crumbly looking surface**, which is covered with crater-like pores.

# Azure vase sponge
*Callyspongia plicifera*

■ **Location** Caribbean Sea

This colourful sponge is a member of the class Demospongia, which includes all the soft, squashy, bath-type sponges. It **lives in sunlit shallow waters** and grows up to 45 cm (18 in) tall. A large specimen can filter thousands of litres of water per hour, extracting algae, plankton, and other tiny particles of food.

# Calcareous sponge
*Sycon ciliatum*

■ **Location** All oceans

Sycon sponges are common members of the calcareous sponge family. They are small, with a **delicate skeleton** made of chalky calcium carbonate. They often grow attached to seaweeds or reef organisms, in order to position themselves in a good feeding current. **A crown of fine spicules** deters predators and helps prevent debris blockages.

# Glass sponge
*Euplectella aspergillum*

■ **Location** Western Pacific Ocean

This tube-shaped sponge is supported by an extraordinary lacy lattice of brittle spicules, which gives it the alternative name "Venus' flower basket". The tube is often **home to pairs of small sponge shrimps,** which enter as juveniles and live their whole lives inside the sponge, eventually growing too big to leave.

# Sea anemones

These "sea flowers" are usually found in shallow waters or tidal pools. Only a few live in the depths of the oceans. Sea anemones look delicate but they are efficient predators that shoot their prey with poisoned barbs. Most sea anemones do not move around much or swim. They stay anchored by a fleshy foot to rocks or dig their soft bodies into sand on the sea floor.

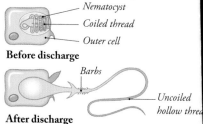

## STINGERS

The tentacles of sea anemones are lined with stinging cells (nematocysts). Each cell contains venom, a barbed needle, and a "trigger" hair. When prey touches the hair, the needle shoots out, injecting the victim with venom. The needle stays attached to the anemone by a thread.

*Nematocyst*
*Coiled thread*
*Outer cell*

**Before discharge**

*Barbs*

*Uncoiled hollow thread*

**After discharge**

## FACT FILE

■ **Sea anemones range in size** from less than 15 mm (½ in) to nearly 1 m (3 ft) in diameter. They can have from 12 tentacles to as many as several hundred.

■ **A sea anemone** is made of a soft body sac, which is attached to the sea bed by a sticky foot. The body is cylinder shaped with a flattened top called an oral disc. A mouth opens in the middle of this disc. The stinging tentacles that surround the mouth can be retracted (pulled in).

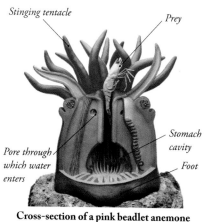

*Stinging tentacle*

*Prey*

*Stomach cavity*

*Pore through which water enters*

*Foot*

**Cross-section of a pink beadlet anemone**

## a anemone
*...opleura elegantissima*

- **...iameter** 2–5 cm (¾–2in)
- **...iet** Small marine animals
- **...ocation** Western Pacific

...emones of this species
...e **in colonies**. They
...often found in
...al pools. When the
...e goes out, they
...ll in their tentacles
...d **cover themselves**
...th sand and
...gments of shell
...prevent themselves
...om drying out.

## Swimming sea anemone
*Stomphia coccinea*

- **Diameter** 1.8–2.3 m (6–7½ ft)
- **Diet** Small marine animals
- **Location** North Atlantic, North Pacific

The swimming anemone behaves
differently from its relatives. If
scared, it bounces off the rock to
which it is attached and **swims
away** by swaying its body back
and forth. When safe, it sinks
back to the sea bed again.

## Long-tentacled sea anemone
*Macrodactyla doreensis*

- **Diameter** 10–15 cm (4–6 in)
- **Diet** Shrimp, small fish
- **Location** Indian Ocean

The tentacles of this anemone are up
to 17 cm (6½ in) long. They are often
twisted, giving the species its other
popular name of **corkscrew anemone**.
This anemone likes to embed its foot into
soft mud on the sea bottom. It has several
**colour variations**, most commonly
shades of grey or purple. The tentacles are
striped with white.

## I'm a **friend**, not prey.
Clown fish like this one often
take refuge within the tentacles
of sea anemones. Mucus on
their skin protects them
from being stung.

# Jellyfish

Jellyfish are simple, free-swimming animals, with stinging tentacles to stun and draw in their prey. The wobbly, jelly-like body is what gives this group of mostly marine invertebrates its name. There are around 300 species.

*The main body of a jellyfish is called the "bell". It surrounds a central cavity, which acts as a gut.*

*The opening into the gut brings food in and takes away waste. It is fringed with stinging tentacles, used for drawing in the food.*

◄ SOGGY BODY *Jellyfish are almost completely made of water. This is fine for life in the ocean, but their lack of a supporting skeleton makes them collapse in a heap if they are washed up on a beach.*

## HOW A JELLYFISH MOVES

READY... *The body of a jellyfish starts to fill with water as it relaxes the ring of muscle cells around the opening of its gut.*

STEADY... *The muscle cells are completely relaxed, and the body is full of water. The jellyfish is now ready to push forwards.*

GO... *The muscle cells slowly contract, forcing water through the opening of the gut. As water leaves its body, the jellyfish starts to move.*

...AND AWAY *The force produced by pushing water away from its bell gently propels the jellyfish in the opposite direction.*

## I make a tasty snack!

So many Nomura's jellyfish get caught up in fishing nets that people in China and Japan have started to eat them instead of the fish.

GIANT JELLY *A diver swims alongside a Nomura's jellyfish off the coast of Japan. These massive sea creatures can grow 2 m (6½ ft) wide and weigh 220 kg (480 lb).*

▼ RED EYE *The red spots at the top of the tentacles of the pencillate jellyfish are simple eyes that it uses to detect light and dark.*

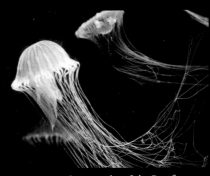

▲ OUCH! *The tentacles of the Pacific sea nettle are covered in thousands of stinging cells that hold on to prey so that it can be drawn into the jellyfish's mouth.*

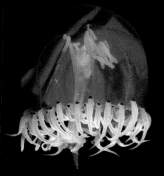

## Nomura's jellyfish

*Nemopilema nomurai*

- **Width** 2 m (6½ ft)
- **Weight** 220 kg (480 lb)
- **Location** Waters surrounding China, Korea, and Japan
- **Diet** Plankton and some crustaceans

Nomura's jellyfish usually drifts in shallow waters but sinks to greater depths to avoid schools of swordfish, tuna, and other predators. The **population of this giant jellyfish has exploded in recent years**, and many are caught up in fishing nets. The sheer weight of jellyfish can then crush the catch and even destroy the nets.

# Corals

There are two types of corals: hard and soft. Hard cora[l]
have an internal skeleton made of limestone. These
types build the huge coral reefs found in tropical
seas. Soft corals, which often look like plants,
have no skeleton. All corals grow from one
tiny animal called a polyp. This animal
produces new polyps, and a colony
slowly develops, forming the cora[l]

## FACTFILE

■ **Number of tentacles:** The
polyps of hard corals have 12 or
more tentacles; those of soft corals
all have eight.

■ **First appearance:** The first
corals appeared on Earth some
540 million years ago.

■ **Reproduction:** Coral colonies
in a reef usually reproduce by
"broadcast spawning", which
means they all release eggs and
sperm into the water at the same
time, often at full moon.

# illar coral
*idrogyra cylindricus*

- **Height** 2 m (6½ ft)
- **Depth** 1–20 m (3–60 ft)
- **Location** Western Atlantic Ocean

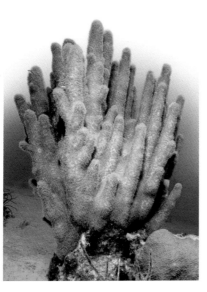

is is a common reef-building
ral. Pillar coral grows straight
wards in **thick spires**. If it is
an area where it is safe from
mage, the coral may become
ry large. Its furry appearance is
used by the **extended tentacles**
its polyps reaching out to feed.

# taghorn coral
*ropora cervicornis*

- **Height** Not recorded
- **Location** Upper to mid-reef slopes
  d lagoons in clear water

here are several hundred
ecies of staghorn coral.
hey all form branching
hapes, like **antlers**. These
orals grow quickly but are
**asily damaged** by rough
aves if the seas are stormy.

# Orange cup coral
*Balanophyllia elegans*

- **Diameter** 1–2 cm (½–¾ in)
- **Depth** 10 m (30 ft)
- **Location** Northwest Pacific Ocean

Often found in tidal pools,
orange cup coral **likes to attach
itself to shady rocks**. The tiny
cups have two ways of feeding.
Sometimes, they put out tentacles to
trap food. Alternatively, the coral keeps its
tentacles withdrawn and catches food simply
by holding open a mouth in the cup.

# Great star coral
*Montastrea cavernosa*

- **Height** Not recorded
- **Depth** 12–30 m (40–100 ft)
- **Location** Atlantic Ocean

Colonies of great star
coral often form **huge
mounds**. In deeper
waters the coral tends to
spread out in flat plates.
The polyps extend their
tentacles to feed at night.

# Mushroom soft coral
*Anthomastus ritteri*

- **Diameter** 15 cm (6 in)
- **Depth** 200–1,500 m (655–5,000 ft)
- **Location** Eastern Pacific Ocean

When this deep-water coral extends
its fragile tentacles to trap food, it
resembles a **strange, underwater
flower**. With the tentacles pulled in,
the coral lives up to its name and
looks more like a mushroom.

# Grooved brain coral
*Diploria labyrinthiformis*

- **Height** Not recorded
- **Diameter** 1.8 m (6 ft)
- **Location** Western
Atlantic Ocean

The polyps that form this rounded
coral arrange themselves in wandering
lines. This gives the coral colony a
**heavily wrinkled appearance**, very
like that of a brain. If sand becomes
trapped between the grooves, the
individual polyps push it out again
to keep the coral clean.

# Worms

Most people think of worms as the squishy, slimy creatures wriggling around in soil. But there are thought to be more than a million different types that are found in a wide range of different places. Some do live in burrows in the ground, but others live in rivers or the sea, and some are parasites that are responsible for causing deadly diseases in humans and other animals.

## FACTFILE

Worms are possibly the most abundant animals on Earth. The main types are:
- **Flatworms** These are flat and ribbon-like. They have no lungs and breathe through their skin. Most are parasites.
- **Roundworms** These have long, thin, rounded bodies. Many live as parasites inside other animals and plants.
- **Segmented worms** These are divided into segments, each with a set of basic organs, that are linked by a long gut. They include earthworms and ragworms.

**Life around deep-sea vents**
On the bottom of many of the deepest oceans are craters, formed by volcanic activity. Many gush out fumes of steaming sea water, rich in nutritious minerals. A variety of animals and plants live around these deep-sea vents, often growing to be much bigger than similar creatures from shallower waters.

## Giant tubeworm
*Riftia pachyptila*

- **Length** 2–2½ m (6–8 ft)
- **Diet** Chemicals from deep-sea vents
- **Location** Pacific Ocean

Peeping out from the top of its hard, **protective white tube**, this bright red worm resembles a giant lipstick. It is found around **deep-sea, hydrothermic vents** on the floor of the Pacific. Here it thrives on a **diet of chemicals** that it absorbs from the water. These chemicals are converted into useable food by **special bacteria** living inside the worm. It has few enemies, but some fish and crabs will nibble at any worm that is protruding from its tube.

# Earthworm

*Lumbricus terrestris*

- **Length** 9–30 cm (3½–12 in)
- **Diet** Decaying plant matter
- **Location** Worldwide

Earthworms move through their burrows just below the soil's surface, feeding as they go. Any undigested matter passes out of their body to form the muddy "worm casts" that are often most noticeable on grass. Segmented worms like this **move in a series of muscular waves** as the segments expand and narrow. Tiny hairs on the segments grip the soil.

*Flaps, or chatae, covered with bristles*

# Peacock worm

*Sabella penicillus*

- **Length** 20–30 cm (8–12 in)
- **Diet** Small marine animals, plankton
- **Location** Europe, North America, Caribbean

This long, thin-segmented worm spends its entire life encased in a **flexible tube** that it builds around itself, using a mixture of sand and mud that it binds together with mucus. It then anchors the tube in position by partly burying it in sand. Surrounding the worm's mouth is a **crown of feathery tentacles**, banded in red, brown and purple. This protrudes from the protective tube when the worm is feeding. When the sea retreats at low tide, **large colonies** of these eye-catching creatures can sometimes be seen on coastal mudflats.

# King ragworm

*Nereis virens*

- **Length** 30–40 cm (12–15¾ in)
- **Diet** Small marine animals, plankton
- **Location** Atlantic Ocean

Few worms are as formidable as this predatory giant. The king ragworm belongs to the **bristleworm** group. It is a marine animal that makes burrows in gravel or soft mud on the sea floor. It is a **good swimmer** and a keen hunter, possessing eyes and sensitive antennae for locating prey, and large **pincer jaws** for seizing its victims. King ragworms may catch and eat small worms of their own species.

*Flexible tube in which the worm lives*

# Sea mouse

*Aphrodita aculeata*

- **Length** 7–20 cm (3–8 in)
- **Diet** Mainly other worms
- **Location** Atlantic, Mediterranean

This marine worm is covered in what looks like dense fur but is, in fact, **bristles**. It also has **long hairs** that shimmer from red to green according to the way light falls on them. Sea mice live in mud or sand on the sea bed, often in deep oceans.

# Medicinal leech

*Hirudo medicinalis*

- **Length** 12 cm (4¾ in) and over
- **Diet** Blood
- **Location** Europe, Asia

The leech has a flattened body with **suckers** at both ends. At the head end there is a mouth with jaws. When a leech bites it **injects chemicals** that numb pain and stop blood from clotting. Leeches may need to feed only every few months.

*The feeding tentacles fan out to catch food*

INVERTEBRATES

# Molluscs

Molluscs belong to a large and incredibly diverse group of invertebrates. They have a huge range of body shapes and sizes, ranging from 2 mm (½ in) snails *(Ammonicera rota)* to the colossal squid *(Mesonychoteuthis hamiltoni),* which is more than 14 m (46 ft) in length and one of the largest animals on Earth.

### Emperor nautilus
*Nautilus pompilius*

The nautilus and its now extinct relative, the ammonite, were once one of the most successful groups of animals found in the world's oceans. However, all except the nautilus became extinct at the same time as the dinosaurs, 65 million years ago.

**We have been on Earth** for 500 million years!

---

## TYPES OF MOLLUSC

**Most molluscs have a shell or at least the remnants of one.** The shell is made out of calcium carbonate and is produced by the mantle, part of a mollusc's fleshy body.

■ **Gastropods,** also called univalves, usually have a single shell. Sometimes they have no shell at all. Snails, slugs, and sea slugs are all gastropods. Gastropods usually have a muscular foot that they use for crawling.

■ **Bivalves have shells made up of two pieces.** When a bivalve needs to close its shell, powerful muscles pull the two halves together, sealing it safely inside. Clams and oysters are bivalves.

■ **Cephalopods** include large invertebrates such as squid. The shells of squid have become internal and support the animal's soft body from the inside. Octopuses have lost the ability to make shells altogether.

Size comparison

*Ammonicera rota*

*Mesonychoteuthis hamiltoni*

Shell made of calcium carbonate

Eye

Tentacle

Muscular foot

# Giant Pacific octopus
*Enteroctopus dofleini*

- **Size** 3–5 m (9¾–16 ft) arm span
- **Weight** 50 kg (110 lb)
- **Diet** Crabs, lobsters, fish, and other octopuses
- **Location** North Pacific Ocean

This is the **largest** octopus in the world. It can change the colour and texture of its skin almost instantly, either to hide from large predators or to warn them away. Along with other octopuses it is the **most intelligent** of the invertebrates.

# Butterfly bubble shell
*Hydatina physis*

- **Length** Shell 45 mm (1¾ in)
- **Diet** Small worms
- **Location** Indo-West Pacific and Atlantic Ocean

This is a **brightly coloured** sea snail with a thin shell. It can withdraw into its shell, although it rarely does as the shell gives little protection. It usually crawls along the sandy sea bed, but unlike most shelled gastropods, **it can also swim.**

# Pyjama sea slug
*Chromodoris quadricolor*

- **Length** 24 mm (1 in)
- **Diet** Sea sponges
- **Location** Mediterranean, western Indian Ocean

Some molluscs have lost all trace of their shells and sea slugs, of which there are 3,000 species, are one of these. To protect themselves, some, like the colourful pyjama sea slug, use **bright patterns** to warn potential predators that they are full of foul-tasting chemicals and are **not pleasant to eat**. If attacked, a sea slug secretes these chemicals from glands just under the skin.

# Blue sea slug
*Glaucus atlanticus*

- **Length** 30 mm (1 ft)
- **Diet** Portuguese man-of-war
- **Location** Worldwide

The blue sea slug is a **predator** and feeds on the poisonous Portuguese man-of-war (commonly thought of as a jellyfish, but actually a colony of hydrozoans). The blue sea slug is immune to the man-of-war's venomous stings. In fact it **stores the stings** in feather-like "fingers" that stick out from its body, it fires these out if it is attacked.

# Flat oyster
*Ostrea edulis*

- **Length** 110 mm (8 in)
- **Diet** Plant and animal matter
- **Location** European Atlantic coast

A bivalve, this oyster spends its life permanently attached to a rock. **It starts as a male**, then becomes female when it is about three years old. Like other oysters, if a tiny piece of food becomes trapped in its shell, the **oyster covers it with a secretion** of minerals and proteins to eventually make a pearl.

# Queen scallop
*Aequichlamys bifrons*

- **Length** 110 mm (8 in)
- **Diet** Plankton
- **Location** Southern Ocean

The shells of this bivalve are usually light purple on the inside. Like all scallops, the queen scallop **moves rapidly** through the water by opening and closing its shell, producing a jet of water that pushes it along. Humans like to eat queen scallops.

# Giant clam
*Tridacna gigas*

- **Length** 1 m (3¼ ft)
- **Weight** 200 kg (440 lb)
- **Location** South Pacific and Indian Ocean

At 1 m (3¼ ft) wide, the giant clam is the **largest bivalve** on Earth. It usually lies in shallow waters. Billions of algae live on its **fleshy lips**. They produce sugars and proteins that the clam feeds on. In return, the clam gives the algae a safe home as well as access to sunlight so the algae can make its own food.

# Slugs and *snails*

Slugs are the slimy, jelly-like creatures that live in gardens and eat plants, and snails are sort of slugs with spiral-shaped shells, but they both belong to a class called gastropoda. All gastropods have a large head and tentacles, plus a soft body they drag around on a single, sucker-like foot.

▲ FLOATING RAFT
*Also known as a bubble raft snail, the violet sea snail floats upside down on the surface of warm seas, anchored there by bubbles of its own mucus. These snails are blind, with a paper-thin shell.*

▶ ROCK CLINGERS
*Limpets cling to rocky shores by sucking on tight with their soft underbellies. When the tide is high, they move slowly, feeding on algae. When the tide is low, they lock into position on the rocks.*

## LAND AND SEA

Some gastropods live on land, while others live in water: all of them lay eggs. The eggs of water-dwelling gastropods develop into larvae and grow in stages to become adults. Land-dwellers hatch as tiny versions of adults. Gastropods have a row of tiny teeth and feed on a widely varied diet.

WARNING SHADES
*Because they don't have shells to protect them, sea slugs carry a sting; their brilliant colouring warns enemies to stay clear.*

## ttuce sea slug
*a crispata*

- **ength** 8 cm (3 in)
- **iet** Plants
- **ocation** Tropical Atlantic waters

...ned for its **ruffled body**, which looks like ...afy lettuce, this sea slug feeds in the same ... as a plant. It eats algae, absorbing and ...king use of the special cells inside that help ...ke sunlight into energy. The ruffles ...ximize its surface area, so it ... absorb as much ...light as possible.

## Dog whelk
*Nucella lapillus*

- **Size** 2–4 cm (1–2 in)
- **Diet** Other gastropods
- **Location** N. Atlantic coasts

Also called the Atlantic dogwinkle, this creature **feeds by boring through the shells of prey**, then sucking out the tissue.

▲ ROCKY NEST
*In spring, dog whelks lay clusters of up to 1,000 eggs, and attach them inside rock crevices.*

## arden slug
*on distinctus*

- **Length** About 3 cm (1¼ in)
- **Diet** Plants
- **Location** North America and Europe

...ated by gardeners across the world, ...e common slug feeds on cultivated ...ants, tubers, and bulbs using a ...sping tongue known as a *radula*. ...ostly **active at night**, they spend ...e day in moist, hidden places. This ...ellowy-grey slug breeds throughout ...ost of the year.

## Garden snail
*Helix aspersa*

- **Diameter** 2.5–4cm (1–1½ in)
- **Diet** Plants
- **Location** Worldwide

Disliked by gardeners, this snail has **a thin shell** with four or five spirals. When it's resting or threatened, it **retracts inside**. The head has **four tentacles**, with eyes in the top two. The garden snail is a close relative of the edible snail, *Helix pomatia*.

## Giant African snail
*Achatina fulicula*

- **Diameter** 30 cm (12 in)
- **Diet** Plants
- **Location** East Africa, southern Asia

The **world's biggest land-dwelling snail**, this creature can cause serious damage to agriculture in the areas where it thrives. Native to the tropics, it's a hardy species that can survive cold or even snowy conditions by hibernating inside its shell. Typically, adults survive for five to six years.

▼ TROPICAL MONSTER
*Giant African snail shells are light brown, banded with dark brown and cream.*

INVERTEBRATES

# Octopuses and squid

Believe it or not, these sea-dwelling creatures are molluscs and related to slugs and snails. They are called cephalopods. Equipped with long arms and a poisonous bite, they have little trouble catching prey. They propel themselves through the sea by taking in water and squirting it out.

OCTOPUS *arms are flexible. The octopus can use them to investigate tight spaces as well as to open shells and hold prey. They "taste" things with their suckers before deciding to eat them.*

## Maori octopus

*Octopus maorum*

- **Length** 23 cm (9 in)
- **Armspan** 120 cm (47 in)
- **Location** Australia, New Zealand

Octopuses eat crabs, lobsters, and molluscs. They have very **good eyesight** and stalk their prey, hiding then pouncing on their victim. They often swim above their prey then fall on to it, using their body **like a net**.

▲ DANGEROUS BITE *The blue-ringed octopus* (Hapalochlaena lunulata) *is found around the coasts of Australia and some Pacific Ocean islands. Its bite can be fatal to humans.*

## You can't **fool** me...

Octopuses are highly intelligent. They have the largest and most advanced brain of any invertebrate. In tests, octopuses have learnt to find their way through a maze and take the lid off a container.

## CHAMPION HUNTERS

Squid and cuttlefish have an internal shell. As well as having eight arms, these animals have two long tentacles, each with a sucker on the end. They use these to grab prey such as fish and other molluscs.

**Size comparison**

◄ COMMON SQUID (Loligo vulgaris)
*Squid live in deep, open water and hardly ever come near the shore. They have a torpedo-shaped body, which helps them to move through the water. Two fins at the end are used for steering. Squid often swim in groups for protection.*

◄ COMMON CUTTLEFISH
(Sepia officinalis) *This animal's flat body is ideal for its life on the seabed. Its internal shell is the familiar cuttlebone that is often found on beaches. Like other cephalopods, cuttlefish change colour and squirt ink to confuse predators.*

# A *world* of shells

Molluscs with shells are divided into two groups: gastropods, which have shells in one piece, and bi-valves, which have shells in two parts. Not all molluscs have shells: octopuses and squid are molluscs, but they have no external shell.

**West Indian worm shell**
*Vermicularia spirata*

**Clear sundial shell**
*Architectonica perspectiva*

**Ocelate cowrie**
*Cypraea ocellata*

**European prickly cockle**
*Acanthocardia echinata*

**Matchless cone shell**
*Conus cedonulli*

**Hebrew cone shell**
*Conus ebraeus*

**Precious wentletrap**
*Epitonium scalare*

**Pacific thorny oyster**
*Spondylus princeps*

**Rayed pearl oyster**
*Pinctada radiata*

**Imperial harp shell**
*Harpa costata*

**Giant razor shell**
*Ensis siliqua*

**Australian trumpet shell**
*Syrinx aruanus*

**Tiger maurea shell**
*Maurea tigris*

**Listers keyhole limpet**
*Diodora listeri*

**Great scallop**
*Pecten maximus*

**Japanese wonder shell**
*Thatcheria mirabilis*

**Common blue mussel**
*Mytilus edulis*

INVERTEBRATES

**Australian scallop**
*Pecten australis*

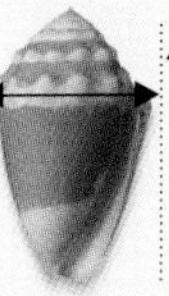

**Pontifical
cone shell**
*Conus dorreensis*

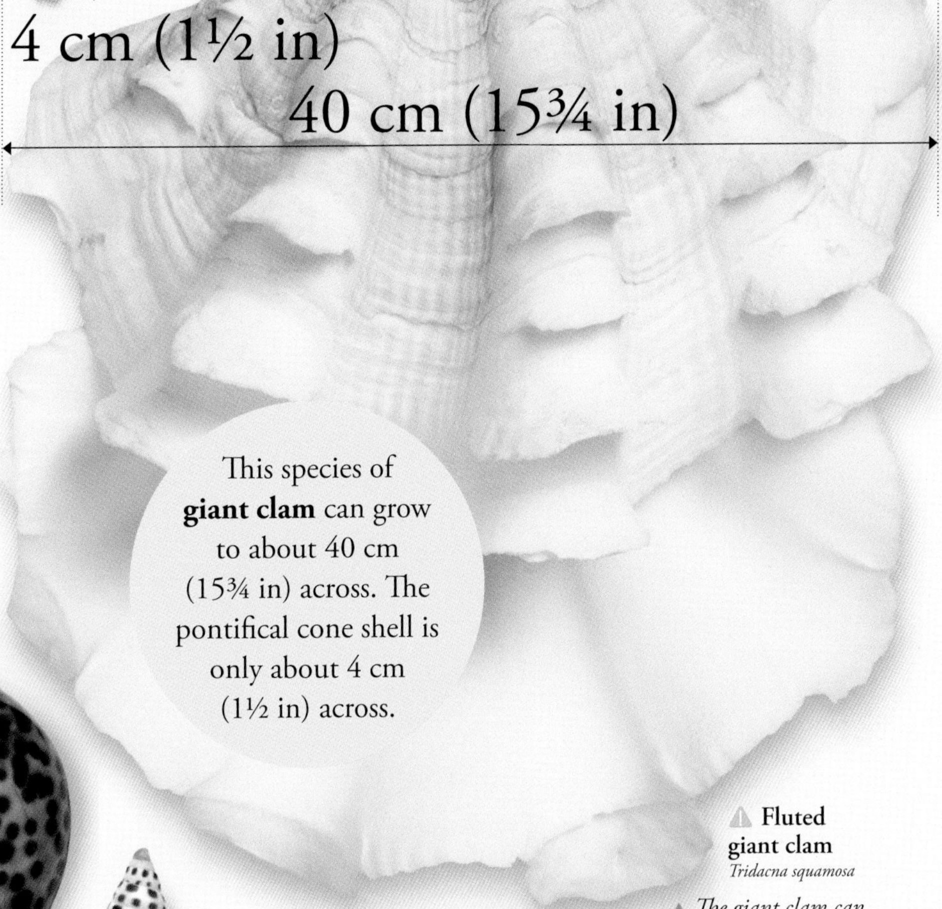

4 cm (1½ in)

40 cm (15¾ in)

**Glory of
the sea**
*Conus
gloriamaris*

This species of
**giant clam** can grow
to about 40 cm
(15¾ in) across. The
pontifical cone shell is
only about 4 cm
(1½ in) across.

⚠ **Fluted
giant clam**
*Tridacna squamosa*

▲ *The giant clam can
close its shell tightly if
it feels threatened by
a predator.*

**Tower screw shell**
*Turritella terebra*

ly-spotted
uger shell
erebra areolata

**Tiger cowrie**
*Cypraea tigris*

**The Junonia**
*Scaphella junonia*

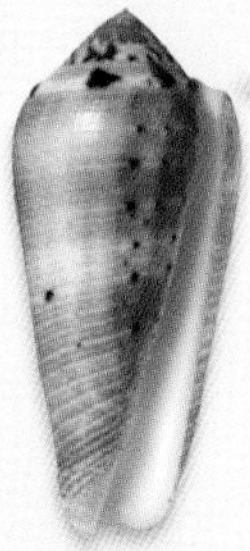

**Circumcision
cone shell**
*Conus circumcisus*

**Triumphant star
turban shell**
*Guildfordia triumphans*

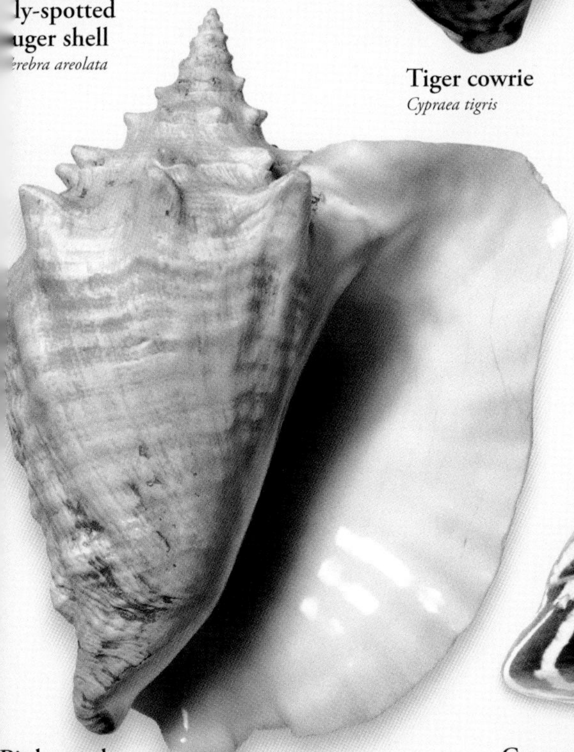

**Pink conch**
*Strombus gigas*

**Commercial trochus shell**
*Trochus niloticus*

**Waved goblet shell**
*Cantharus undosus*

**Flinders' vase shell**
*Vasum flindersi*

# Arthropods

More than 80 per cent of all the animals we know about on Earth are arthropods. They are a diverse group of animals ranging in size from microscopic gall mites to Japanese spider crabs that measure up to 4 m (13 ft) across – that's the same length as a car. Arthropods are found in almost every habitat imaginable, from seals' noses and pools of petrol to crushing depths and frozen glaciers.

## DEER TICKS (*Ixodes ricinus*)

- **Ticks cannot jump like fleas**. Instead, they wait for their host to walk by, and then grab hold. Ticks live in shrubs and tall grass.
- Ticks use their **legs** to tightly **grip** on to the chosen host. They can detect heat given off from a host.
- Although they mainly target deer, these **parasites** will nestle on any large mammal, including humans.
- Ticks carry **several diseases** and can pass these on to their host.

*The tick stabs her harpoon-like mouthparts into the flesh until she hits a blood vessel.*

*She will now expand to almost 200 times her original size as she gorges on blood.*

SHEDDING ITS SKIN
*The Pacific lobster, like most arthropods, has a hard exoskeleton, which it sheds as it grows. The new exoskeleton takes time to harden, leaving the lobster vulnerable to predators.*

INVERTEBRATES

# Arthropods

| Insects | Centipedes and millipedes | Spiders, scorpions, ticks, and mites | Sea spiders | Crabs, lobsters, and shrimps | Horseshoe crabs |
|---|---|---|---|---|---|

Butterfly

Wasp

Grasshopper

Centipede

Millipede

Raft spider

Gold scorpion

Deer ked

Sea spider

Crab

Squat lobster

Prawn

Horseshoe crab

*Insects are one of the most adaptable and diverse groups of animals on Earth, with over a million species.*

*These many-legged arthropods have long, segmented bodies. They also have a pair of poisonous claws.*

*This group is known as arachnids. They have two body sections, but don't have wings or antennae.*

*Despite the name these marine arthropods aren't spiders. Species range in size from 1 mm to 75 cm (¹⁄₃₀–30 in).*

*Crustaceans are mainly aquatic. They have a hard exoskeleton, two pairs of antennae, and a pair of compound eyes.*

*These aren't true crabs; they are closer to arachnids. They have the rare ability to regrow lost limbs.*

## Imperial scorpion
*Pandinus imperator*

- **Length** 12–23 cm (4¾–9 in)
- **Location** Africa

Relying on its size and **powerful, serrated pincers** the imperial scorpion has no need for deadly venom. Instead, it sneaks up and grabs, crushing its prey's external skeleton or **cutting through its flesh.** Small, pincer-like mouthparts then pull it to pieces. A female scorpion gives birth to live young. She protects, feeds and carries them on her back until they are able to fend for themselves.

*Once gripped by the pincers, prey can be stabbed repeatedly with the stinger.*

*A scorpion will crush its prey with powerful pincers.*

## Horseshoe crab
*Limulus polyphemus*

**Length** 28–60 cm (including tail) (11–24 in)
**Weight** 4.5 kg (10 lb)
**Location** East coast of North America

These crabs haven't changed much in nearly 300 million years. They are considered **living fossils** and are close living relatives to the now extinct trilobites. Despite their common name, **they are not crabs,** but are related to arachnids. A female horseshoe crab will lay between 15,000 and 60,000 eggs. Horseshoe crabs grow slowly and it can take 12 years for the young crabs to become adults.

## Sea spider
*Colossendeis australis*

- **Leg span** 50 cm (20 in)
- **Location** Worldwide oceans

Sea spiders are found all over the world, from coastal tropical waters to the poles. *Colossendeis australis* are **giant deep-sea inhabitants**, with leg spans reaching more than 50 cm (20 in). They **suck the juices** from soft-bodied invertebrates, or graze on small aquatic animals. Other sea spider species are smaller and can be found in coastal waters and reefs.

■ **Number of species:** 5,000
■ **Key features:** All have a long, thin body that is perfect for flying. Two pairs of large transparent wings are held either out to the side (dragonflies) or folded along the back (damselflies) when resting. Their huge compound eyes can see really well. They are ferocious hunters. The larva, known as a nymph, lives entirely underwater.

# Dragonflies
## *and damselflies*

If you had been alive around 300 million years ago, you would have seen insects flying around that were almost identical to today's dragonflies and damselflies. The adults, with their striking colours and amazing flying skills, are a familiar sight. But these elegant, eye-catching insects spend most of their lives as water-dwelling larvae, or nymphs, well hidden in the murky depths of rivers and lakes.

## Southern hawker
*Aeshna cyanea*

■ **Length** 6.5–7 cm (2½–2¾ in)
■ **WIngspan** 7–8 cm (2¾–3 in)
■ **Location** Europe

The nymphs take up to three years to gain their wings, but an adult has just a few weeks which to mate before it dies. The males zoom off at speeds of up to **30 kph (19 mph)** to establish their breeding territories, fiercely driving off intruders and any rival males.

## Emperor dragonfly
*Anax imperator*

- **Length** 7–8 cm (2¾–3 in)
- **Wingspan** 10–11 cm (4–4¼ in)
- **Location** Europe, C. Asia and N. Africa

This is one of the biggest and most powerful dragonflies. It also **holds the record for being the fastest** and can swoop and dive through the air at speeds of up to 38 kph (24 mph). Adults seize and eat their prey, which include butterflies and other flying insects, on the wing. The larvae, or nymphs, take up to a year to become winged adults, but then live for only around 10 days. Males often fight to the death over territory.

## Common darter
*Sympetrum striolatum*

- **Length** 38 mm (1½ in)
- **Wingspan** 58 mm (2³⁄₁₀ in)
- **Location** Europe and W. Asia

Common darters are given their name because they **fly in an unpredictable way**. They are often colourful and have strong and thick bodies. They prefer to live in wet areas. In order to lay their eggs females hover above water and then release them into the water.

## Four-spotted chaser dragonfly
*Libellula quadrimaculata*

- **Length** 4–4.5 cm (1⅔–1¾ in)
- **Wingspan** 7–7.5 cm (2¾–3 in)
- **Location** Europe, N. Asia, North America

Chaser dragonflies can **see colour** and their eyes are also very sensitive to movement. These aggressive creatures can spot prey from several metres away. They then swoop up from under their target, tearing into it using the **sharp spines** on their legs.

## Common blue damselfly
*Enallagma cyathigerum*

- **Length** 3–3.5 cm (1¼–1½ in)
- **Wingspan** 3.5–4 cm (1½–1⅓ in)
- **Location** Europe

The moment a female lands in his territory, a male blue damselfly will fly over to her and hover just in front of her. By flashing his **brightly coloured wings**, he is hoping to impress her and prove that he is a suitable mate. He may also hover over and make several landings on the water that runs through his territory. He does this to convince the female that it is a good place for her to lay her eggs, so that the nymphs that hatch out have the best chance of survival.

---

### MAYFLIES

The ancestors of mayflies were probably among the first insects to take to the air about 354 million years ago and, like their dragonfly cousins, have changed little since then.

- **Adult mayflies never eat.** Only the larvae, known as nymphs, feed. It can take as long as three years for a nymph to develop fully into an adult. But once it is an adult, it may live for just a few hours.

- **Number of species:** 2,500

- **Key features:** Adult mayflies have two pairs of transparent wings, which are held upright above the body. Two or three long tails project from the tip of the abdomen. Like dragonflies, their antennae are short, but their eyes are slightly smaller.

*3 tails*

## Common mayfly
*Ephemera danica*

- **Length** 1–3.5 cm (⅜–1½ in)–excluding tail filaments
- **Location** Europe

The artificial flies used for trout fishing are modelled on these mayflies, which are also **known as greendrakes**. Eggs are laid in rivers and lakes. Nymphs chew their way into the silt on the bottom and feed on tiny plants and animals that live there.

INVERTEBRATES

# Stick and leaf insects

These remarkable insects bear an uncanny resemblance to the twigs and leaves on which they live. The stick insects, or walking sticks, are found around the world but, like leaf insects, most species live in dense vegetation in tropical regions. Thanks to their odd appearance, many people like to keep these unusual insects as pets.

**LEAF-LIKE INSECTS**
*Found in the humid rainforests of Southeast Asia, the leaf insect* Phyllium celebicum *has a pattern of lines on its body that look exactly like the veins of a leaf.*

# Leaf insects
Family Phylliidae

- **Length** 3–11 cm (1¼–4¼ in)
- **Species** Around 30
- **Diet** Leaves
- **Location** Australasia, Southeast Asia, Mauritius, the Seychelles

Leaf insects **mimic leaves** with their flat, round bodies and dull green and brown coloration. Some leaf insects have spots and blotches that add to the effect, while others simply look like dead, wrinkled leaves.

## MASTERS OF DISGUISE
True to their name, stick insects have slender, twig-like bodies to blend in with their surroundings and avoid being eaten. Some sway in the breeze to add to the disguise.

RECORD BREAKERS
*Stick insects come in different shades of green and brown, with bumps on their bodies to make them look more like twigs. They are the longest insects in the world. The longest species lives in Borneo and grows up to 30 cm (12 in) in length.*

## I can **change colour**.
Some young leaf insects change colour after they hatch. They take on their distinctive green colour after the first moult, which is around a week or more after hatching.

INVERTEBRATES

251

# Grasshoppers and cricket.

With more than 20,000 species, there is a huge variety of these insects, both in behaviour and appearance. Most communicate with a chirping noise called their "song" and, during the breeding season, this sound fills the air in many warm parts of the world.

**Roesel's bush cricke**
*Metrioptera roeselii*

## GROWING UP

All grasshoppers and crickets undergo incomplete metamorphosis. This means that young insects change gradually as they mature, moulting several times. Those species that develop wings have tough forewings that protect delicate hindwings. Crickets grow much longer antennae than grasshoppers, often longer than their bodies.

▲ EARDRUM *Bush crickets hear using drum-like membranes on their forelegs. Grasshoppers have membranes on their sides for hearing. The membranes pick up the songs of potential mates. Grasshoppers sing by rubbing their legs against their wings, while crickets rub their wings together.*

## One, two, three, **jump**.

Grasshoppers and crickets have long, powerful hindlegs. Even those species that have wings often jump away from danger instead of flying. It makes it more difficult for a predator to catch them.

### FACTFILE

■ Many grasshoppers have colourful wings to startle predators. Others use camouflage as a defence.

■ Locusts are grasshoppers that form swarms. They can cause great damage to crops.

■ Crickets eat a variety of food, from plants to kitchen scraps. Many are hunters or scavengers.

■ Weta crickets have enormous, spiny back legs, which they show to predators to warn them to keep away.

# ilkweed grasshopper
*nateus morbillosus*

**ength** 70 mm (2¾ in)
**ocation** South Africa

les of this species of
sshopper can fly a short
tance, but females do not
even though they have wings.
is is probably because females
too heavy to get off the ground.
is insect's **bright colours act as a
rning** to predators to leave it
ne. If it is attacked it will give
**foul-tasting foam**.

▲ DIET *This
species feeds on a
variety of plants.*

# Stripe-winged grasshopper
*Stenobothrus lineatus*

■ **Length** 18 mm (¾ in)
■ **Location** Central and southern Europe
to western Asia

This species of grasshopper has a narrow
white stripe along the edge of its forewings.
This grasshopper is usually green but it can
come in a **variety of colours**, from green to
yellow, brown, and red. The insect has one of
the **quietest songs** among grasshoppers.

# uropean mole cricket
*yllotalpa gryllotalpa*

**Length** 45 mm (1¾ in)
**Location** Europe

ole crickets have short, broad, toothed
ont legs for digging. Females dig chambers
the soil to lay their eggs. Males dig
urrows, from where their songs sound
uder. There are about 60 species of mole
icket. They are covered with **short, velvety
airs**, like the burrowing mammal from
hich they get their name.

# Desert locust
*Schistocerca gregaria*

■ **Length** 60 mm (2¼ in)
■ **Location** Africa, western Asia

The desert locust is known for forming **huge
swarms** that can stretch for hundreds of square
kilometres and contain 40 to 80
million locusts. The
locusts **change
colour** from green
to brown when they
are overcrowded.
They can be solitary, but
lack of food makes them
swarm. The swarms fly up to
130 km (80 miles) a day.

# Speckled bush cricket
*Leptophyes punctatissima*

◄ **Length** 18 mm
¾ in)
■ **Location** Europe

As its name suggests,
this cricket's body is
covered with tiny black
speckles. It **cannot fly
but can jump a long way**
on its long, slender legs. The
male's song is difficult for
humans to hear because it is
so high-pitched. But female
crickets can hear it, and they
answer with their own song.

# African cave cricket
*Pholeogryllus geertsi*

■ **Length** 38 mm (1½ in)
■ **Location** Northern Africa, southern Europe

Cave crickets can be recognized by
their **humped backs**, and they are
sometimes known as camel crickets.
They have **extra-long hindlegs**
for jumping, and even longer,
sensitive antennae. They use
their antennae to help them
detect predators. There are
about 500 species of
cave cricket around
the world.

253

# Mantids

With a triangular-shaped head and the curious ability to turn it around to see behind, mantids are strange-looking creatures. The common name "praying mantis" comes from the prayer-like appearance of its forelegs, not from its skill as an accomplished predator.

If prey thinks it hasn't been spotted, it had better think ag The praying mantis has the unique ability to turn its hea 300 degrees – this means it can see who is lurking behind it.

# Devil's flower mantis

*Idolomantis diabolicum*

- **Length** 14 cm (5½ in)
- **Location** Sub-Saharan Africa

The African devil's flower mantis is **one of the biggest mantises in the world**. It lives in the dry, bushy scrublands of eastern Africa. Here it lurks about pretending to be a nectar-bearing flower – a very attractive sight to a lot of insects.

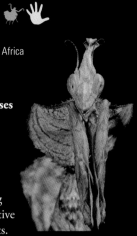

## ▲ PRAYING IN WAIT

*Mantids are ambush predators. Hunting during the day with their specially adapted vision, they patiently lie and wait for their prey to get close.*

## ▲ LASH AND GRAB

*Mantids use their powerful spiked forelegs to lash out at fantastic speed and grab their prey. The mantis body remains amazingly still and steady.*

## ▲ A NASTY BITE?

*Mantids do pinch and bite, but they don't possess a poisonous venom. They rely on their size and camouflage to defend themselves.*

INVERTEBRATES

# Cockroaches

These robust, leathery insects have flat, oval bodies so they can squeeze into tight spaces to escape predators or find food. Most roaches live in dark, damp places and come out at night to feed. In their natural habitat they eat fallen fruits, leaves, and other plant material, but some will also eat the remains of dead animals. A few roaches are pests that infest houses and spread disease.

▲ EGG-LAYING MACHINES *An adult American cockroach lives for a year or more, but in this short time the female will produce an average of 150 young. The young roaches, or nymphs, hatch from egg cases called ootheca The nymphs mature into adults within a year.*

LIVE BEARERS *Cockroaches such as the giant hissing cockroach give birth to live young. The female lays eggs in an egg case but then draws it back inside her abdomen so the young develop inside her body.*

## FACTFILE

- **Number of species:** The cockroach order Blattodea has 6,000 species divided into seven groups or families.
- **Key features:** Flat, oval, leathery bodies with long, whip-like antennae.
- **Size:** Cockroaches grow quite big – the giant cave cockroach can reach 10 cm (4 in) in length.

Size comparison

# Giant hissing cockroach

*...phadorhina portentosa*

 **3**

- **Length** 5–7.5 cm (2–3 in)
- **Weight** 23 g (⅘ oz)
- **Location** Madagascar

...s large roach lives on the ...st floor among the leaf ...er and rotting logs. It ...nes out at night to feed ...fruit and plant material. ...en fighting or mating ...makes a hissing noise by ...cing air through its breathing ...es. Hissing is also used as an **alarm** ...to the rest of the colony. Males hiss ...re often than females.

# Giant burrowing cockroach

*Macropanesthia rhinoceros*

 **10**

- **Length** 8 cm (3¼ in)
- **Weight** 35 g (1 oz)
- **Location** Australia

A true giant, this is the **heaviest species** of cockroach in the world. Giant burrowing cockroaches construct and **live in burrows** up to 1 m (39 in) under the ground. They come out at night to collect leaf litter and other dead plant material, which they take back to their burrow to eat.

*Leathery segmented abdomen*

# ...ustral ellipsidion

*...ipsidion australe*

- **Length** 2.5 cm (1 in)
- **Location** Australia

...ese bush cockroaches are active during the ...y, where they can be found wandering over ...ants in Australia. The younger nymphs are ...ually **striking**, with bands of bright yellow ...ts running across the abdomen. Like all ...ckroaches, the nymphs grow into adults by **shedding their outer skin** in stages. This species feeds on pollen, honeydew, and mould fungus.

# German cockroach

*Blatella germanica*

- **Length** 12–15 mm (½–⅝ in)
- **Location** Worldwide, except for cold climates

German cockroaches are found wherever there is human habitation, but they do not like the cold. In the wild, they live in warm, dark, damp crevices. Although they have wings, they **rarely fly**. They are most active at night, when they scavenge for food. **Unfussy eaters**, they will eat soap, glue, toothpaste, or even each other when food is scarce.

# Death's head cockroach

*Blaberus craniifer*

**2**

- **Length** 4–6 cm (1½–2½ in)
- **Location** Central America; introduced to southern USA

This roach takes its common name from the **"skull"** or "vampire" markings on the pronotum – part of the thorax just behind the insect's head. The nymphs lack wings, while adults have wings but do not fly. These roaches cannot climb up glass so they **make good pets** for open aquariums. They feed mostly on plant material, but will eat other foods that may be available.

# Green banana cockroach

*...anchlora nivea*

- **Length** 2.5 cm (1 in)
- **Location** Caribbean and US Gulf Coast

These **small, green roaches** are also known as Cuban cockroaches, reflecting their Cuban origins. They have since spread to the United States on shipments of Caribbean fruit. As nymphs, these roaches burrow under logs and other debris, but the adults are usually found crawling on shrubs and trees. They **emerge at night** and are drawn to bright lights.

# American cockroach

*Periplaneta ame ricana*

**1**

- **Length** 2.5–4 cm (1–1½ in)
- **Location** Worldwide

This **pest thrives** in warm, moist conditions indoors as well as outdoors. These roaches are common in basements, sewers, and buildings where food is prepared, such as bakeries and restaurants, as well as in houses. This species is large and **slow to develop**. In cool weather it will often seek warmth and food inside a house. Like the German cockroach, it will eat anything.

# Bugs

To a biologist, the word "bug" means a very particular group of insects, also know as hemipterans. Bugs come in an enormous variety of shapes and live very varied lifestyles, but they share a special way of feeding and have a distinctive wing structure.

**STAB AND SUCK** A close look at a bug reveals it has no mouth, only a stout "beak" shaped like a reinforced drinking straw. This is used to stab prey or tap into plants and suck up body fluids or sap. Bugs cannot bite or eat solid food.

**CLASSIC BUG** *This fore[st] shield bug shows typical bu[g] characteristics: toughened front wings covering small, delicate hindwings, and sto[ut] drinking-straw mouthparts*

---

### FACTFILE

■ **Number of species:** Entomologists have so far described over 80,000 species of bug, and there may be at least as many still to be discovered.

**TWO TRIBES** *Bugs can be grouped into two main types. The plant-feeding heteropterans have front wings with hardened bases and membranous tips, while the homopterans have uniform wings and often suck fluids from other animals.*

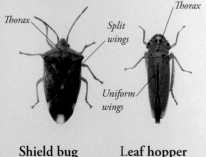

Thorax
Split wings
Thorax
Uniform wings

**Shield bug**
*predatory homopteran*

**Leaf hopper**
*typical heteropteran*

INVERTEBRATES

## ottony cushion scale

*a purchasi*

- **ength** about 5 mm (1/5 in), including egg sac
- **tatus** Pest
- **ocation** Originally from tralia, now worldwide

ese small sap-sucking ects are a **major pest citrus crops** such as nge and lemon oves. Males are found casionally, but most les are hermaphrodites d are able to reproduce thout mating.

## Periodic cicada

*Magicicada septemdecim*

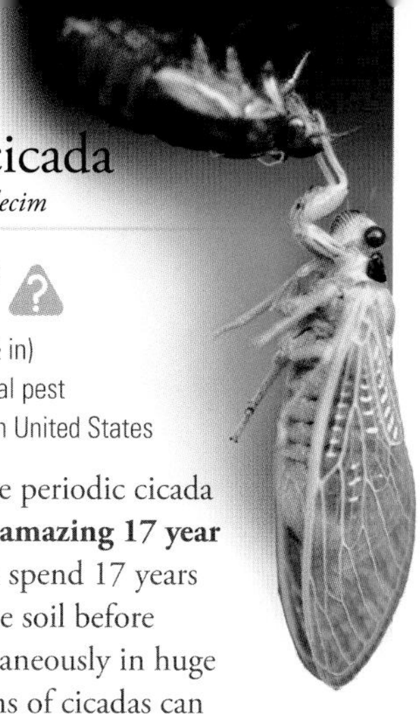

- **Length** 4 cm (1½ in)
- **Status** Occasional pest
- **Location** Eastern United States

The largest of the periodic cicada species, with an **amazing 17 year lifecycle.** Larvae spend 17 years developing in the soil before emerging simultaneously in huge numbers. Swarms of cicadas can damage young trees and **have been known to stop traffic and cause accidents**! Newly emerged adults mate, produce eggs and die within a few weeks and all is quiet for a further 17 years.

## Assassin bug

*Eulyes illustris*

- **Length** 2 cm (8/10 in)
- **Status** Neutral
- **Location** Philippines

The black-spotted red assassin bug shown here is just one of thousands of species of assassin bug. As the name suggests, these insects are **predators**. Some live by sucking blood. Assassin bugs are found worldwide, especially in tropical and subtropical regions. They make their homes in plants, on the ground, and in leaf litter. Some can **transmit diseases to humans** through their bite.

## ond skater

*rris lacustris*

- **Length** 8–20 mm (3/10–8/10 in)
- **Status** Neutral
- **Location** Worldwide

ond skaters are **predatory bugs** at stalk the surface film of still ools and ponds. Their long in legs allow them to spread eir weight over a wide area and ater-repellent hairs on the feet revent them from sinking. They use he water surface as a spider uses a web, sing vibrations to track down potential rey. Pond skaters leave the water to **ibernate in winter**.

## Cabbage aphid

*Brevicoryne brassicae*

- **Length** 1.5–2.5 mm (6/10–1 in)
- **Status** Pest
- **Location** Originally from Europe, but spreading

Like other aphids, this species **feeds on plant sap** and can occur in such vast numbers that the plant host is destroyed. Cabbage aphids also **transmit a number of plant diseases**. They are one of about 250 aphid species listed as plant pests.

## Forest shield bug

*Pentatoma rufipes*

- **Length** 14 mm (½ in)
- **Status** Occasional pest
- **Location** Worldwide

This **common species** occurs in natural forests and plantations. It is associated with oak trees, but can become a nuisance in commercial fruit orchards. It eats plant juices and insects. Females lay eggs in crevices on tree bark during the winter. The larvae hatch the following spring.

## Lantern bug

*Fulgora lanternaria*

- **Length** 3 cm (1 1/5 in)
- **Status** Neutral
- **Location** Peru

One of a large group of strange-looking insects with a **greatly enlarged head** section. The species is also known as the peanut-headed lantern fly. The hindwings bear large eyespots to deter predators and further protection is given by plant poisons extracted from tree sap and stored in the lantern bug's body.

## Water scorpion

*Nepa cinerea*

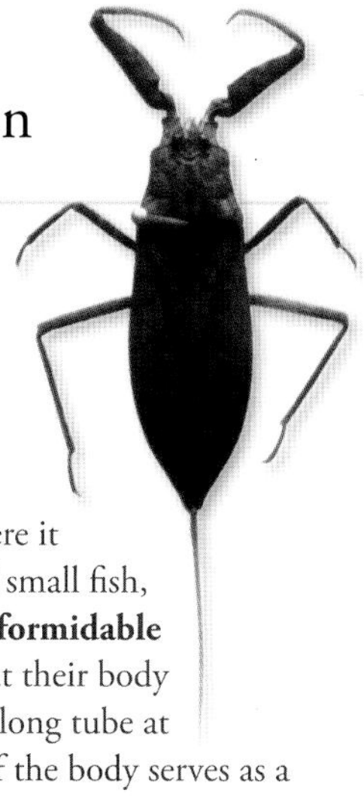

- **Length** 2 cm (4/5 in)
- **Status** Neutral
- **Location** Europe

This leaf-shaped bug inhabits still pools, where it hunts other insects and small fish, trapping them with its **formidable pincers** and sucking out their body fluids. The long tube at the back of the body serves as a snorkel – every 30 minutes or so the scorpion reverses up to the surface to replenish its air supply.

# Treehoppers

Treehoppers first appeared on our planet about 50 million years ago. Entomologists (scientists who study insects) think there are up to 3,200 species that live in warmer regions worldwide, especially in tropical forests. Many of these insects have large, thorny projections on the thorax, which give them their alternative common name of thorn bug.

## FACTFILE

- **Number of species:** Around 3,200
- **Distribution**: Worldwide
- **Diet:** Treehoppers suck sap from plants. Any undigested sap passes through the treehopper's body as honeydew. Ants love honeydew and will stand guard over the insect to protect it.

MASTER OF DISGUISE
*From a distance, the distinctive thorn-like projection on the thorax of the treehopper helps to break up the shape of the insect. Predators might think that the treehopper is part of the plant upon which it is resting.*

INVERTEBRATES

# Thorn bug
*Umbonia crassicornis*

- **Length** Up to 1 cm (½ in)
- **Diet** Plant sap
- **Location** Central and South America and southern Florida

The **distinctive bump** on the back of the thorn bug is so sharp that it can pierce through a shoe and puncture human skin. **This treehopper is a pest** in many parts of its range thanks to the damage it does to the plants on which it thrives.

◄ HORNY ISSUES
*Adult thorn bugs have just one bump on their backs, but the nymphs start off with three. The shape, size and colour varies widely between individuals.*

▲ CHEMICAL PROTECTION
*Would-be predators usually steer clear of treehoppers and their nymphs (above) because the bodies of these distinctive bugs contain foul-tasting chemicals. The females even protect the eggs by coating them with a frothy substance that contains the same noxious chemicals.*

## Don't step on me!
Tread on the sharp thorax of the treehopper, and the resulting wound could easily become infected thanks to the tiny micro-organisms that feed on the honeydew.

▲ NYMPHS
*Female treehopper bugs lay hundreds of eggs and then guard them until they hatch about 20 days later. The female will then look after the brood. Treehoppers and their nymphs carpet the twigs and branches on which they live.*

INVERTEBRATES

261

# A *world* of beetles

About one third of all insects are beetles. They range in size from those just visible to the naked eye to giants that are 19 cm (7½ in) long. Beetles are found all over the world in every sort of habitat, on land and in fresh water. They have hard forewings called elytra, which close over the hind wings to protect them.

**Snout beetle**
*Cyrtotrachelus dux*

**Malaysian brentid beetle**
*Eutrachelus temmincki*

**Hercules beetle**
*Dynastes hercules*

**Jewel scarab beetle**
*Chrysina resplendens*

**Click beetle**
*Semiotus angulatu*

**Malayan frog beetle**
*Sagra buqueti*

**Jewel beetle**
*Sternocera aequisignata*

**Ladybird**
*Coccinella 7-punctata*

At up to **19 cm** (7½ in) long, the male Hercules beetle is one of the **world's longest** beetles. Ladybirds are 5 mm (¹/₅ in) long.

**King stag beetle**
*Phalacrognathus muelleri*

**Longhorn beetle**
*Callipogon barbatus*

**Longhorn beetle**
*Batocera rufomaculata*

**Pie-dish beetle**
*Helea subserratus*

**INVERTEBRATES**

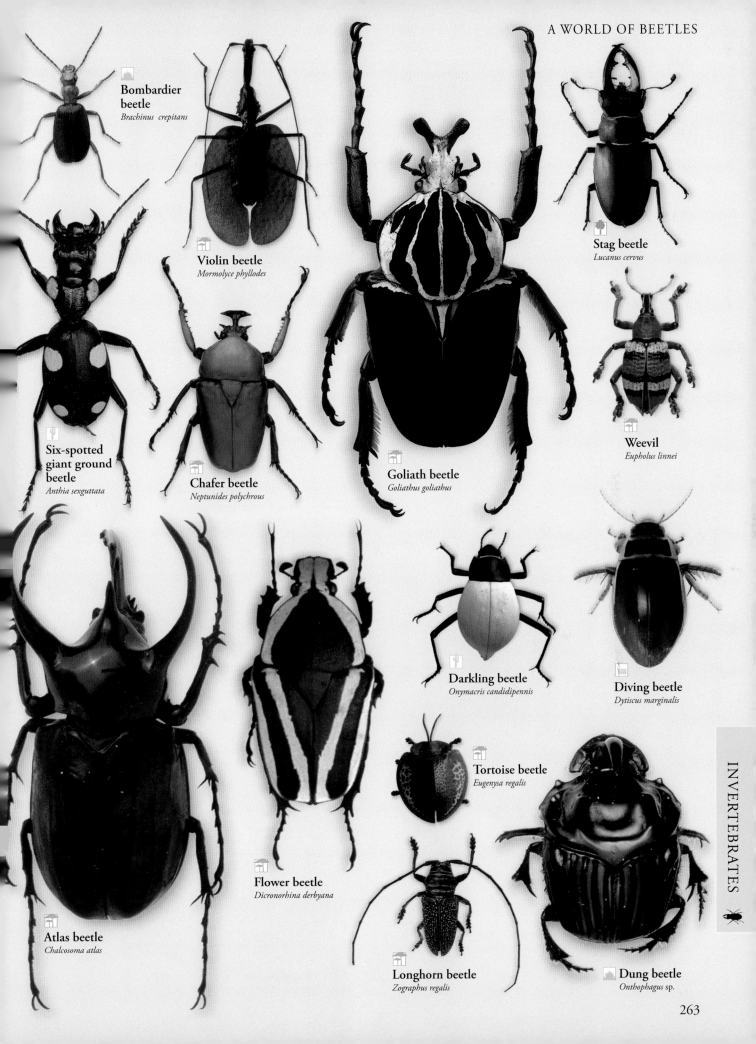

**Bombardier beetle**
*Brachinus crepitans*

**Violin beetle**
*Mormolyce phyllodes*

**Stag beetle**
*Lucanus cervus*

**Six-spotted giant ground beetle**
*Anthia sexguttata*

**Chafer beetle**
*Neptunides polychrous*

**Goliath beetle**
*Goliathus goliathus*

**Weevil**
*Eupholus linnei*

**Darkling beetle**
*Onymacris candidipennis*

**Diving beetle**
*Dytiscus marginalis*

**Tortoise beetle**
*Eugenysa regalis*

**Flower beetle**
*Dicronorhina derbyana*

**Atlas beetle**
*Chalcosoma atlas*

**Longhorn beetle**
*Zographus regalis*

**Dung beetle**
*Onthophagus* sp.

# Wetas

The flightless weta of New Zealand is one of the world's most ancient species still alive today. The different types vary in size, with the giant wetas being among the biggest insects on Earth. The word "weta" derives from the native Maori, *wetapunga*, meaning "God of Ugly Things".

MOUNTAIN STONE WETA
*New Zealand offers a varied climate and the mountain stone weta has adapted to this. During winter at high altitudes, the mountain stone weta can survive being frozen at temperatures of -10°C (14°F).*

264

# Poor Knights weta
*Deinacrida fallai*

- **Length** 15–20 cm (6–8 in)
- **Status** Vulnerable
- **Location** Poor Knights Islands, New Zealand

Poor Knights wetas are one of 11 giant weta species. They split their time between the trees and ground, where they lay their eggs. **Nocturnal**, they **feed on fruit and fungi**, with insects forming a minor part of their diet. Though large, the crown of heaviest weta has gone to the wetapunga of Little Barrier Island, where a pregnant female weighed a staggering 70 g (2½ oz).

## ⚠ CONSERVATION

Giant wetas have become increasingly threatened. One main reason for this is the introduction of predators, such as rats and mice, into their natural habitats. Giant wetas are listed as vulnerable and conservationists have set up captive breeding programmes around New Zealand.

**Giant wetas aren't the only weta group in New Zealand.** There are also about 10 species of tree weta and as their name suggests, they are mainly located crawling about in trees. Smaller than the giant wetas, tree wetas live in small groups and can be found in the wooden burrows made by wood-boring beetle larvae. Watch out, though; they may be small, but tree wetas possess a nasty bite!

# A **mammal** role for an **insect**.

Millions of years ago, the New Zealand archipelago broke away from the main landmass. Because few mammal species made it onto the islands, the weta evolved behaviours usually associated with small rodents, such as burrowing and preying on smaller insects.

▲ THREATENING BEHAVIOUR
*The weta definitely puts the creepy into creepy-crawly. But it's not as scary as it looks and can feel threatened itself. To protect itself the male bush weta adopts a defensive posture. It stretches its large jaws, raises its spiny legs above its head, and hisses aggressively.*

# Ants

Ants are found on almost every land mass on the planet, except the frozen Arctic and Antarctic. They live in highly organized colonies, usually with one queen or breeding female and an army of female workers. The workers build shelters, find food, and defend their nests.

## Dinosaur ant
*Dinoponera gigantea*

- **Length** 40 mm (1½ in)
- **Diet** Insects and earthworms
- **Location** South America

One of the biggest ants in the world, dinosaur ants live in relatively **small colonies** of around 100 individuals. Their nests are found under mounds of soil. Inside are **networks of connecting tunnels**. The ants mostly forage for food at night, and feed on small, live animals.

## KEEPING ON TOP

Dinosaur ants do not have a queen – instead they have a breeding worker called a mother ant. If a rival challenges her position, she marks it with a chemical sting, then leaves it for her workers to kill and dispose of.

▼ DINOSAUR ANTS
*cut up large pieces of food using their serrated jaws, known as the mandible.*

INVERTEBRATES

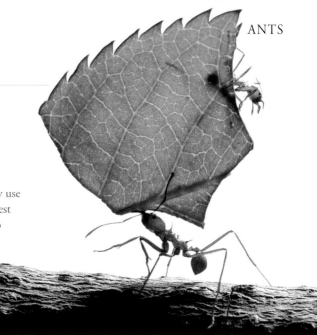

# Leaf-cutting ant
*Atta cephalotes*

- **Length** Queen 35 mm (1⁵⁄₁₀ in)
- **Diet** Fungus
- **Location** Southern USA, Central America, South America

These ants have **sharp jaws** that they use to cut leaves from plants in their forest homes. They carry the leaves back to their nests where the leaves decay. Fungus grows in the decaying leaves, and the ants eat this fungus. **More than 1,000,000 ants may live in each nest**.

# Honeypot ant
*Myrmecocystus mimicus*

- **Length** Queen 13 mm (⁵⁄₁₀ in); workers 10 mm (½ in)
- **Diet** Insects and nectar
- **Location** Southern USA and Mexico

These ants **survive hot, dry habitats** by using workers as food storage pots. The workers, called "repletes", **gorge on nectar** until their abdomens are stuffed and swollen. They then act as living larders, feeding other ants in the colony. When two colonies meet, they put on "tournaments" of display fighting. The colony with the most ants wins. The losers run away.

# Wood ant
*Formica rufa*

- **Length** 10 mm (½ in)
- **Diet** Aphids, flies, caterpillars, beetles, honeydew
- **Location** Europe

An aggressive hunter, the wood ant **feeds on other insects**. It also "milks" aphids by stroking each individual until the aphid releases a droplet of sweet honeydew. Wood ants live in nests containing up to 1,000,000 inhabitants. If the nest is disturbed, the ants **swarm out and bite** the intruder.

# Fire ant
*Solenopsis invicta*

- **Length** Queen 8 mm (³⁄₁₀ in)
- **Diet** Young plants and seeds, insects
- **Location** South America, USA, Australia, New Zealand

This tiny, **stinging ant** lives in a soil nest, often on lawns, pastures, or roadsides. If disturbed, the ant releases a chemical that alerts other fire ants nearby. These then rush to attack. Their sting is extremely painful – similar to burning – and **can cause death** among people who are sensitive to the sting.

# Weaver ant
*Oecophylla smaragdina*

- **Length** Queen 15 mm (⁷⁄₁₀ in); workers 11 mm (½ in)
- **Diet** Honeydew
- **Location** Asia and Australia

Weaver ants build their nests by pulling the leaves of trees together and **"weaving"** them with silk produced by the ants' larvae. A colony made up of 500,000 ants may stretch over 10 or more trees.

# Bulldog ant
*Myrmecia gulosa*

- **Length** 21mm (⁹⁄₁₀ in)
- **Diet** Honeydew, nectar, small insects
- **Location** Australia

A bulldog ant has good eyesight, **large serrated jaws**, and a powerful sting. Bulldog ants remain perfectly still until prey comes into range, then **ambush** it. All the prey they catch is taken back to the nest where it is fed to the growing larvae.

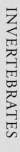

# Termites

Relatives of the cockroach, some termites build huge mounds that dominate the landscape. They feed on plant matter. Termites are often considered pests as they eat crops and infest houses, chewing through wooden walls and beams until the house is destroyed.

**1,000,000 termites** live in this cathedral termite mound. They all work for th good of the colony and will protect it with their lives.

## FACTFILE

- **Number of species:** 2,800
- **Key features:** Six legs. No obvious body divisions. Workers are usually small and pale coloured. Soldiers are bigger, often with large jaws. Neither usually have eyes. All live in colonies.

**Relative sizes**

Queen

Worker    Soldiers    King

## Magnetic mounds

In northern Australia, termites build mounds up to 4 m (13 ft) high. These are likened to magnetic compasses as the narrow sides face north and south and the wide sides face east and west. This ensures that only a small area of the mound faces the hottest mid-day sun.

## Cathedral termite mounds

Cathedral termites of the *Macrotermes* species build cement-hard mounds from soil and saliva. The mounds are ventilated by a network of tunnels and holes that can be opened to let in air, or blocked up with mud to stop heat escaping. The mounds protect the colony from predators such as ants, spiders, and lizards.

# Cathedral mound termite

*Macrotermes bellicosus*

 10

- **Length** Workers 10 mm (½ in);
soldiers 12 mm (⁶⁄₁₀ in);
queen 140 mm (6½ in)
- **Diet** Fungus, wood, and
dry plant matter
- **Location** Africa

Like all termites, cathedral mound termites are **social insects**. They live in highly organized colonies, like ants or bees. Their **main food is fungus**, which grows in chambers inside their nests. The fungus feeds on chewed-up wood that has passed through the termites' bodies.

## ▲ WORKERS

*Most termites in the colony are workers. Their job is to build and maintain the nest, find food, and look after the eggs.*

## ▲ BECOMING QUEEN

*The only termites capable of having young are the reproductives. Once a male and female mate, the female lays eggs and a new colony begins. The female is now a queen (above). Her mate is the king.*

## ▲ THE QUEEN'S BODY

*As the queen gets older, her abdomen expands and she is able to produce increasing numbers of eggs. A fully grown queen can produce more than 2,000 eggs in a day.*

*Cross section of a cathedral termite mound. Food stores and nurseries are mostly underground.*

Ground level

Food stores

Fungus grown in gardens inside the nest

Nurseries containing eggs

King and queen's royal chamber

INVERTEBRATES

# Bees and wasps

Alongside the humble ant, bees and wasps form one of the most plentiful groups of animals on Earth. The honey bee and common wasp are a familiar sight on a summer's day and humans have become reliant on them for the predation of pests, pollination, and for honey production.

## FACTFILE

- **Number of species:** There are 160,000 species of wasp and 20,000 species of bee.
- **Key features:** Both bees and wasps possess two pairs of wings and large compound eyes. Most species live in colonies, though some live a solitary life. Wasps are generally predatory and hairless, whereas bees have hair and feed on pollen and nectar.

Honey bees' nest
(at left and below)

## FRIEND OR FOE

The bee is widely seen as the gardener's friend because of its role in pollination, though the wasp's role shouldn't be forgotten. As a predator, it acts as an efficient pest control agent. In fact, almost every pest insect has a species of wasp that preys on it.

### Honey bee
*Apis mellifera*

- **Length** 8–15 mm (⅓–⅗ in)
- **Location** Originally Asia, now worldwide

Honey bees were first domesticated by the ancient Egyptians more than 4,500 years ago. This taste for honey hasn't waned and the art of bee-keeping, known as apiculture, is still practiced the world over. Wild honey bees live in colonies, which can be made up of more than **50,000 worker bees** and just **one fertile queen**. The queen can live up to two years, unlike the workers who only survive for about one month.

POLLEN COLLECTOR *Bees land on flowers to collect nectar, which is used to make honey, and pollen, which is used to feed the bee larvae. When they land on each flower, pollen sticks to their legs. It is stored in pollen baskets on their hind legs.*

INVERTEBRATES

270

## ant horn-tail wasp

*erus gigas*

**ngth** 40 mm (1⅗ in) + 17 mm (⅔ in) ovipositor
**cation** Europe

name and appearance of the giant horn- conjures up a fearsome vision, though it is **te harmless**. The sting-like projection seen a female is known as an ovipositor, it is ally part of her reproductive organ and it is d to **bore into trees**, so she can lay her eggs. grubs that hatch will feed on the wood.

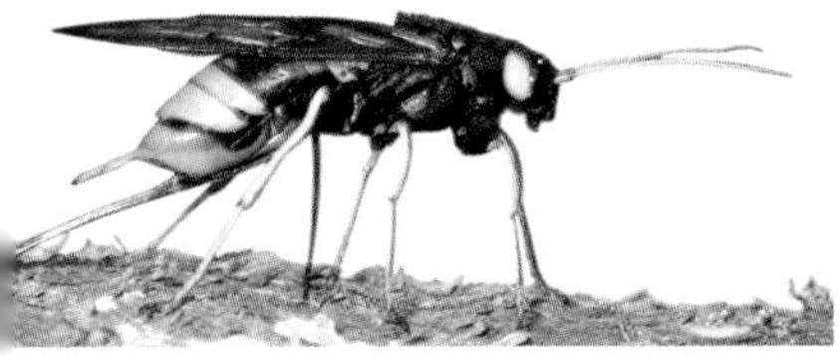

## Tarantula hawk wasp

*Pepsis formosa*

- **Length** 40–50 mm (1⅗–2 in)
- **Location** USA and Mexico

The tarantula hawk wasp is one of the biggest wasps in the world. It gets its name from its **ability to hunt down large tarantula spiders** and paralyse them with a powerful venom. It uses the spiders as food for its grubs. The tarantula hawk wasp possesses a 7 mm- (¼ in-) long sting to inject its venom, which is said to be the **most painful sting** of any insect.

## uff-tailed bumble bee

*mbus terrestris*

**Length** 12–22 mm (½–⅞ in)
**Location** Europe

ne buff-tailed bumble e is usually the first umble bee to emerge ter winter. The oung, fertilized ueens have **thick ir** to protect them uring the cold nonths. They est below ground.

## Carpenter bee

*Xylocopa violacea*

- **Length** 20–23 mm (⅘–1⅖ in)
- **Location** Europe

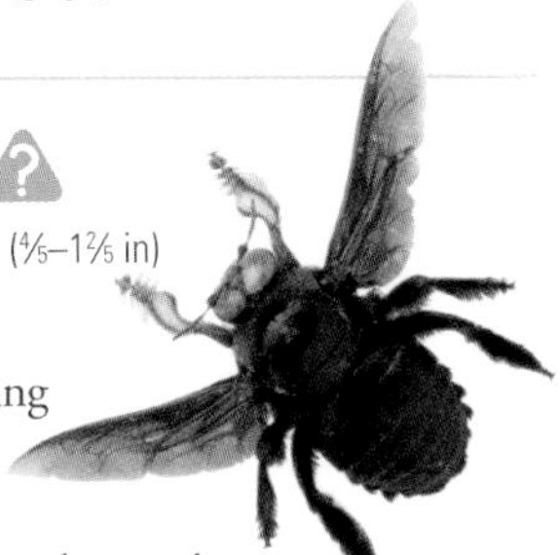

These wood-working bees use their **powerful jaws** to bore tunnels in wood to make their nests. They don't eat the wood, they discard it or use it to create partitions. The male bees aggressively guard the nest, buzzing loudly and dive-bombing anything that comes near. Though it is all for show, they don't pose any real threat as the **males cannot sting**. The females can sting, but aren't aggressive.

## Giant ichneumon wasp

*Rhyssa persuasoria*

- **Length** 40 mm (1⅗ in) + 30 mm (1¼ in) ovipositor
- **Location** Northern hemisphere

The giant ichneumon is a **parasitic wasp**. The female hunts down giant horn-tail wasp grubs by sensing the vibrations they make when chewing through wood. Using her long ovipositor, she drills through the wood and lays her eggs on the grubs. Her babies will grow, slowly **eating their grub host**.

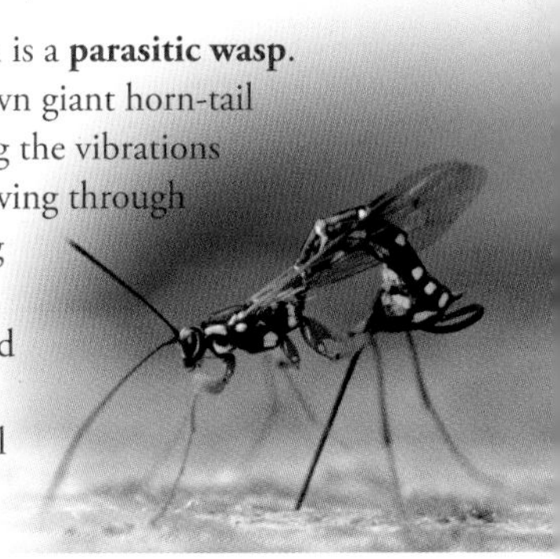

## Hornet

*Vespa crabro*

- **Length** 20–35 mm (⅘–1⅖ in)
- **Location** Europe, Asia, and North America

The hornet is a **social wasp and lives in a colony**, normally upwards of 500 insects. The hornet shoulders a bad reputation because of its imposing look and **aggressive-sounding buzz**. In truth, it rarely stings unless seriously provoked.

## Potter wasp

*Eumenes fraternus*

- **Length** 13–18 mm (½–5⁄7 in)
- **Location** North America

This crafty little wasp gets its name from the **pot-shaped nests** it builds out of mud and water. Inside, it lays a single egg and packs it full of food, usually paralysed caterpillars. Adult potter wasps are **solitary** and feed on nectar.

# Flies

Flies are a large group that covers common house flies to exotic mosquitoes. Most flies have just one pair of wings. But they also have the shrunken remains of a second pair of wings. These are called halteres and act as flight stabilizers, allowing these insects to fly with incredible skill and agility. Flies will eat almost anything, including flesh, blood, faeces, urine, rotting plants, sweat, and nectar.

## FACTFILE

- **Number of species:** 122,000
- **Key features:** Most have large compound eyes. Some have sharp mouths for piercing prey; others have fleshy mouths that suck food.
- **Size:** Examples range from tiny gnats to Australian bottle flies with their 8 cm (3 in) wingspan.

Size comparison

Sucking mouthparts

## Leaf-mining fly
From the Agromyzidae family

- **Length** 1–6 mm (1/32–1/4 in)
- **Diet** Plants, leaves, stems, seeds, and roots
- **Location** Worldwide

Many farmers consider these flies to be a **major pest**. Their larvae will munch their way through the leaves of any plants that they happen to come across and can often destroy an entire crop in this way.

*Mosquito can be dea Females use syringe-like mouthparts to s blood from other animals. Anophele gambiae mosquitoes (below) bite humans, passing on the parasite that causes malaria.*

**Malaria mosquito**
*Anopheles gambiae*

INVERTEBRATES

272

# House fly
*Musca domestica*

- **Length** 5–6 mm (⅕–¼ in)
- **Diet** Organic waste, including leftover food, rotting flesh, and faeces
- **Location** Worldwide

The house fly is **found almost everywhere**, feeding on any food that humans and other animals leave lying around. They help to **spread more than 100 diseases**, including cholera and typhoid. But without them huge amounts of organic waste would not decompose and would just pile up.

# Crane fly
*Tipula paludosa*

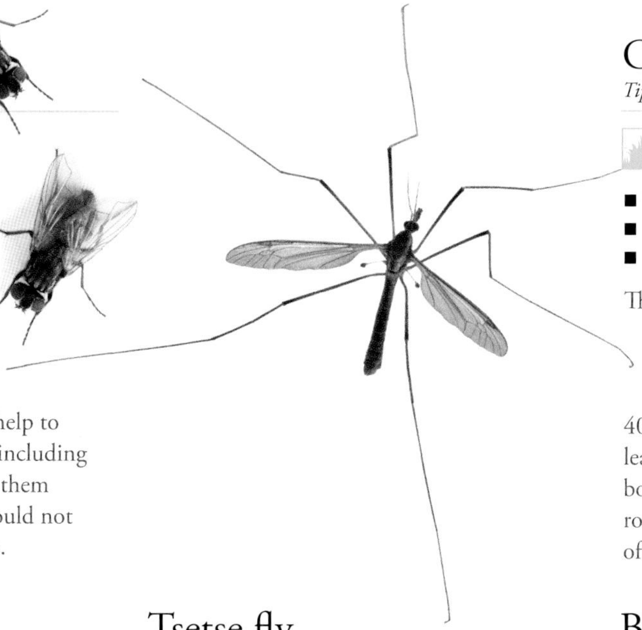

- **Length** 18–25 mm (¾–1 in)
- **Diet** Plant roots, nectar (adults)
- **Location** Worldwide

These **fragile flies** are sometimes known as daddy-long-legs. Despite their large wings, they are **poor fliers** and rarely get very far from the ground. The tough-looking, 40 mm (1½ in) long larvae are called leatherjackets. They live in rotting wood, bogs, and damp soil, where they eat plant roots, especially those of grass. Crane flies often make a tasty snack for passing birds.

# Stalk-eyed fly
*Cyrtodiopsis whitei*

- **Length** 7–10 mm (⅓–⅖ in)
- **Diet** Fungi, bacteria, rotting plants
- **Location** South East Asia

To prove who is the best and therefore most likely to attract a mate, male stalk-eyed flies literally **go eyeball-to-eyeball with each other**. The male with the widest ranging eye stalks usually wins. The loser normally flies off unhurt to search for another male, hopefully smaller than himself, that he can challenge for the right to mate.

# Tsetse fly
*Glossina morsitans*

- **Length** 7–15 mm (⅓–⅔ in)
- **Diet** Blood
- **Location** Africa

Adult tsetse flies are **bloodsuckers**. They use their piercing mouthparts to suck blood from humans and other animals. They can drink up to three times their weight in blood in one sitting. By feeding in this way, tsetse flies help to **spread a fatal sleeping sickness** that affects people and cattle.

*Abdomen swollen with blood after feeding*

*Before feeding*

# Blue bottle fly
*Calliphora vomitoria*

- **Length** 10–15 mm (⅖–⅔ in)
- **Diet** Rotting meat and plants, faeces
- **Location** Europe, North America, and Northern Asia

These flies can **sniff out any rotting flesh or faeces that is lying around**, even from as far away as 8 km (5 miles). Their **disgusting diet** means that blue bottles do an important job in helping to clear away a lot of undesirable organic waste. The female fly lays her eggs, up to 2,000, while she is feeding.

# Hornet robber fly
*Asilus crabroniformis*

- **Length** 20–25 mm (⅘–1 in)
- **Diet** Insects, decaying organic matter
- **Location** Europe

Huge eyes, a long, thin body, and grasping spined legs make this fly an **excellent aerial hunter**. Its dagger-like mouthparts inject paralysing saliva into its prey, which it sucks up.

# Bee fly
*Bombylius major*

- **Length** 12–15 mm (½–⅔ in)
- **Diet** Nectar, bee grubs
- **Location** Europe, North America, Northern Asia

With its stout, furry body and high-pitched whine the bee fly does a good job of **mimicking a bee**. But the long, rigid proboscis (feeding tube) held out in front of its head gives the game away. A bee's proboscis curls up when not in use. Bee fly larvae live as parasites in the nests of solitary bees. Here they feed on stored nectar and bee grubs.

*Proboscis*

*Halteres*

# Butterflies and moths

The marvellous patterns and brilliant colours of their wings mean that butterflies are a more welcome sight than most insects. But many members of the huge group of animals to which they belong are in fact tiny, hairy, brown moths. These delicate-looking creatures are also much tougher than they appear. Some can survive in deserts and even the freezing Arctic.

## FACTFILE

- **Number of species:** 168,000
- **Key features:** Four wings and large compound eyes. Most have a long, coiled feeding tube (proboscis).
- **Size:** Largest moth: Atlas (*Attacus atlas*); smallest butterfly: Western pygmy blue (*Brephidium exilis*).

Size comparison

MONARCH BUTTERFLY *Every winter, tens of millions of these butterflies migrate from the cold of Canada and the eastern United States to the warm sunshine of Mexico and California. Some fly over 4,000 km (2,500 miles).*

METAMORPHOSIS *When a butterfly's or moth's egg hatches, a caterpillar crawls out. Its main job is to eat and grow, until it is as big as it can be. Then it stops eating and a tough, leathery coat forms around it. It is now a pupa. Inside this protective coat, the caterpillar changes into a winged adult. When it is ready, the new moth or butterfly emerges and flies away.*

Caterpillar hatches

Pupa forms

New butterfly emerges

Ready for take-off

## Atlas moth
*Attacus atlas*

- **Wingspan** 20–28 cm (8–11 in)
- **Location** S. China, S.E. Asia

This giant is the **largest species of moth** in the world. But being so big does not seem to stop many other animals from ~~t~~empting to hunt it down and make a meal of ~~it~~. To help scare off predators, this moth's wings ~~ha~~ve **special protective markings** that look very ~~sim~~ilar to those found on a highly poisonous ~~cob~~ra snake. The atlas moth secretes a wool-like ~~sil~~k that is used for cloth in parts of China.

## Postman butterfly
*Heliconius melpomene*

- **Wingspan** 8–10 cm (3–4 in)
- **Location** Central and N. South America

This colourful butterfly lives for six months or more. Most moths and butterflies only live for a few weeks and the **long life** of this species may be due to its highly nutritious diet. Like all butterflies and moths it sucks up nectar from flowers using its **long proboscis**, or feeding tube. At the same time, it takes up large amounts of pollen, which is particularly rich in health-giving nutrients.

## Indian leaf butterfly
*Kallima inachus*

- **Wingspan** 6–8 cm (2½–3 in)
- **Location** N. India, W. China

This butterfly is **difficult to see** when it is at rest. This is because the colouring on its underside makes it **look like a leaf**. But if it is disturbed, it rapidly opens its wings, flashing the bright blue and orange of its upper surface. This change confuses predators, giving the butterfly a few seconds to escape being eaten.

## ~~P~~eacock butterfly
*~~In~~achis io*

- **Wingspan** 5.5–6 cm (2–2½ in)
- **Location** Europe, N. Asia

~~A~~dult peacock butterflies **hibernate all winter** ~~in~~ sheltered spots, such as a hollow in a tree, a cavity in a building, or even a garden shed. On the first sunny days of spring, the females emerge and fly off to look for stinging nettles on which they lay their eggs. Each **female lays about 500 eggs.**

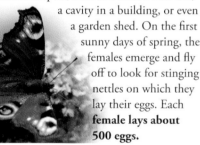

## Death's head hawk moth
*Acherontia atropos*

- **Wingspan** 9–12 cm (3½–4¾ in)
- **Location** S. Europe, W. Asia

This moth **loves honey** and breaks into beehives to get at it. The bees sometimes attack, but usually they ignore it, possibly because this moth can give off a scent that makes it **smell like a bee**. It is also quite noisy. The caterpillar makes a clicking sound by grinding its jaws and the adult squeaks loudly.

## Morpho butterfly
*Morpho peleides*

- **Wingspan** 9–11.5 cm (3½–4½ in)
- **Location** Central and South America

The scales on this butterfly's wings are actually transparent, not blue, and act **like prisms**. The blue colouring is caused by the way these "prisms" split up sunlight falling on the wings into its component colours. The wings are so **bright** that they are visible from 1 km (⅝ mile) away.

## ~~S~~unset moth
*~~C~~hrysiridia croesus*

- **Wingspan** 9–11 cm (3½–4¼ in)
- **Location** East Africa

This is one of the few moths that **flies during the day**. Like other day-flying moths, it is brightly coloured. Like the morpho butterfly, its **dazzling colours** are not due to special pigments, but are caused by having prism-like scales on its wings. In this case, these scales split up the sunlight striking them into a rainbow of colours.

## Orange-barred sulphur butterfly
*Phoebis philea*

- **Wingspan** 7–8.5 cm (2¾–3¼ in)
- **Location** S. USA, Central and South America

At the height of summer, thousands of these shimmering, golden-yellow butterflies **gather together** on the banks of dry riverbeds. They are there to **suck up the mud**, which has large quantities of nutritious minerals dissolved in it. This unusual activity is known as "mud puddling".

INVERTEBRATES

# Moths and Butterflies

There are about 170,000 species of butterfly and moth and 90 per cent of them are moths. It can be difficult to tell a moth from a butterfly. Most butterflies fly during the day and most moths fly at night. Moth antennae range from single strands to feathery branches. Butterflies have clubbed antennae.

**Goat moth**
*Cossus cossus*

## MOTHS

**African moon moth**
*Argema mimosae*

**Owl moth**
*Brahmaea wallichii*

**Provence burnet moth**
*Zygaena occitanica*

**Oak eggar**
*Lasciocampa quercus*

**Madagascan sunset moth**
*Chrysiridia rhipheus*

**Hoop pine moth**
*Milionia isodoxa*

**Buff-tip**
*Phalera bucephala*

**Hieroglyphic moth**
*Diphthera festiva*

**Magpie moth**
*Abraxas grossulariata*

**Garden tiger moth**
*Arctia caja*

**White witch moth**
*Thysania agrippina*

**Pale tussock**
*Calliteara pudibunda*

**Hornet moth**
*Sesia apiformis*

**Verdant sphinx hawk-moth**
*Euchloron megaera*

INVERTEBRATES

# BUTTERFLIES

**Peacock butterfly**
*Inachis io*

**Small copper**
*Lycaena phlaeas*

**Cocoa mort bleu**
*Caligo teucer*

**Chequered skipper**
*Carterocephalus palaemon*

**Queen Alexandra's birdwing**
*Ornithoptera alexandrae*

The Queen Alexandra's birdwing is the **largest butterfly** with a wingspan of up to 28 cm (11 in). The small copper has a wingspan of 2.5 cm (1 in).

**Lesser grass blue butterfly**
*Zizina otis*

**African giant swallowtail**
*Papilio antimachus*

**Japanese emperor**
*Sasakia charonda*

**Viceroy**
*Limenitis archippus*

**Blue morpho**
*Morpho menelaus*

**Cairns birdwing**
*Ornithoptera priamus*

**Hewitson's blue hairstreak**
*Thecla coronata*

**Great spangled fritillary**
*Speyeria cybele*

**Great orange tip**
*Hebomoia glaucippe*

INVERTEBRATES

277

# Scorpions

The scorpion's thick armour plating makes it the arachnid equivalent of a battle tank. It has four pairs of legs, two strong pincers, and a long, curling tail. The tail carries a venomous sting. This is mainly a weapon of defence but can also be used to paralyze prey. The venom of some species is lethal to humans. Scorpions spend most of the day in the shade, coming out to hunt at night.

## They think I'm a **taxi** service!

Scorpions give birth to live young. After they emerge, the female carries the whole brood on her back wherever she goes. Sometimes there can be as many as a hundred babies holding on. Until a young scorpion develops its own hard shell and tail stinger, it needs its mother to protect it against predators.

### PINCER MOVEMENT
*Scorpions use their pincers to catch and hold on to prey. If the prey is small enough, the scorpion simply crushes it to death.*

# Giant desert hairy scorpion

*Hadrurus arizonensis*

■ **Length** 10–15 cm (4–6 in)
■ **Location** USA

This is the largest native scorpion in North America. It gets its name from its size, and the brown hairs on its tail and legs. These **hairs detect air and ground vibrations** and are useful in finding prey. Usually this scorpion lies in wait, ready to ambush a suitable victim. Although this scorpion's **eyesight is poor**, its senses of hearing and touch are excellent.

▲ DEFENCE TACTICS *When threatened, a scorpion lifts its two pincers and waves them aggressively at its attacker. If this doesn't work, it will bring its tail forward to sting the aggressor.*

▼ RANGE OF SIZE *The emperor scorpion is one of the largest species and grows to more than 20 cm (8 in) in length. Originally from Africa, these scorpions are sometimes kept as pets, despite their painful sting. Numbers are threatened by over-collection. The European scorpion is only about 3 cm (1⅕ in) long and shelters in wall crevices. Its sting is only mildly painful.*

EUROPEAN
SCORPION

EMPEROR
SCORPION

INVERTEBRATES

# Spiders

Spiders creep about on eight long legs. Most of them have eight eyes as well. The size of a spider ranges from a few millimetres to 30 cm (1 ft). Spiders can be found in a wide variety of habitats. Many live in burrows in the ground. Others find their way into our homes.

▲ WATER SPIDER *(Argyroneta aquatica)* *This is the only species that lives under water. It survives by spinning an air-bell to live in. Females wrap their eggs in silk and spend most of their time inside the bell.*

▼ CRAB SPIDER *(Misumena vatia) This spider, often sitting like a crab, waits on flowers for its prey. It catches large meals, including butterflies and bees.*

## SILK SPINNERS

Spiders have many different uses for the silk they make. Lots of spiders spin webs as a trap for their prey. Then they can sit and wait for their food to arrive. Silk cocoons are made to protect spiders' eggs. Spiders also use silk to line and seal their burrows.

**Female king baboon spider**
*Citharischius crawshayi*

▶ BABOON SPIDER
*Like other tarantulas, the king baboon spider comes out at night to hunt. It feeds on a variety of animals including lizards, large insects, and mice.*

### FACTFILE

- **Number of species:** There are about 40,000 species of spider.
- **Key features:** Predatory animals that have two body segments and eight legs. All spiders produce silk, but not all use it to trap their prey. Most have venom, though only 200 species of spiders possess a bite that is harmful to humans.

Size comparison

# Northern black widow
*Latrodectus variolus*

- **Length** 15–40 mm (⅗–1½ in)
- **Location** North America

Black widows possess a **potent neurotoxic venom.** The bright hourglass markings warn its predators not to eat it. The female is bigger, lives longer, and is more venomous than the male. Over a summer, a female will produce 6–9 sacs of eggs, each containing 200–400 eggs.

# European cave spider
*Meta menardi*

- **Length** 40–50 mm (1½–2 in)
- **Location** Europe

The **adult cave spider is photophobic,** meaning it doesn't like light and searches for caves, tunnels, and dark holes. In complete contrast, the baby cave spiders are attracted to light. This is thought to allow the species to spread beyond the home cave. Cave spiders **prey on smaller invertebrates**, especially slugs. They possess venom, but it isn't strong. This, coupled with their lack of aggression, has landed them the tag of "gentle giants".

# Brown huntsman spider
*Heteropoda venatoria*

- **Length** 75–125 mm (3–5 in)
- **Location** North America, Asia, and Australia

The brown huntsman gets its name from its **ability to hunt its prey using speed** and its powerful mouth parts. It does have the ability to spin a tangle web, but the web is only used to slow down prey. This spider **feeds on cockroaches**, which makes it a welcome visitor to households. It does have a **venomous bite**, although it isn't too powerful, and it is more likely to flee when disturbed.

# Indian ornamental spider
*Poecilotheria regalis*

- **Length** 180–230 mm (7–9 in)
- **Location** India

The Indian ornamental spider belongs to the tarantula family. It usually lives high in trees, its **long legs** helping it to climb. The female is a silver-grey and is larger than the brown male. In the wild, the Indian ornamental spider is **lightning fast** and has a strong venom. It preys on large insects, lizards, and birds.

# King baboon spider
*Citharischius crawshayi*

- **Length** 120–200 mm (4¾–7⅘ in)
- **Location** Eastern Africa

This is an **aggressive** spider. It will attack with little reason and inject venom through its long fangs. When threatened, it rears up to show its fangs and **hisses**. It is active at night, searching for prey and excavating its burrow, which can go down more than 2 m (6½ ft).

# Spiny-bellied orb weaver
*Gasteracantha cancriformis*

- **Length** 2–9 mm (⅟₁₃–⅓ in)
- **Width** 9–13 mm (⅓–½ in)
- **Location** North and South America

The spiny-bellied orb weaver is easily identified by its **brightly coloured and pointy body**. The females are larger than the males, and they live a **solitary life** within their webs. The web can be 1–6 m (3¼–19½ feet) off the ground and is a series of loops and spirals. The webs have a catching area of up to 60 cm (2 ft), trapping whiteflies, moths, and beetles.

# Spider *silk*

Spiders are known for producing silk. The silk
is made from protein and is produced by small
organs called spinnerets. Many spiders use silk to
catch prey, usually by building a web into which
insects fly and get stuck. Other spiders use silk
to transport themselves on the breeze.

## FACTFILE

- Spider silk never decays or dries out.
- The silk thread of an orb-web spider can be stretched by up to 50 per cent of its original length before it breaks.
- Some trapdoor spiders lay "signal" threads outside their burrow. If something touches a line, the spider rushes out to catch its victim.
- The bolas spider *(Mastophora cornigera)* throws a thread with a sticky ball on the end at its prey. The prey then gets stuck to the ball.

▲ IN A SPIN *Orb-web spiders build webs that radiate out from a central hub. They then fill in the gaps between the strong framework strands with a long spiral of sticky silk thread.*

▲ DECORATION *The spider* Cyclosa insulana *decorates its web with bands of silk. No-one is sure why it does this, but it may be to hide the spider from view, to strengthen the web, or to stop birds flying into it and breaking it.*

**TARANTULAS** Many tarantulas use silk to line their burrows. This may be to stop the burrows falling in and to keep them moist. Some tarantulas also produce sticky silk on their feet that helps them grip when climbing vertical surfaces.

◄ ZIGZAGS *The silver argiope spider* (Argiope argentata) *can be found from the USA down to northern South America. It is known for the dense, zigzag-shaped webbing that it makes on plants. Sometimes these spiders sit in the middle of their web with their legs in the shape of an X.*

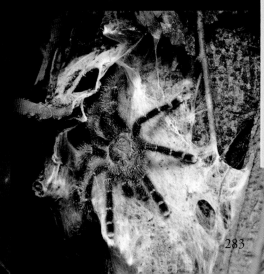

# Crustaceans

This large group of arthropods includes the familiar, the colourful, and the tidy. Most crustaceans live under water, either fresh or marine, though some have joined us on land. This move isn't for everyone – some hitch a ride on other animals, while others cling for life on rocks.

## A PARASITIC LIFE

Some crustaceans live attached to other animals. These are known as parasites. Some parasitic crustaceans, such as sea lice, cling to the skin of fish, but can swim independently. Others, like the tongue worm, are more dependent on their hosts. It attaches its tongue-shaped body to reptiles, birds, and mammals using five mouth-like appendages. Tongue worms rely on the host's blood supply to provide them with food to live and reproduce.

### FOLLOW THE LEADER
*This mysterious single-file migration of the Caribbean spiny lobster is triggered by a drop in water temperature. The exact reason for the migration is unknown, but biologists believe it is to mate and find warmer waters.*

## Caribbean spiny lobster
*Panulirus argus*

15

- **Length** 20–60 cm (8–24 in)
- **Location** Western Atlantic Ocean

The Caribbean spiny lobster is a **shy, nocturnal crustacean** that hides among reefs and coral during the day for protection. Unlike most lobsters its claws are weak, so it relies on chemical receptors or antennae to locate food. It ventures out at night to **scavenge for food**, feeding on the remains of dead sea creatures and plants it finds on the seabed.

# dpole shrimp
*os cancriformis*

■ **ength** 20–40 mm (⅘–1⅗ in)
■ **ocation** Europe

dpole shrimps have hardly
nged for 220 million years, and
considered **living fossils**. They
born survivors and multiply in
ge numbers in perfect conditions,
ile their eggs can survive freezing
mperatures and drought. They also
the award for the crustacean with
e **most legs**, with up to 35 pairs.

# Peacock mantis shrimp
*Odontodactylus scyllarus*

■ **Length** 12–18 cm (4–7 in)
■ **Location** Indo-Pacific

This rainbow-coloured shrimp may look
pretty, but it harbours a **nasty surprise**. It
loiters in its burrow using its super-sensitive
eyesight to locate lunch. It then
**ambushes** at lightning speeds
grabbing with its
powerful
claws.

# Water flea
*Daphnia pulex*

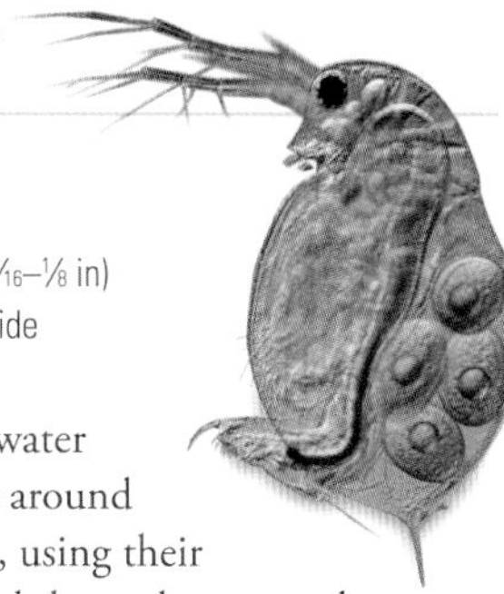

■ **Length** 2–5 mm (¹⁄₁₆–⅛ in)
■ **Location** Worldwide

These small freshwater
crustaceans move around
in a jerky fashion, using their
antennae to propel themselves towards
their lunch. They prey on smaller
crustaceans, though are generally **filter
feeders**, sucking up single-celled organisms.
Water fleas have to mate to reproduce, and
the young fleas are **reared in a pouch** inside
the adult's exoskeleton.

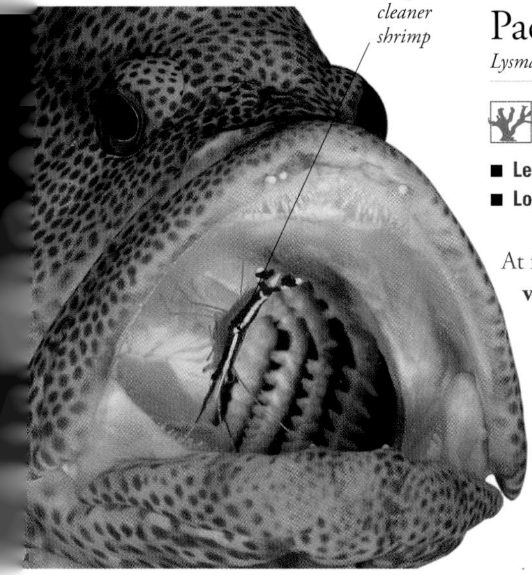

*Pacific cleaner shrimp*

# Pacific cleaner shrimp
*Lysmata amboinensis*

■ **Length** 60–70 mm (2½–3 in)
■ **Location** Red Sea and Indo-Pacific

At first glance these helpful little shrimp looks
**very well trained** or possibly mad. They
gather together to provide **"cleaning
stations"** on coral reefs, where they
remove dead tissue and parasites from
various fish (including some that are the
shrimps' **natural predators**). Cleaner
shrimp have a selfish motive though –
they are **scavengers**, and they naturally
feed on the material they remove.

# Robber crab
*Birgus latro*

■ **Length** 100–150 cm (40–60 in) (outstretched legs)
■ **Location** Indian and Western Pacific oceans

Robber crabs only live
28 days in the sea before
opting for a life on land.
**Living in burrows**, they
have been found up to
6 km (2 miles) inland.
They are also known
as coconut crabs for their love of coconuts.
Good climbers, they have **powerful claws** that
allow them to crack open their favourite food.

# Common woodlouse
*Oniscus asellus*

■ **Length** 10–16 mm (⅖–⅗ in)
■ **Location** Western and Northern Europe

These are one of the biggest woodlice in
Europe. They thrive in damp, dark
environments, and happily **eat dead plants**
and rotting animals. They are known as
decomposers, and they **help to decay and
recycle vast amounts of organic waste**.

# Goose-necked barnacle
*Pollicipes polymerus*

■ **Length** 10–15 cm (4–6 in)
■ **Location** Northern and Eastern Pacific

The name "goose-necked" comes
from the fleshy, **leathery stalk**
that the barnacle uses to cling
to rocks. It is a **filter feeder**
and catches smaller crustaceans
and plankton. In the Middle
Ages, people thought these
barnacles were young geese
trapped on the riverbed.

# Spider crabs

Spider crabs are instantly recognizable by their triangular shell, or carapace, and their long, thin legs. They pick up sponges, seaweed, anemones, and even bits of wood, which they attach to hairs on their body and legs to act as a disguise. They will swap their decorations to match new surroundings.

## It gets **chilly** down here!

With a body the size of a large dinner plate, and its long, extendable legs, the Japanese spider crab walks across the sea floor like an enormous mechanical spider. It lurks in the deepest parts of the ocean, often around hot-water vents in the Earth's crust.

## Japanese spider crab

*Macrocheira kaempferi*

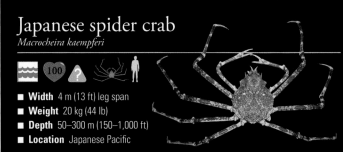

- **Width** 4 m (13 ft) leg span
- **Weight** 20 kg (44 lb)
- **Depth** 50–300 m (150–1,000 ft)
- **Location** Japanese Pacific

These crabs are the largest members of the crab family and the biggest living arthropod. They usually have a **knobbly orange body** and legs with **white spots**. The biggest specimens have a body 37 cm (15 in) wide, with each leg measuring up to 2 m (6½ ft) long.

▶ NASTY NIPPERS

*Male Japanese spider crabs are bigger than females, and their front legs grow longer. Both sexes have a pair of pincers that are capable of prising open mollusc shells. The crab's other eight legs end in spikes that it uses to dig into the sea floor.*

A TASTY LUNCH
*Although the Japanese spider crab is the biggest crustacean in the ocean it is still preyed upon by even larger predators, such as the giant octopus. It is also caught by fishermen.*

## PICKY EATERS

Despite their long limbs, these leggy crustaceans don't break any speed records. Often too slow to catch speedy live prey, they pick a way across the sea bed looking for dead animals or slow invertebrates. Some have been seen to eat plants and algae. The front claws are used to pick lunch to pieces and pass it into the mouth.

◄ PORTLY SPIDER CRAB
*(Libinia emarginata) The portly spider crab is a species of crab found in river estuaries. This crab grows a "garden" of sponges and seaweed across its back. The carapace is shiny and covered with short hairs. These trap microscopic sea creatures that then set up home here. The portly spider crab is slow moving, and eats what it can find.*

# Centipedes and millipede

Despite looking similar, centipedes and millipedes have evolved in very different directions. Millipedes have become slow-moving, heavily armoured herbivores, while centipedes are fast, lightweight predators. Anothe major difference is in the number of legs – millipedes have two pairs on each segment, centipedes only one.

**Giant African millipede**
*Archispirostreptus gigas*

## PILL MILLIPEDE

■ **At first glance the pill millipede** looks similar to a land crustacean called a woodlouse. However, the millipede has a large shield-like plate behind its head, more legs, and a glossy black appearance.

◄ *Pill millipedes have thirteen smooth body segments. A woodlouse has eleven rough segments.*

▶ *If attacked by a predator the pill millipede can roll itself into an armour-plated ball.*

## My feet **really** hurt...

The front pair of legs in all centipedes has evolved into hollow fangs through which they inject poison into their victim. The walking legs of the giant desert centipede are also tipped with sharp claws that can cut human skin and drip poison into the wound.

# at-backed cyanide llipede
*aphe haydeniana*

- **ength** 30–40 mm (1½–2 in)
- **ocation** North America

h its black and yellow **warning colours**, this ipede has few predators. If it is threatened ecretes pungent-smelling, highly toxic rogen cyanide through pores in its side. So only one ground beetle has been discovered t can deal with this **defence mechanism**. males have 31 pairs of legs while males have y 30 pairs of legs.

# Giant desert centipede
*Scolopendra heros*

- **Length** 130–150 mm (5–6 in)
- **Location** USA

Giant desert centipedes are extremely efficient predators. They are **capable of sprinting** at speeds of up to 0.5 m (1⅗ ft) per second and use all of their 21 pairs of legs to ensnare their prey before delivering a **paralysing bite**. Centipedes can kill large prey such as lizards and mice. Females will protect their eggs and watch over juveniles until they can fend for themselves.

*Claw-tipped leg*

*Segmented body*

# arden centipede
*hobius forficatus*

- **Length** 20–30 mm (¾–1½ in)
- **Location** Europe

his **common species** is found in rdens. **At night they hunt** for all invertebrates that hide under cks and fallen logs. In gardens, e underside of a plant pot akes a good place for them go in search of food. If ey are uncovered they will uickly run for shelter.

# Cave centipede
*Scutigera coleoptrata*

- **Length** 30–60 mm (1½–2½ in) including legs
- **Location** Europe, Asia and North America

Perfectly evolved for life in caves, this centipede has **long legs and antennae** that allow it to feel for its prey in the pitch black. Once the prey is located, the centipede swiftly pounces and injects a **potent venom** to kill it. They are also found in the basements and cellars of houses, where they feed on spiders, ants, cockroaches, and other pests.

# Red-legged millipede
*Epibolus pulchripes*

- **Length** 110–150 mm (4¼–6 in)
- **Location** Africa

Found mainly in grassy areas near the coast, the red-legged millipede prefers to **forage at night**. It does this because it is cooler and there is less chance of it dehydrating, a danger for all terrestrial invertebrates. Like all millipedes the red-legged millipede feeds on vegetable matter, and can **cause damage** to seedlings and crops.

*Red legs*

# Giant centipede
*colopendra hardwickii*

- **Length** 260–350 mm (10¼–13½ in)
- **Location** South America

Few animals will try nd tackle a fully rown giant centipede. However, if another creature does try to make a meal of one of these it will have to deal with its **venomous** bite, 46 powerful clawed legs, and a pair of **needle-tipped appendages** at the rear end.

▼ ON THE ATTACK
*Giant centipedes have been known to attack prey that is almost as big as themselves, including mice and bats.*

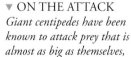

289

# Echinoderms

Echinoderms are found in seas and oceans all over the world. They include starfish, sea urchins, brittlestars, sea cucumbers, and sea lilies and featherstars. Many are vividly coloured. This is because of special pigment cells in the skin. In some species, these cells are sensitive to light and the animal changes colour as night falls.

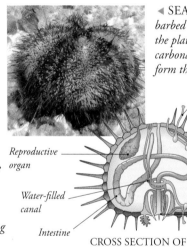
## Brittlestar
*Ophiura ophiura*

- **Length** 8–10 cm (3–4 in) leg span
- **Diet** Molluscs, crustaceans, sea worms, plankton
- **Location** N.E. Atlantic Ocean

Like all brittlestars, of which there are several thousand species, this one has five long, **flexible arms** that radiate out from a disc-like body. It uses these snake-like limbs to swim away from danger. Brittlestars often feed on decaying matter, but this one is also an **active predator**. To snare its prey, it loops its long arms around its victim.

## Violet sea apple
*Pseudocolochirus violaceus*

- **Length** 15–17 cm (6–6½ in)
- **Diet** Plankton (filter feeder)
- **Location** E. Indian Ocean, W. Pacific Ocean

This is a type of sea cucumber. Its soft body can be a variety of different colours, although its feet are always yellow and the area around its mouth is usually blue or violet. It feeds by extending the ring of **feathery tentacles** that surround its mouth, using them to trap bits of food and tiny organisms that are flowing past in the sea current. It then pulls the tentacles into its mouth, drawing in its catch. If a violet sea apple is injured or disturbed, it often reacts by **releasing a poison** that can kill many small fish and other small sea animals.

INVERTEBRATES

## ue sea star
*kia laevigata*

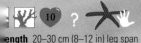

- **ength** 20–30 cm (8–12 in) leg span
- **iet** Decaying organic matter, plankton, molluscs
- **ocation** Indian Ocean, W. and C. Pacific Ocean

**striking colour** makes this sea star one he most eye-catching inhabitants of the al reef. Some individuals are also bright nge. Like all echinoderms, the blue sea r can **re-grow any lost limbs**. But the lity of this species to do this is particularly pressive. If the animal is pulled apart by redator, any legs that do not get eaten grow into a completely new sea star.

## Cotton-spinner sea cucumber
*Holothuria forskali*

- **Length** 20–25 cm (8–10 in)
- **Diet** Plankton (filter feeder)
- **Location** N.E. Atlantic Ocean

If a cotton-spinner is attacked, it has an extraordinary defence mechanism. It **expels its internal organs**, including its entire digestive, respiratory, and reproductive systems. This sticky mass not only confuses a predator, but can trap and entangle it as well. Over time, **new replacement organs** grow back inside the cotton-spinner's body.

## Common starfish
*Asterias rubens*

- **Length** 20–50 cm (8–20 in) leg span
- **Diet** Molluscs, crustaceans, sea worms, plankton
- **Location** N.E. Atlantic Ocean

**Huge groups** of common starfish are often found in places where the feeding is good. Sometimes as many as 800 can be seen packed together in a single square metre. Starfish enjoy eating bivalve molluscs, such as mussels and clams. The starfish grabs its prey and uses its tube feet to prize open the bivalve's shell. Then it **pushes its stomach out of its body** and into the shell, where it digests the now defenceless animal.

## eather star
*tedon petasus*

- **Length** 17–23 cm (6½–9 in)
- **Diet** Plankton (filter feeder)
- **Location** N.E. Atlantic Ocean

his feather star has **ten arms** and likes to nake its home in sheltered places, half-hidden y rocks, or in a wreck. All feather stars spend the first months of their lives attached by a stalk to a pebble, or seaweed. They break free and swim off as soon as their arms have fully developed.

## Crown-of-thorns starfish
*Acanthaster planci*

- **Length** 30–40 cm (12–16 in) leg span
- **Diet** Corals, molluscs, sea urchins, algae
- **Location** Red Sea, Indian Ocean, Pacific Ocean

This is the world's **largest starfish**. For protection it has a dense coat of thorny spines. If it is touched or stepped on, these **spines release a toxin** that can cause severe pain, nausea, and vomiting. Corals are this starfish's favourite food. Its voracious appetite has **damaged many coral reefs**, including the vast Great Barrier Reef off the coast of Australia.

# Glossary

**Aerial** relating to air.

**Agile** able to move quickly and easily.

**Amphibian** a type of cold-blooded vertebrate, such as a frog or newt. Most amphibians develop from larvae that live in water and breathe through gills, and become land-dwelling adults that breathe air through lungs.

**Anal** of fins, near the tail.

**Antenna** movable sense organ on the head of animals such as insects and crustaceans.

**Antler** bony growth, often branched, on a deer's head. Unlike horns, antlers usually grow and are later shed every year.

**Aquatic** living or growing in or near water.

**Arachnid** a type of animal, such as a spider or scorpion, that has a two-part body and four pairs of legs.

**Arboreal** living in or connected with trees.

**Artery** a vessel that carries blood away from the heart.

**Arthropod** an animal with a segmented body, jointed limbs, and a hard, outer covering.

**Australasia** a term used to describe the area that includes Australia, New Zealand, Papua New Guinea, and neighbouring islands in the Pacific Ocean.

**Baleen** brush-like fringe that some whales have at the back of their mouth to strain food from the water.

**Beak** a set of narrow, protruding jaws, usually without teeth.

**Blowhole** nostril on top of the head of whales, dolphins, and porpoises; hole in the ice that aquatic mammals breathe through.

**Blubber** the thick layer of fat that protects some animals (like whales and seals) from the cold.

**Bovid** animal family with hooves divided in two (called cloven hooves).

**Breed** to produce young.

**Bristles** short, stiff, coarse hairs.

**Buoyancy** the tendency of a body or an object to float in water.

**Burrow** a hole in the ground that some animals (such as rabbits) live in.

**Camouflage** colours or patterns on an animal's skin or fur that allow it to blend with its surroundings.

**Carnivorous** often used to describe animals that eat meat, but also refers to animals in the order Carnivora, such as bears and cats, all of which have long, sharp teeth.

**Carrion** the remains of dead animals.

**Cartilage** firm, flexible tissue that is part of the skeleton of vertebrates. In fish such as sharks, the entire skeleton is made of cartilage.

**Cell** the smallest existing unit of living matter.

**Claw** pointed, horny nail on an animal foot.

**Cnidarian** a type of simple aquatic animal such as a sea anemone.

**Colony** a group of animals (such as penguins) that live together.

**Comb** fleshy crest on a bird's head.

**Coniferous** referring to a tree with scaly cones that contain seeds.

**Courtship** the process by which animals attract their mates.

**Crèche** a group formed by the chicks of some birds such as flamingos, terns, and ostriches.

**Crustacean** a type of arthropod, mainly aquatic, that has a hard shell.

**Dabbling** the action of a waterbird when it upends to reach food deep down in the water with its beak.

**ciduous** referring to a tree that sheds
leaves in autumn and grows new ones
spring.

**n** a safe resting place for an animal.

**urnal** active during the day.

**hinoderm** a type of symmetrical
arine animal such as a starfish.

**holocation** locating distant or
visible objects by bouncing sound waves
them.

**nvironment** the natural world all around
, including land, air, and living things.

**xotic** dramatically unusual; introduced
om another country.

**xtinct** no longer existing on Earth.

**alconry** the sport of training falcons or
sing them to catch game.

**ang** the tooth an animal uses to seize
nd tear its prey.

**lank** the side of an animal between the
ibs and the hip.

**Flipper** an aquatic mammal's paddle-
shaped limb.

**Flock** a group of birds or mammals
assembled together.

**Fluke** a rubbery tail flipper on whales
and similar creatures.

**Forage** to wander in search of food.

**Forelimb/forefoot** a limb or foot at the
front of an animal's body.

**Gam** a large group of whales that travel
together.

**Gills** feathery structures on the side of a
fish's head that extract oxygen from the water.

**Gnaw** to bite or nibble continuously.

**Graze** to feed on growing grass and other
green plants.

**Grooming** describes an animal's
behaviour when it cleans itself or another
animal.

**Habitat** the place, or type of place, where
a plant or animal lives naturally.

**Harem** often used to describe a group of
female animals under the protection of
one male.

**Hatch** to emerge from an egg or a pupa;
to keep an egg warm so it will hatch.

**Hatchling** recently hatched young (for
example, a turtle).

**Heath** a large area of uncultivated land,
usually with peaty soil; see moor.

**Herd** a large group of animals that feed
and travel together.

**Hibernate** to go into a deep sleep-like
state, usually during the winter.

**Hindlimb/hindfoot** a limb or foot at the
rear of an animal's body.

**Hooves** the horny feet that animals such
as horses and reindeer have.

**Horn** a hard, pointed growth, usually
hollow, on some mammals' heads.

**Immune** having a high level of resistance
to one or more diseases.

**Incisor** in mammals, a flat tooth at the
front of the jaw used for slicing or
gnawing.

**Insectivores** animals that eat insects.

**Invertebrate** an animal without a
backbone.

**Keratin** a tough protein found in hair,
nails, claws, hooves, and horns.

**Lair** a home or resting place of a wild
animal.

**Larva** the immature wormlike form that
hatches from the egg of many insects.

**Litter** a group of young animals born to
the same mother at the same time.

**Lodge** the den or lair of a group of
animals such as beavers.

**Luminous** giving off light; bright.

**Mammal** a warm-blooded animal that
feeds its young on milk produced by the
female.

**Mane** the long, thick hair that grows on
the neck of some animals, such as horses
and male lions.

**Marine** connected with the sea.

**Marsupial** a type of mammal with a pouch on the female's abdomen to hold developing young.

**Migration** moving from one place to another according to the seasons, usually to find food or to breed.

**Mollusc** a type of invertebrate that has a soft body without segments, and – usually but not always – a shell.

**Monotreme** an egg-laying mammal such as a platypus.

**Monsoon** seasonal wind accompanied by heavy rain.

**Moor** a large area of uncultivated land, usually with peaty soil; see heath.

**Mudflat** muddy area of ground exposed at low tide, but under water at high tide.

**Muscle** a type of living tissue that contracts and relaxes to produce movement.

**Mustelid** one of a family of predatory mammals such as weasels, ferrets, or badgers.

**Mute** silent.

**Necking** a mating ritual of male giraffes in which they lock necks and sometimes clash heads.

**Nectar** sweet liquid, produced by flowers; some birds and insects feed on nectar.

**Nest** a structure built by birds or insects, usually to lay eggs in.

**Nocturnal** active at night.

**Nursing** referring to a female mammal feeding her young on her milk.

**Offspring** the young of a person, animal, or plant.

**Operculum** the body flap that covers a fish's gills.

**Organism** an individual member of a biological species.

**Ossicone** small horn covered with skin.

**Pacing** a distinctive walk in which both legs on the same side move together, then both legs move together on the opposite side; seen in camels and their relatives.

**Pack** a group of animals that join together for activities such as hunting.

**Passerine** a perching songbird such as a warbler or a thrush.

**Patagium** a skinflap, such as a bat's wing, used for flying or gliding through the air.

**Pectoral** of fins, behind the head.

**Pelvic** of fins, on the underside.

**Perch** to settle or rest, often briefly.

**Photophore** a light-emitting organ, especially one of the luminous spots on some marine fish.

**Pigment** a substance that colours other materials.

**Pinniped** one of a group of mammals, such as seals and walruses, that have flippers instead of feet.

**Placenta** the organ inside the womb of a female mammal that nourishes the developing young.

**Plankton** the mass of tiny plants and animals that float around in the sea and provide food for marine animals.

**Plumage** a bird's feathers.

**Predator** an animal that hunts, kills, and eats other animals.

**Preening** when a bird cleans and smoothes its feathers with its beak.

**Prehensile** adapted for seizing or grasping; often used to describe a tail.

**Prey** an animal that is hunted, killed, and eaten by a predator.

**Pride** a group of lions.

**Primate** an animal that has hands or feet that can grasp, and a relatively large brain.

**Pronking** behaviour seen in some antelopes in which they bounce up and down on stiff legs when they are frightened or excited.

**Protected** (species) a type of animal whose life or habitat is safeguarded by law to save it from extinction.

**pil** the round, dark opening in the eye t gets bigger and smaller to control the ount of light that enters.

**gmy** a very small example of its kind, h as a pygmy shark.

**uill** the hollow, horny centre of a ther.

**ainforest** dense, tropical woodland that ts very heavy rainfall.

**aptor** a bird of prey.

**egurgitate** bring back food that is not mpletely digested from the stomach to e mouth.

**eptile** a class of vertebrates that breathe r and are usually cold blooded, such as ogs and lizards.

**Reservation** an area of land set aside for he protection of particular animals or abitats.

**Rodent** gnawing mammals such as mice nd rats.

**Roost** to settle down for rest or sleep, or o perch.

**Ruminate** to regurgitate food and chew it again – sometimes called "chewing the cud".

**Scales** small, overlapping plates that protect the skin of some animals such as fish and reptiles.

**Scavenge** to feed on the carcasses of other animals.

**School** a large group of fish swimming close together.

**Sett** the burrow of a badger.

**Sheath** a close-fitting covering.

**Shoal** a large group of fish swimming together in a loose formation.

**Sirenian** an order of mammals, including the dugong, that have a flat tail, paddle-like front limbs, and no hind limbs.

**Skeleton** the rigid framework (usually bone or cartilage) of an animal's body.

**Snout** a long, projecting nose.

**Social** involving interaction with other animals.

**Solitary** likely to live alone.

**Sonar** the process of detecting an underwater object, such as prey or a fellow creature, by using sound waves.

**Spawn** to produce or deposit eggs; used of aquatic animals.

**Spherical** in the shape of a sphere or round ball.

**Spine** an animal's supporting column or backbone.

**Stoop** the action of a bird when it dives down very quickly, usually to attack prey.

**Suckle** to feed milk to young from a teat or breast.

**Talon** the sharp claw on a bird of prey.

**Tentacle** a long, bendy, arm-like body part that aquatic animals such as squid and octopus use for touching and grasping.

**Temperate** moderate, not extreme.

**Terrestrial** relating to land.

**Territory** an area occupied and defended by an animal, or a group of animals.

**Toxic** relating to a poison or a toxin.

**Troop** a gathering of one kind of primate, such as monkeys.

**Tropical** relating to hot, humid regions.

**Tusk** a hard, tooth-like horn. Elephants and walruses have tusks.

**Vein** a vessel that carries blood towards the heart.

**Venom** poisonous liquid produced by some animals such as snakes and scorpions.

**Vertebrate** an animal with a backbone.

**Wetland** tidal flat or swamp where the soil is permanently wet.

**Whiskers** long, sticking-out hairs or bristles that grow near an animal's mouth.

**Wing span** the measurement from the tip of one wing to the tip of the other when the wings are outstretched.

# Index

# Acknowledgements

...publisher would like to thank the ...wing for their kind permission to ...oduce their photographs:

(...r: a-above; b-below/bottom; ...ntre; f-far; l-left; r-right; t-top)

...rie Abbott: 17cl; **Alamy Images:** ...ique R Aguirre Aves 139tr; AfriPics. ...a 109tr; Alaska Stock LLC 223br; ...an & Cherry Alexander 131tr; ...dyLim.com 235cl; Heather Angel ...r; Arco Images 14b, 145tc, 177bl, ...b, 283tr; Auscape International ...tr; Bill Bachmann 117br; Peter ...ritt 133bl; Blickwinkel 124cl, ...clb, 163cr, 177bc, 179tr, 185c, ...r, 198 (Malabar), 200l, 202l, 206l, ...l, 210l, 212l, 214l, 216l, 218l, ...l, 222l, 246cr, 257cr, 271cr; Steve ...om 11br, 109cra, 129tl, 144b; Rick ...Nora Bowers 166tr, 191c; John ...ancalosi 125br; Nigel Cattlin/Holt ...udios International Ltd 227br, 257c; ...andon Cole Marine Photography ...tl, 290bl; Bruce Coleman Inc 179c; ...ark Conlin 304; Andrew Darrington ...5l; Danita Delimont 117tr, 121br; ...homas Dobner 249cl; Matthew ...oggett 161cl; Redmond Durrell 300, ...1; Karin Duthie 181cl; Florida ...mages 169cr; FotoNatura 127bl; ...ephen Frink Collection 180b, 235cr, ...85cl, 291br; Johan Furusjö 129bl; ...im Gainey 274b; Guillen ...hotography 287br; Blaine Harrington ...II 124b; Mike Hill 149br; Bjorn ...Holland 286-287; Friedrich von ...Horsten 91cr; Chris Howes/Wild ...Places Photography 232c; Iconotec ...239cr; imagebroker 43br; ...INTERFOTO Pressebildagentur 167tr; Jonathan Samuel Gregg Irwin 162c; Andre Jenny 125bl; Steven J Kazlowski 7tl, 120bl, 120-121; Kevin Schafer 127tr, 130-131, 163bl, 187tr;

Holt Studios International Ltd 259cr; Juniors Bildarchiv 179bl, 182-183, 186t, 259bl; William S. Kuta 259tc; Kuttig-Animals 183tr; LMR Group 129tr; John E Marriott 15tl; Chris Mattison 171c, 197bl; Mediacolor's 246tr; Melba Photo Agency 49br; Louise Murray 264-265; N:id 281bl; Eyal Nahmias 275tr; NaturePics 259tl; David Noble Photography 19c; Rolf Nussbaumer 139bc; David Osborn 131br; Papillo 170, 198 (Emerald), 227clb; Jacky Parker 157cr, 157tr; Robert C Paulson 249tr; Wolfgang Polzer 181br; Premaphotos 181c; Adam Seward 10c; Martin Shields 179cl, 189c; Marco Simoni 133cl; Terry Sohl 142cr; tbkmedia.de 107br; David Tipling 136-137; Tom Uhlman 50-51; Duncan Usher 12c; Ariadne Van Zandbergen 21crb; John van Decker 135bl; Travis VanDenBerg 235tr; Visions of America, LLC 120cla; Visual & Written SL 25br, 247br, 284; David Wall 18-19c; John Warburton-Lee Photography 213tc; Dave Watts 148l; Petra Wegner 227tr; Maximilian Weinzierl 12-13c; Wildlife GmbH 18l, 196t, 210crb, 211cr, 211cra; Anna Yu 43c; Jim Zuckerman 7tc, 176bl, 176-177t; **Ardea:** Kathie Atkinson 195br; Ian Beames 45bl; Hans & Judy Beste 27cl; Leslie Brown 140-141; Julie Bruton-Seal 85tc; Piers Cavendish 25cr; Bill Coster 119br; Johan De Meester 66; Steve Downer 32br; Jean-Paul Ferrero 42t; Kenneth W Fink 33bl, 137tr; François Grohier 23r, 46tr, 102bl, 102cl, 126b, 271tr; Greg Harold 198 (Turtle); John Cancalosi 17cla, 39cl, 123cr; Ken Lucas 39br, 189t, 289tr; Geoff Moon 21cr; Hayden Oake 75cb; Pat Morris 44bc, 193br, 193c, 199tr, 229br; Jadgeep Raiput 88; Sid Roberts 149cr; Geoff Trinder 45br; David & Katie Urry 229tr; M Watson

11tl, 25tr, 44t, 132b; M. Watson 40-41, 41br, 94br, 101cr; Doc White 10tl; Jim Zipp 118l; Andrey Zvoznikov 30tl; **Kevin Arvin:** 271br; **Bill Blevins:** 199 (Woodhouse); **Lia Brand Photography Inc:** 19tr; **Monika Bright, University of Vienna, Austria:** 236b; **Meng Foo Choo:** 19cra; **Corbis:** Remi Benali 18bc; Niall Benvie 153bl; Jonathan Blair 164bl; Brandon D Cole 52l, 231cl; Kevin Fleming 76b; Michael & Patricia Fogden 260cl; Martin Harvey 143tr; Kevin Schafer 133tr, 174ca; Frans Lanting 111c; Danny Lehman 21c; Joe McDonald 11crb; Arthur Morris 142tr; Joel W Rogers 223cr; Jeffrey L Rotman 286br; Galen Rowell 11c; Josef Scaylea 137br; Paul A Souders 4-5b, 183br, 296-297; Herbert Spichtinger 148r; Kennan Ward 105cb; **Tammyjo Dallas:** 8 (snake); **Christoph Diewald:** 16b; **DK Images:** American Museum of Natural History 180cl; Peter Chadwick/ Courtesy of the Natural History Museum, London 148bc, 151crb; Malcolm Coulson 129tc; Philip Dowell 129cr; Dudley Edmonson 62crb; Exmoor Zoo, Devon 135tl; Frank Greenaway/Courtesy of the Natural History Museum, London 127cr, 257br, 275bl, 275c, 275crb, 276cl; Rowan Greenwood 129br; Colin Keates/Courtesy of the Natural History Museum, London 275tc; Mike Linley 196c; Maslowski Photo 151cl; National Birds of Prey Centre, Gloucestershire 118br, 119bl, 119cr; Natural History Museum, London 113c, 113tl; Stephen Oliver 113tr, 151bl; David Peart 20cl, 167cl; Barrie Watts 16-17; Jerry Young 62cr, 274t, 275cra; **Tolis Flioukas:** 9 (hermit crab); **FLPA:** Michael & Patricia Fogden/Minden 146-147; J W Alker 228r; Terry Andrewartha 105bl; Fred

Bavendam 242bl, 242-243t; Matthias Breiter 51cr; Richard Brooks 123br; Wendy Dennis 149cl; Reinard Dirscherl 240b; Richard Du Toit/ Minden Pictures 62b, 100-101; Michael Durham 34br; Gerry Ellis/ Minden Pictures 69cra; Peter Entwistle 249cl; Yossi Eshbol 31tl; Katherine Feng/Globio/Minden Pictures 69br, 69cr; Foto Natura Stock 93b, 93cl; Tony Hamblin 118tr, 142bl; David Hosking 265br; Mitsuhiko Imamori 269br; Jurgen & Christine Sohns 30br, 42b, 43bl, 176br; Gerard Lacz 63cl; Frans Lanting 6-7, 31br, 37br, 81t, 123bl, 160-161, 292-293; Hans Leijense 60-61, 93cr; S & D & K Maslowski 28bl, 28c; Chris Mattison 198 (Monte); Phil McLean 139tl; Claus Meyer/Minden Pictures 38tr, 279-279; Michio Hoshino/Minden Pictures 38br, 64-65, 104-105t; Minden Pictures/ZSSD 65br; Patricio Robles Gil/Sierra Madre/Minden Pictures 86-87; Mark Moffett/Minden Pictures 197br, 256b, 267bl; Yva Momatiuk/John Eastcott/Minden Pictures 76-77; Piotr Naskrecki 253t; Chris Newbert/Minden Pictures 229tl; Flip Nicklin 54-55; Pete Oxford 71cr; Panda Photo 189br; Fritz Polking 109br; Michael Quinton/Minden 105cr; Len Robinson 155bc; Walter Rohdich 162bl; Cyril Ruoso/Minden Pictures 68-69; Malcolm Schuyl 33br, 33tl; Chris & Tilde Stuart 102-103; Roger Tidman 67br; Jan Vermeer/Foto Natura 78b; Larry West 190tr, 281tl; Terry Whittaker 32bc, 77b, 139c; D P Wilson 140bl; Martin B Withers 2 (Dingo), 62tl; Norbert Wu 2tl, 26r, 229cr, 235bl; Zhinong Xi 107cr; **Getty Images:** AFP 156-157, 233bc; Ingo Arndt 133cr; Pete Atkinson 151tl; Gary Bell 169tl; Gary Benson 94t; Walter Bibikow 17c; Emanuele Biggi

**ACKNOWLEDGEMENTS**

273br; Kathy Collins 271cl; DAJ 5tl, 154bl; Flip De Nooyer/FotoNatura 127br; Roger Deha Harpe 165br; Georgette Douwma 201c; Michael Dunning 180tr; Nicole Duplaix 173cr; Michael Durham 190b; Danny Ellinger 135tr; Tim Flach 267tr; Larry Gatz 3 (hammerheads), 201l, 206-207; George Grall 197c; Gavin Hellier 1; Kevin Horan 116-117; Jeff Hunter 58-59; Gavriel Jecan 275tr; Rene Krekels 7tr, 188; Tim Laman 254-255; Timothy Laman 28tl, 191tr; Patrick Landmann 261cr; Cliff Leight 86t; Michael Melford 222-223; Michael Nichols 22-23, 89br; Patricio Robles Gil/Sierra Madre/Minden Pictures 89bl; Mark Moffett 196b; Piotr Naskrecki 261br; Paul Nicklen 86b; Michael & Patricia Fogden 186cl, 194-195; Michael Redmer 184-185; Jeff Rotman 233bl; Tui De Roy 133bc, 133tl, 149tl; SA Team/Foto Natura 167c; Kevin Schafer 59crb; Chris Schenk 126tr; Yomiuri Shimbun 232-233; Tom Stoddart 91br; Ben Van Den Brink 270cl; Wim van Egmond 285tr; Tom Vezo 63br; Norbert Wu 213bc, 218-219; Minden Pictures/ZSSD 110-111; **Jack Goldfarb/Design Pics Inc:** 199 (Couch's spadefoot); **Andreas Graemiger:** 11cra; **Thor Håkonsen:** 255tr; **Chod A. Hedinger:** 15tr; **imagequestmarine.com:** Jim Greenfield 291c; Takaji Ochi 290-291; Peter Parks 239c; **iStockphoto.com:** Omar Ariff 215br; Bostb 186br; Marshall Bruce 10bl; Michel De Nijs 17cra; Alan Drummond 10br; Mike Golay 15bl; Hazlan Abdul Hakim 10bc; Andrew Howe 153cr, 154bc; Frank Leung 111cr; Jurie Maree 18ca; Peter Miller 10tr; Phil Morley 12cra; Dawn Nichols 125tr; Katrina Outland 285br; Lorenzo Pastore 91t; Matej Pribelsky 112l; Achim Prill 192; Proxyminder 270b; Ryan Saul 208cr; Steve Snyder 273cr; Jan Will 17crb; Mark Wilson 10fbr; **Stephen Kelly:** 16c; **Ray Macey:** 257cl; **Earl F. Martinelli:** 19tl; **Ric McArthur:** 11cla; **Sean McCann:** 257bl; **Taco**

**Meeuwsen:** 153c; **Cheryl Moorehead:** 227ftl; **National Geographic Image Collection:** Darlyne A Murawski 282-283; **Natural Visions:** 69tr, 104bl; **naturepl.com:** Ingo Arndt 38l; Peter Blackwell 72br, 171br; Brandon Cole 169tr; Bruce Davidson 97br, 280-281bl; Doug Perrine 92-93, 93t, 167br, 230-231b; Jurgen Freund 165bl, 235br, 238t; Nick Garbutt 31cl; Tony Heald 98t; Kim Taylor 34cr, 256t; Eliot Lyons 83b; Tom Mangelsen 106br; Luiz Claudio Marigo 251cr, 283br; George McCarthy 67tl; Rolf Nussbaumer 138; William Osborn 153br; Pete Oxford 37bl, 57b, 79br, 97cr; Pete Cairns 79cr, 106-107; Constantinos Petrinos 285tc; Tony Phelps 279t; David Pike 41tr; Premaphotos 251br, 283cr, 289cr; Peter Reese 265tr; Jeff Rotman 238-239tc; Jose B Ruiz 155tc; Andy Sands 273bl; Phil Savoie 154c, 273cl; Peter Scoones 234; Anup Shah 36, 98b, 99tl, 164br; Igor Shpilenok 31cr; Sinclair Stammers 280t; Lynn M Stone 70-71, 80-81, 173bc; David Tipling 85tr; Jeff Vanuga 105cl; Tom Vezo 288b; Doc White 81b; Staffan Widstrand 99br, 122b; Mike Wilkes 101br; Simon Williams 268-269; Solvin Zankl 239tc; **NHPA/Photoshot:** Bryan & Cherry Alexander 85cr; ANT Photo Library 28-29; Daryl Balfour 72-73t, 73bl; Anthony Bannister 30tr, 175bl, 269cr; Bill Coster 135br, 155cr; Laurie Campbell 135cl; Gerald Cubitt 37tl; Lee Dalton 115cb; Stephen Dalton 112t, 249tl, 260-261, 279br, 279cb; Nigel J Dennis 143br; Nick Garbutt 23c, 83tr, 97tr, 147cr; Ken Griffiths 267br; Adrian Hepworth 147br; Daniel Heulin 143c, 174b, 191br, 199c; James Warwick 96-97, 97ftl, 150-151; B Jones & M Shimlock 228l; Rich Kirchner 51br; Stephen Krasemann 70l, 137cr; Martin Harvey 183cr, 268b; Dr Eckart Pott 129c; Cede Prudente 173br; Steve Robinson 82b, 97tl; Andy Rouse 44l, 108-109; Jonathan & Angela Scott 109crb; Taketomo Shiratori 84c; M. I. Walker

229bl; Dave Watts 27br; Martin Wendler 169br; **Photolibrary:** Animals Animals/Earth Scenes 174tr; Kathie Atkinson 26cl, 257tr; David Courtenay 81c; Daniel Cox 79bl; David M Dennis 237tc; IFA-Bilderteam GmbH 61r; Juniors Bildarchiv 46b; London Scientific Films 227bl; Stan Osolinski 51tr; Oxford Scientific Films 147tr; Werner Pfunder 104br; Mary Plage/OSF 99c; Survival Anglia 155r; Konrad Wothe 25crb; **Stuart Plummer:** 19bc; **Guido & Philippe Poppe–www. poppe-images.com:** 231cr; **Stefano Prigione:** 14tl; **PunchStock:** Design Pics 193tr; Digital Vision 173bl; Digital Vision/Caroline Warren 164-165t; Jupiter 239br; **Raymond Racaza:** 19cl; **Mike Robles:** 9 (blue starfish); **Science Photo Library:** Charles Angelo 235tl; Nigel Cattlin 258; John Devries 134b; Eye of Science 12br; Pascal Goetgheluck 266; Richard R Hansen 250-251, 251tr; Sinclair Stammers 9tr; Barbara Strnadova 269tr; Jean-Philippe Varin 267tl; Jerome Wexler 12bl; **SeaPics.com:** 2 (Dolphins), 5tc, 20-21, 23l, 52r, 200-201, 201cr, 203bc, 203bl, 203br, 208b, 208tl, 209br, 209tl, 210-211, 214-215, 215tr, 216bl, 216br, 216c, 216cr, 216tr, 217bl, 217br, 217clb, 217tl, 219br, 219tr, 220, 221bl, 221br, 221c, 221cl, 221cr, 221tl, 221tr, 231cr, 239tr, 286bl; **Shutterstock:** Kitch Bain 4tl; Joe Barbarite 226bl; Lara Barrett 226cl; Mircea Bezergheanu 226clb; Stephen Bonk 3 (Newt); Sandra Caldwell 2 (Echidna); Ivan Cholakov 3 (Iguana); EcoPrint 226tl; Richard Fitzer 225br; Josiah J. Garber 227cr; Mark Grenier 4tc; Peter Hansen 3 (Snake); Lavigne Herve 227cl; Eric Isselée 298-299; Ivanov 290cl; Mawroidis Kamila 224bc; Cathy Keifer 3 (Mantis); Kelpfish 3 (Starfish), 226-227b; K L Kohn 3 (Frog); DJ Mattaar 3tr, 4tr, 224bl, 302-303; Mayskyphoto 3 (Parrot); David Mckee 2 (Ape); Mishella 4ftr; rsfatt 174cl; Vishal Shah 294-295; Johan Swanepoel 18cb; Morozova Tatyana 234b; Florin Tirlea

224-225; Alan Ward 5tr; Richard Williamson 3 (Anemon); **Chanda Singh:** 11tr; **Still Pictures:** John Cancalosi 172bl; Martin Harvey 7... 90-91; **Kayla Swart:** 19clb; **www.▮ no:** Erling Svenson 291bl; **Brian Valentine:** 248-249, 272, 272t; **Ni▮ van Veelen:** 9 (sponge); **Warren Photographic:** 84tl, 85bl, 246b, 2... Jane Burton 109bl; Kim Taylor 252... 289c, 289cl; **Tom Weilenmann:** 19... **Wikimedia Commons:** Holger Gröschl 271tl; Rowland Shelly, PhD North Carolina State Museum of Natural Sciences 289tl; **Sergey Yeliseer:** 154tr;

**Jacket images:** _Front:_ **Alamy Imag...** Juniors Bildarchiv bc; **Corbis:** Ma... Harvey br; **Getty Images:** Georget... Douwma fbr; Ralph Hopkins bl; Oxford Scientific Films/Photolibra... t. _Back:_ **Corbis:** Jenny E. Ross tc; **FLPA:** Frans Lanting b; Larry West... **Getty Images:** Michael Melford ftr... **Brian Valentine:** tl. _Spine:_ **FLPA:** Frans Lanting b; **Getty Images:** Oxford Scientific Films/Photolibra... t. _Back Flaps:_ **SeaPics.com**

All other images © Dorling Kindersley
For further information see:
www.dkimages.com

**Dorling Kindersley would also like to thank:**

**Editorial assistance:** Amy-Jane Beer, Alex Cox, and Leon Gray
**Design assistance:** Natalie Godwin, Emma Forge, Tom Forge, Sophie Pelham and Vicky Wharton
**Picture researcher:** Romaine Werblov...
**Proofreaders:** Lee Wilson and Kevin Royal
**Indexer:** Chris Bernstein

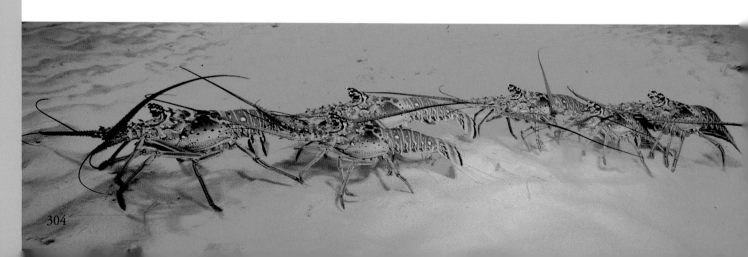